SLEEPING with the

100 great places to stay in *Costa Rica*

**Includes charming small inns,
bed & breakfasts,
luxury villas, jungle lodges, birders' retreats,
beach paradises, decadent spas
and many other fantastic places
you need to know about
in Costa Rica**

Chris Fields and Alison Tinsley

D1208007

HayFields Publications
Santa Fe, New Mexico

Copyright © 2007 by HayFields Publications, a Division of HayFields Science Incorporated, PO Box 5929, Santa Fe, NM 87502. All Rights Reserved.

To our parents:
Carolyn Tinsley who gave her love of travel to Alison
Joan and Bert Fields who gave their love of language to Chris

First Printing: 2007

Library of Congress Control Number: 2007925669

All photographs not otherwise attributed are Copyright © Alison Tinsley. All photographs used by permission.

Cover art by Pat Redding Scanlon.

Printed in the USA on Forest Stewardship Council (FSC) certified paper.

4 wheel Suv car + gas

-1000
$$\overline{\$2560}$$

+ airfare,
  food

+ San Jose — 2 nights / 1 night
  Could arrive, spend 1 night to
  whitewater rafting trip on Pacuare River
  $96 each return us to La Fortune
  stay in subub

Hotel Casa Alegra 90×3 90
Hampton Inn 144×3 90
Hotel Bougainviller 130×3 90

$$\overline{\$2830}$$

Arenal   x 3 nights
           Tabacon Grand Spa for 3 ? $395
                                          395

           Villa Decary   150
           fishing for 2 - 3   half day   150
Monteverde 2 nights
           Hotel Fonda Vela   130
                                           130

Manuel Antonio - 2 nights   360
Arenas   360

Drake   4 nights   4500
        La Paloma

Contents

Introduction

This book is the one we wish we'd had when we first came to Costa Rica. We arrived with a pile of conventional guidebooks but no clear ideas about what the various places we'd planned to visit, or hotels we'd arranged to stay in, would be *like*. We made some good guesses on that first trip, as well as some not-so-good ones. We never imagined, for example, that our hotel for the first two nights, a "boutique" little place conveniently near Juan Santamaria airport, would be a recovery destination for plastic surgery patients. Imagine our surprise at breakfast when everyone but us appeared in stitches!

Now we live here. We still carry three or four guidebooks around with us, but we mainly trust our own – and our traveling friends' – impressions of what it's like to stay here or there around the country. What it's like is what this book is about. After all, you're on vacation: you're not just looking for a room, you're looking for an experience. And if you're like us, a medical experience is not what you had in mind.

What makes a Great Place to Stay?

We've both been business travelers, and have stayed in countless big-name corporate hotels, including several of the "resort" variety. As much as we might appreciate the familiar consistency of these places after 16 hours of air travel and meetings, it's not what we want on a vacation. We want hot water, and an in-room coffee maker is nice, but we're not looking for a place where we know exactly where everything is located because it's just like the last place we stayed. We want to be charmed – we want someone to have taken the time to make a place unique and appealing, to give it a personality. We have a natural bias toward small inns, boutique hotels and B&Bs, but have included some mid-size hotels that use design, services, landscape, or other features to create a distinctive experience.

 Costa Rica is about nature, and we're not impressed by structures or attitudes that might be cool, but don't fit at all with the local environment. Snap-to, stand-at-attention service is nice where it belongs, but it hardly matches the relaxed atmosphere and easy-going mannerisms typical of Costa Ricans (or *Ticos* as they call themselves). Paris or New York manners are out of place in Costa

Rica. We like to have WiFi, but we're not fond of television, and hearing the neighbor's TV or having to endure CNN or music videos in a public area is always a black mark in our book.

A principal objective in any hotel is to sleep, and the quiet and darkness necessary to sleeping are important criteria for us. We value privacy and are especially fond of truly private outdoor spaces, where you can neither see nor be seen by other guests.

Costa Rican lodgings come in all price ranges, and price alone is no guide to charm or character. We don't expect a $75 room to have fancy high-count sheets or handmade organic bath soaps; near the coasts, we don't even necessarily expect hot water. We do expect inexpensive places to be well-equipped and pleasant, and to be interesting, fun places to stay. If, however, a hotel claims to have four or five stars or costs more than $250 per night, it had better be perfect. And it had better not be the least bit pretentious. Nothing is worse than an upscale hotel that makes you feel like they're doing you a favor to let you through the door.

The Costa Rican government tourism department (ICT) assigns ratings of one to five stars to hotels that request an official evaluation, using criteria that seem heavily weighted toward the American-style resort hotel model. Many smaller hotels have not bothered filing the required paperwork to get a rating, and the star ratings of those that have bothered don't necessarily correlate with whether we find them charming. A criterion that does matter is whether the owner operates the place him- or herself and/or has hired a competent and fully-empowered manager. We've encountered several places where an absentee owner micromanages the staff, and no one on site has any real authority. Few of them have made it into this book.

Our only overtly hostile reception was at Punta Islita, reputedly the most upscale place on the Nicoya Peninsula, and one of the hardest to find. After driving around for an hour following their less than consistent road signs, we finally reached the front gate and explained that we were travel writers who just wanted to look around the hotel. The guard

chatted for while on the phone with the front desk, then explained that we would be admitted provided we left our passports in his care. I've visited sensitive military installations and government labs, and any number of security-crazed corporations, and I've shown my passport or other IDs to a lot of parking-lot guards, but I've never had one ask to *keep* my passport! We politely declined, and you won't find Punta Islita in this book. There may be people out there who appreciate this level of extreme paranoia, but we're not them, and we expect you aren't either.

Sustainable Tourism

On top of all of our other criteria, we look pretty closely at how a hotel relates to its environment and its community. We had never even heard of "sustainable tourism" when we first came to Costa Rica, but we were impressed by the number of hotels that had programs in place to support local schools, assist with community-based recycling programs, or contribute in other ways to local economic development and environmental preservation. These are hotel keepers who are not just in business for themselves; they are using their businesses effectively as fund-raising tools to engage in broader social development. They are using tourism income to preserve and strengthen the things tourists come to see in Costa Rica, and indeed in Central America in general: a different and more pristine environment, and a vibrant culture less based on consumerism than those in the U.S. or Europe.

In the late 1990s, Costa Rica developed a formal program to encourage sustainable tourism, the Certification for Sustainable Tourism (CST), which has been implemented by the government's tourism department (http://www.turismo-sostenible.co.cr). The CST program evaluates hotels based on criteria including hiring practices (from the local community is best), recycling and alternative energy programs, efforts in guest education and engagement. Many of Costa Rica's best hotels participate in this program; all three that have achieved the highest rating (five Leaves) – Lapa Rios, Finca Rosa Blanca, and Villa Blanca – are profiled in this book.

We have, however, also found that many smaller hotels and B&Bs with robust sustainability programs have not been evaluated and hence do not have CST certificates. Several hotel keepers have told us that they do not have the time and resources to prepare the required materials, arrange the on-site evaluations, and make the multiple trips to San José that may be required. Our advice is to expect larger hotels to have CST certificates with at least two leaves, but not to hold the absence of a certificate against a smaller hotel, lodge, or B&B. Whether you see a certificate or not, ask your hosts about sustainability, and what work they are doing for their communities and the environment. You'll find yourself having some very interesting conversations, and you may get an unexpected tour of a local school or a home-made hydroelectric plant. And you'll probably find yourself thinking about how you, too, can help make the tourist economy more sustainable in countries like Costa Rica, and at home as well.

Room Cost Codes

Gone are the days when Costa Rica was an inexpensive destination. Price ranges for lodgings here are comparable to the U.S. or Europe. Different parts of the country have different average prices; the Caribbean coast and the mountains are typically less expensive than the Pacific, the north and south of the country are cheaper than the center, and Monteverde is still surprisingly reasonable given its popularity. We represent price ranges by dollar-sign codes ($ up to $$$$). Lots of places are priced near price-code cutoffs (no matter where you put them), so don't be afraid to cross categories if your budget is near a cutoff point.

We use the following cost codes:

$	Up to $75 U.S.
$$	$76 - $150 U.S.
$$$	$151 - $250 U.S.
$$$$	$251 U.S. and over.

Cost codes are based on high-season, double-occupancy rates for the most moderate rooms up to the most expensive. For example "$$" means all the rooms for two, counting taxes, are between $76 and $150. A cost code of "$ -$$$" means the lodging has rooms for two starting below $76 and going up to somewhere between $151 and $250. A cost code in red (e.g. $$$) indicates that all meals (breakfast, lunch, dinner) are included in the rate. Some places include drinks too!

Many Costa Rican lodgings quote prices exclusive of taxes, which are roughly 16% (for the 2006 – 2007 season). We have added 16% to pre-tax rates to assign cost codes. Some establishments charge 5% or more for credit-card payments. Our cost codes are based on cash prices.

Prices change unpredictably. Avoid surprises – always check websites for current prices and confirm in writing the *total* price you will be expected to pay.

Keywords

Costa Rican lodgings typically advertise a vast array of activities, and most can arrange essentially any activity even at a distant site through third-party tour operators. We use the following keywords to summarize our take on the best attributes and activities at our favorite places, counting only those activities available at or directly organized by the lodging itself.

Adults Only: These are lodgings that do not permit children, usually defined as anyone under 16. Check website or call to confirm.

Art/Architecture: Some places display interesting art collections; others are works of art themselves. A few are both.

Birding: You can see interesting birds almost anywhere in Costa Rica and we carry our binoculars wherever we go. We award this keyword to places where an interesting variety of birds are plentiful on the property, and the lodgings provide extensive species lists, knowledgeable birding guides, books and identification charts, and a pleasant environment for watching.

Destination Restaurant: We tend to avoid lodgings that do not have good restaurants at least nearby. This keyword is for places that have a truly great restaurant on site, the kind you'd drive a long way to get to even if you weren't staying at the hotel.

Downtown: Although they may not be located in a large city, these lodgings are within walking distance to restaurants, nightlife, shopping, and other "town" attractions.

Fishing: Almost anyplace near the water can organize a fishing trip; this keyword is for lodgings with their own guides and boats or with a focus on fishing as a primary guest activity.

Happening Place: This designates places with an evening scene where you have a good chance of meeting people other than your fellow guests. All these places have lively bars; some show movies.

Hiking: Lodgings with scenic and well-maintained trails on the grounds or with proximity and easy walking access to lovely, traffic-free country roads or public trails receive this keyword. This notation is also given for hotels close to National Parks.

Honeymoons: Almost everyplace offers a "honeymoon suite," but some are dramatically better than others. Privacy and a romantic setting are musts to receive this notation; great food and a touch of the exotic help.

Horseback Riding: Places with their own horses, guides, and great trails receive this designation.

Kid-friendly: This designation includes places that have special activities or play areas for children.

Oceanfront: Lots of places say they're "beachfront" but we really mean it – it's only "oceanfront" if the ocean is a few easy steps from your room. You'll also find that a lot of Costa Rican "beaches" are, in fact, mainly rock, usually with a stretch of sandy beach nearby.

Relax/Get Away: These are quiet, tranquil places to just kick back and chill. You don't have to be doing something every minute, do you?

Spa: Alison tries out every spa she sees (someone has to do it!). We keyword the best.

Surfing: You'll find surfers on almost any beach in Costa Rica, but this designation is for surfing destinations with good waves and on-site expertise, often with boards for rent and classes on offer. We're happiest when the hotelier is him/herself an active surfer.

Wildlife: This keyword is awarded to great places for seeing monkeys, crocodiles, sloths, sea turtles, or other memorable critters.

Yoga/meditation: It's easy to find yoga platforms and a business card for a local instructor. We award this keyword for lodgings with a beautiful setting, a designated yoga facility and, generally, an on-staff or regularly-associated instructor.

Getting Around

Costa Rica is a small country (51,000 km^2 or 20,000 square miles), bigger than Maryland or Switzerland but smaller than West Virginia or Iceland. The most frustrating mistake many travelers make, however, is to assume that they can get around Costa Rica at U.S. or European speeds. You can, but only if you fly.

If you only have a week in Costa Rica and you want to visit far-flung destinations like Tortuguero or the Osa Peninsula, plan to take one of the regional airlines (SANSA or Nature Air) from San José to wherever you're going and back. Round-trip fares are typically in the neighborhood of $150, so unless you were planning on driving with a car full of people, flying is not much more expensive than car rental and gas. And it is much, much faster: one hour to get to Puerto Jiménez, for example, not ten.

The reliable and inexpensive way to get around is by public busses, which are clean, frequent, and not much slower than driving yourself. Point-to-point fares are typically a few dollars. For an extensive guide with schedules, see John Wood's *Costa Rica by Bus*.

A final alternative to consider before renting a car is hiring a driver. This is what tour companies do. There are many independent drivers, some with 4-WDs. Many speak at least some English or other second language. A good way to find drivers in the areas you're planning to visit is through your hotels – most have relationships with trustworthy and knowledgeable drivers.

Driving in Costa Rica

OK, you've evaluated your alternatives and decided to test your skill and patience on Costa Rica's roads. Be advised: this is nothing like driving in the U.S. or Europe, or even Mexico. You simply cannot go fast. Highway speed limits are typically 60 or 80 kilometers per hour, i.e. 37.5 or 50 mph, but averaging 30 mph between point A and point B is making really good time in Costa Rica. Traffic on the famous *Interamericana*, the main road called Highway 1 north of San José and Highway 2 to the south, is often moving at 10 mph or less, as lines of heavy trucks struggle up and down the mountains. If you think it will take an hour to get where you're going, count on two (or maybe three or four).

Driving in Costa Rica can be fun, but you need a good highway map (we like the *National Geographic* AdventureMap best), an alert navigator, and a lot of patience. Be prepared for typical Costa Rican highway conditions: no shoulders, minimal signage, one-lane bridges, abrupt changes from paved to unpaved road, lots of potholes. Keep in mind that busses and disabled vehicles stop on the road, not off it, and that road construction often takes precedence over traffic. Don't be surprised if you have to wait in a line that may be over a mile long while a road crew does some paving or fells a tree into the middle of the highway. Keep a sharp eye out for pedestrians (slow down – they will not get out of your way), farm animals, and wildlife of every kind. Always carry drinking water, a good spare tire, a compass, and a flashlight. Don't speed (you *will* get a ticket), and DO NOT DRIVE AT NIGHT.

With two or three exceptions, Costa Rican highways do not have highway-number signs. Signs at intersections point to destinations, and often to hotels or attractions, not towns. Your best way to navigate to some cities – e.g. Tamarindo – is to follow the signs to the larger hotels. We give directions from prominent towns or other landmarks, and use highway numbers so that you can reference them to your map, not to the road itself.

There are several roads that look great on the map but aren't. Avoid Highway 141 from Naranjo to Ciudad Quesada; it is a major truck route and is excruciatingly slow. The *Interamericana* from San Ramón to Esparza is narrow, curvy, typically fog-bound, and jammed with truck traffic; take Highway 3 from La Garita to San Mateo, then Highway 131 to Esparza instead. Highway 21 east of the junction with Highway 18 in central Nicoya is wretched; if you're going to southern Nicoya by car, take the ferry from Puntarenas to Paquera (*not* to Playa Naranjo). Highway 32 from San José to Limón is mostly good road, but don't expect to make good time – every east-bound shipping container goes via this road. Highway 34 down the central Pacific coast is beautiful, except for the stretch between Quepos and Dominical, which is bone-jarringly unpaved (be patient, they're working on it).

There are also some great roads – Highway 6 from just north of Cañas to Upala, Highway 142 from San Ramón to La Fortuna, Highway 10 from Paraíso to Turrialba. Even the *Interamericana* is pretty, as long as you're not staring at the truck bumper in front of you. And many of the unpaved roads are stunningly beautiful, just slow. So have a granola bar, quit worrying about when you're going to get there, and enjoy the ride.

Glossary

You'll encounter plenty of special Costa Rican vocabulary traveling here, starting with *Tico* – what Costa Ricans call themselves. Here are some of the most common Costa Rican-isms, as well as a few ordinary Spanish words you might find worth knowing.

Banco: 1) a bank; 2) a bench for sitting, usually built into a wall

Calle: street, road

Carablanca (or *mono carablanca*): white-faced monkey

Casona: a big house, typically the main house on a farm

Cerveza: beer

Congo (or *mono congo*): howler monkey

Cordillera: mountain range

Extranjero: foreigner, anyone not Costa Rican

Finca: farm or ranch

Gallo Pinto: literally "spotted rooster" – the national breakfast dish of beans and rice

Hermosa: beautiful

Mono: monkey

Palapa: an open-sided structure, often with a thatched, umbrella-shaped roof supported by a single central pole

Peligro: danger; *peligroso*: dangerous

Playa: beach

Pura Vida: literally "pure life" – a Costa Rican greeting, exclamation of enthusiasm, and informal motto

Rancho: 1) a large palapa; 2) an open-air restaurant

Ropa: clothing; *Ropa Americana*: shop selling bulk-imported clothing for very low prices

Soda: 1) a small, inexpensive restaurant serving Costa Rican fare; 2) sparkling water or club soda

Tico/Tica: (n) a Costa Rican (masc./fem.); (adj) typically Costa Rican

Tienda: small shop

Tipico: typical, used especially for food or handicrafts

Tortuga: turtle, especially a sea turtle

Volcán: volcano

San José and Escazú

We know plenty of ex-pats who won't go near San José, at least not voluntarily, but we kind of like it. It's a working city: sprawling, not particularly clean or well-maintained, and certainly not spruced up for tourists. Marseilles or maybe Toulouse – not Paris; Birmingham or Manchester – not London. But it's also the unrivaled political, economic, and cultural heart of Costa Rica, and spending some time in San José is revealing about the country and its people. Besides, there are some fun places to stay here and some great restaurants.

San José didn't really get off the ground until the late 1700s; there's nothing colonial about this city. The grand civic structures, like the opera house and the splendid old post office, date from the late 19th or early 20th centuries. While the downtown is dominated by 30- and 40-year-old buildings that can only really be described as ugly, the nearby neighborhoods of Amón and Yoses include lots of examples

of what might be called European-early-modern-meets-tropical architecture. Except for the fabulous Grano de Oro, the places we like to stay are in these neighbor-hoods and most feature this pleasing fusion of designs.

We don't like particularly like driving in San José. The roads are narrow, most corners have no street signs, and the traffic is fierce. It's hard to find where you're going, and even harder to park once you're

there. Red taxis are plentiful and it's often easier to just take one. Addresses here, as in most of Costa Rica, are given by compass directions and distances in meters from some local landmark. (Our address is "two km NW of the Red Cross in Atenas.") A city block is often called "100 meters" (even though it's usually much shorter), while a half-block is called "50 meters." *Avenidas* run east-west, on the long axis of the city; *calles* run north-south. You can usually see the huge grey Banco Nacional (BN) tower, which is a fair marker for the center of town. Some parts of the city are unsafe – our advice is to stay out of any area that looks questionable or just to stay in the areas immediately north (Amón) or east (Yoses) of downtown or in the well-patrolled city center itself. You'll need a good city map; we like the one by Jiménez and Tanzi ("Jitan") the best. You can find them at 7th Street Books, two blocks from the Gold Museum in the center of downtown.

The western suburb of Escazú, on the other side of the big La Sabana Park, is the polar opposite of San José. This is where lots of North Americans and other ex-pats live, and where you'll find American-style shopping malls (with lots of U.S. chain stores), fancy boutiques, and shops full of imports from all over the world. Escazú has a nice old church and a charming parade of traditional, brightly-painted ox carts, but it's mainly a chunk of the no-kidding developed world plunked into Central America. You can find just about anything you might want here, but it's not *really* Costa Rica. For that, head back to San José, or better, out into the countryside beyond.

Cinco Hormigas Rojas $

Central San José – Barrio Amón   Downtown

Photo © Alison Tinsley

Contact Information:
506-257-8581 (voice); 506-255-3412 (fax)
info@cincohormigasrojas.com
www.cincohormigasrojas.com

Essentials:
4 Rooms
English, Spanish
Cash Only
On-street or public lot parking
Continental breakfast included, Restaurants nearby
Room Amenities: Internet available in office

How to get here:
Ask your cab driver to go to the Café Mundo Restaurant. Cinco
Hormigas Rojas is just across Calle 13 – look for the gate with all the
trees behind it.

Remember that hippie artist from back in the 70's? She had the little gallery next to the café, with lavender walls, a multitude of hanging plants, and sort of free-form paintings of nude women with lots of breasts? Well, she lives in San José now, and her home is a B&B: Cinco Hormigas Rojas.

A diminutive wooden Indian Chief greets you when you walk through the gate, and a yellow crocodile. Mayra has planted thick stands of bamboo in her front yard, as well as trees and all kinds of vines. Orchids and bromeliads hang in baskets in the shade. On a block of nondescript houses, hers stands out as a green oasis, and she carefully feeds and nurtures the birds, bats, and squirrels that have migrated to her little private reserve. Multi-colored hand-lettered signs guide you to the front door and the stairs going up to the guest rooms. Odd little objects found who-knows-where are tucked into corners or sit under trees or on the lips of birdbaths. The yard is a living multi-media collage, with the animals – and now you – as temporary participants.

Upstairs, you have your choice of three bedrooms that share a bath (families or groups sometimes rent all three) or a two-bedroom suite with its own bath plus what evidently used to be a small kitchen. The walls are all brightly painted green, blue, purple, or lavender. There are lots of drawings and paintings, as well as hanging silk sarongs and beaded curtains. The common area between the rooms is festooned with dried bamboo, wicker and bamboo furniture and big floppy pillows. There's a little upstairs porch and windows looking into the green outdoors. Hummingbirds chase each other through the flowering vines, and parakeets you can't quite see squawk somewhere.

The location here is just about perfect. The street is quiet, but you're only two blocks from the National Cultural Center with its contemporary art museum, all located in the sprawling grounds of the old national liquor factory. Shady parks with big trees and splashing fountains flank the museum complex on both sides, and the center of downtown is just another five minutes away. In fact, most of the sights that visitors come to San José to see are within a ten minute walk.

Mayra will make you breakfast, and for lunch or dinner one of our favorite spots is right across the street. Café Mundo is a hangout for students and young professionals; it has a full bar and great lunch specials every weekday. It will remind you of that place by your old college, but with a contempo urban edge. Pick a table on the broad front porch, order one of their full glasses of wine, and take in the scene. You'll understand why San José is such a vibrant, young-feeling city.

Posada del Museo

Central San José

$-$$

Downtown

Photo © Alison Tinsley

Contact Information:
506-258-1027 (voice); 506-257-9414 (fax)
posadadelmuseo@racsa.co.cr
www.hotelposadadelmuseo.com

Essentials:
11 Rooms
English, Spanish, French, Italian
Cash only
Off-street or public lot parking
Breakfast included, Café open for lunch, Restaurants nearby
Room Amenities: TV, Free WiFi

How to get here:
Ask your cab driver to take you to the Museo Nacional. The Posada is right across Avenida 2 from the museum entrance.

The hotel Posada del Museo is so close to the turreted Bellavista Fortress, now the National Museum of Costa Rica, that one of its round towers appears on the hotel's business card. The Posada occupies an old, two-story wood-frame house right across the street from the Fortress, on the new pedestrian mall that runs from the Ministry of Justice and Supreme Court up to the center of the Parque Nacional. It's not much to look at from the outside, but walk in the door, and you're in a space that will remind you of a grand home in old New Orleans. The main room extends up to the ceiling, with a mezzanine on the second floor above. The walls are a soft yellow with white trim; there is a splendid old brown-and-gold tiled floor. You'll be greeted by Sylvia, the Argentinean Innkeeper; she designed the renovation and brought the antique furniture and each room's colorful curtains from Buenos Aires. There's a sense of reserve and somewhat down-at-the-heels elegance here, as if the aristocrats had fallen on hard times but their home was still being carefully tended.

The rooms here are light and airy, with big windows, wood floors, and colorful walls and window dressings. Local art hangs on the walls, mostly nature-themed but with some fun contemporaries adding humor and just a bit of an edge. Sylvia holds exhibits in the hotel and her husband's adjacent café and keeps a few favorite pieces from previous shows up as well. The furnishings are simple but elegant, and some rooms have unexpected delights like the French-style painted ceiling in Ave de Paraiso, the downstairs suite. Many of the rooms have lovely old French doors with framed glass transoms above; the narrow panes in the doors have been painted for privacy, but it's intriguing to imagine what the halls must have looked like before when they were all open or hung with light veils of curtain. The best room in the house is Mariposa, the upstairs master suite on the south side, away from the traffic on 2nd Avenue.

Make sure to spend some time across the street at the museum while you're here. The first thing you'll notice about the Bellavista Fortress is the vast number of pock marks in the walls, especially on the southeast tower across from the Posada. In 1948, this was the Army Headquarters, and the bullet holes mark the defeat of the federal army in the brief Costa Rican civil war. The old fortress was converted to house the museum after the army was formally disbanded and now stands as a monument to Costa Rica's determined national stance as a non-militarized, peace-loving country. While the *museo* captures the politics of the past, the mall running past the Posada attracts the politics of the present. One night we could hear chanting well into the evening as a crowd informed the National Assembly, right next to the museum, of its feelings about free-trade agreements and globalized economies. For seeing the people's Costa Rica, you can't get a better front-row seat than this.

Hotel Le Bergerac $$

San José – Barrio Yoses　　　　　　　　　Destination Restaurant

Photo © Hotel Le Bergerac

Contact Information:
506-234-7850 (voice); 506- 225-9103 (fax)
bergerac@racsa.co.cr
www.bergerachotel.com

Essentials:
28 Rooms
English, Spanish
All major credit cards accepted
Secure parking
Breakfast included, Restaurant serves dinner only.
Room Amenities: TV, Ceiling fan, Refrigerator, Private outdoor space
　　(Superior rooms only)

How to get here:
Ask your cab driver to take you to the intersection of Paseo Ruben
Dario – the eastward extension of Avenida Central – and Calle 37.
This intersection is four blocks east of where Ruben Dario joins with
Avenida 2. Turn south (right if coming from the center of town) on
Calle 37, then right again at the first side street. Hotel Le Bergerac
will be on your left.

Hotel Le Bergerac reminds us of places we have stayed in Paris – modernist, spare, tastefully-decorated, and a bit reserved but with tropical gardens and much larger rooms than you would find in Paris at any reasonable price. Built around three formerly private houses and a split-level main building, all connected by lush gardens with covered passageways, the hotel has many pleasant, intimate spaces for conversations, reading, or just relaxing from your day. Its location, in the upscale Los Yoses suburb between downtown San José and the main campus of the University of Costa Rica, is ideal for its principal clientele of businesspeople and Spanish-language students.

There are four classes of rooms – standard, superior, deluxe and grande – all clean and white and spacious, but a little bland. The closets, however, are knock-your-socks-off. Bring your entire wardrobe! (Okay, I know we're reaching when we talk about the closets, but the reason to stay at the Bergerac is not really for the rooms). The bathrooms, too, are large but somewhat antiseptic feeling. A few primary colors would go a long way. Ask for a superior room so that you'll have a private garden and make sure it's back from the street.

The main reason to stay at the Bergerac is dinner: dinner at the justly-famous Ile de France restaurant of Chef Jean Claude. The Ile de France serves classic bistro dishes, including such standards as stewed rabbit, duck *confit*, and steak *tartare*. We chose beef – *forestiere* and *au poivre vert* – and were rewarded with beautiful steaks, extremely tender and very rare. The wine list is extensive and the service is classically French: the staff hangs around quietly talking, completely nonchalant, but they never let a wine glass reach empty. Dessert was exquisite.

After a dinner like this, you won't want to have to go anywhere else – certainly not by driving through the heart-stopping, potholed chaos of San José. Even a taxi ride would be an injustice to your meal. Tucked as it is onto a small side street, the Bergerac offers the one key essential of urban hotels – a quiet place to sleep. Breakfast at the Bergerac is served in the restaurant or outside in the garden, with hot, obviously just-prepared croissants complementing the standard Costa Rican fare. Room rates include breakfast – we were not even asked for a room number.

The Bergerac would do well to upgrade its bed linens, and we wondered why anyone would still charge even a nominal fee for internet access. But these are minor complaints given our pleasant stay.

Fleur de Lys $$
Central San José   Downtown

Photo © Alison Tinsley

Contact Information:
506-223-1206 (voice); 506-257-3637 (fax)
reservaciones@hotelfleurdelys.com
www.hotelfleurdelys.com

Essentials:
31 Rooms
English, Spanish, German
All major credit cards accepted
Public lot parking
Breakfast included, Restaurant serves dinner only
Room Amenities: TV, Ceiling fan, Refrigerator/minibar (Suites only),
    Jacuzzi tub (Suites only)

How to get here:
Ask your cab driver to take you to the Museo Nacional. The Fleur de Lys is the pink building on Calle 13, half a block off Avenida 2. Your driver will need to go around the block, as Calle 13 is one-way toward Avenida 2.

One of San José's frequent tremors rattled the windows a bit after midnight and woke us up. Costa Rica likes to remind you that the earth is neither firm nor fixed under your feet, so if you are terrified of earthquakes, this may not be the best vacation spot for you. My first realization, after the quake racket subsided, was that the traffic had also stopped. The Fleur de Lys is only half a block from 2nd Avenue, and we'd gone to sleep to a steady background drone punctuated by occasional sirens and fireworks. Now it was quiet.

You've probably stayed in hotels just like the Fleur de Lys if you've traveled much in Europe; it's the kind of solid, middle-class-neighborhood establishment one finds in the staid, non-touristy parts of any European city, often near a university. An older gentleman in an impeccable grey suit greets you at the door and insists on carrying your luggage. The walls are half-paneled in dark wood. The stairs are grand and creak just a little when you step on them. The conversations going on around you are in three or four different languages. Staff and guests are all nicely dressed, so if you're wearing shorts or a T-shirt with some kind of silly slogan on it you feel like an oaf, but everyone politely ignores your discomfort.

The Fleur de Lys occupies two classic old houses, one finished with wood paneling, the other with plaster. Numerous vertical light shafts penetrate the buildings, so every room has windows. We stayed in Daisy (the rooms are all named for flowers) which is built around three light shafts all painted bright yellow. The room positively glows. All the rooms are different and each has its own ambiance; Guaria Morada is the pre-Columbian art room with a glass case full of statuettes and a large diamond-shaped window looking out over the rooftops, while Gloxina – our favorite – is light and airy and has its own private third-floor terrace. There are some odd quirks: two-person fiberglass Jacuzzi tubs are plunked incongruously into the sitting areas of the Master Suites and all the rooms have somewhat disconcerting spray-nozzle bidets built into the toilets. The rooms feature original art; some is lighthearted, but some is positively morose. You may want to ask for a room with happy art. All of the public spaces are filled with art as well, most of it Central American Contemporary but with one roomful of Cubans. All of it is for sale; talk to Thomas, the General Manager, if you're interested.

The Hotel's Restaurant Obelisco is small and intimate and only serves dinner, but it's a dinner worth coming back for. Christian, the German chef, is fond of figs, and his steak with black fig sauce is excellent. There are several other options nearby if you're here on a Sunday when the Obelisco is closed, but why not arrange your hotel schedule around dinner? It's very romantic and your room's right upstairs. Who knows, the earth may move for you, too.

Raya Vida Villa $$
San José – Barrio Amón   Downtown, Art/Architecture

Photo © Raya Vida Villa

Contact Information:
506-223-4168 (voice); 506-223-4157 (fax)
rayavida@gmail.com
www.rayavida.com

Essentials:
4 Rooms
English, Spanish
Visa and MasterCard accepted (7% surcharge); Cash preferred
Secure parking
Breakfast included, Restaurants nearby
Room Amenities: TV, Ceiling fan, Internet available in office

How to get here:
Ask your cab driver to take you to the Hospital Calderón. Continue
past the hospital entrance on Calle 17, then turn right on Avenida 9,
left after one block onto Calle 19, and left again onto Avenida 11. Go
all the way to the end of Avenida 11 (there will be a drop-off in front
of you) and turn right into an alley. The Raya Vida is behind the
black gate at the end of this alley.

The first thing I saw after ringing the bell by the Raya Vida's impressive black gate was Foss the dachshund, racing toward me at full yell. Once inside I realized why this place was so hard to find – it's a truly aristocratic house bearing little resemblance to the surrounding neighborhood. Michael, the owner and innkeeper, later explained that during the social troubles of the 1930's, this grand house and its extensive grounds were guarded by two Panamanian pumas that were released every night to prowl the coffee fields and gardens looking for tasty intruders. We were relieved that Luna, the current watchdog, seemed pretty laid back, and that the Raya Vida's three feline inhabitants were fat and pampered and mainly wanted their ears scratched.

The Raya Vida is a classic B&B, with four guest rooms intermingled among Michael and Tina's own living quarters, but it kind of feels like staying in a museum. Works by European masters grace the walls, together with a substantial collection of Costa Rican artists and various pieces of historical interest. The house itself dates from 1897, and has been renovated with doors, chandeliers, and an antique piano from the home of Adela Jiménez, Costa Rica's famous architect, anti-cancer crusader, and suffragette. Michael can tell you the provenance and significance of every work, as well as the tales of the house and of the various people who contributed to it. Many B&B's embody history lessons, but we've seldom met an innkeeper who seemed to relish the role of curator quite as much as Michael does.

Each of the four rooms has its own private bathroom, and each has a different theme. The Garden Room downstairs and Pineapple Room upstairs where we stayed are the more private. The rooms have comfortable queen beds and (of course!) appropriate artwork. The masks, alas, have gone from the Mask Room, replaced by Currier & Ives prints, but these are *original* Currier & Ives, and are complemented by a lovely Amish quilt – very New England. If you tire of admiring paintings and sculpture, there is a reading room with a large book collection and a TV room with movies. You can sit up on the balcony with a cat on your lap and contemplate the city below. The Raya Vida is backed by the Simon Bolivar Park, part of the San José zoo, so it is one of the quieter places in all of San José.

Michael and Tina don't serve dinner, but for a real treat in that department head over to Bakea just a few blocks away. Chef Camille Ratton is busy inventing her own take on Classic French meets the tropics and doing a lovely job of it. Try the steak *frites* with morel sauce and don't miss the "Cahuita and Caramel," an amazing combination of dense chocolate and caramel ice cream served on a double-sided plate. You'll find yourself planning a trip back to San José just for that.

La Gioconda House $$

San José – Barrio La California   Downtown

Photo © La Gioconda House

Contact Information:
506-248-9422 (voice); 506-223-7522 (fax)
lagioconda@costaricahousehotel.com
www.costaricahousehotel.com

Essentials:
5 Rooms
English, Spanish, French, Italian
All major credit cards accepted
Secure parking lots nearby (about $15 per night)
Breakfast included, Restaurants nearby
Room Amenities: TV, Ceiling fan, Internet (in office), Guest kitchen

How to get here:
If you're taking a cab, tell the driver that La Gioconda is on the corner of Calle 25 and the north side of Paseo Ruben Dario (which is the extension of Avenida Central) right across Ruben Dario from the Nicaraguan Embassy.

A print of *La Gioconda* – the Mona Lisa – smiled down on Antonella and Vincenzo as they sat in their favorite restaurant the night they heard that their offer to buy the old house on Calle Central had been accepted. A year of renovations later, the former residence, bar, and office building, just three blocks from the National Museum, is styled in contemporary Italian with an open-air interior garden, a fountain with lilies and fish, and art on every wall. A portrait of La Gioconda herself smiles enigmatically over the pool table in the reception area, and a larger image provides a landmark to taxi drivers outside.

La Gioconda has an urban edge – unlike many places in San José, there's nothing the least bit dowdy or old-fashioned here – but at the same time maintains a refreshing informality. We arrived about 11 a.m. to find Berta, the cat, curled up between the silk-covered pillows of our just-made bed. You need to like animals to stay here; Berta and Sheila – maybe the world's most laid-back German shepherd – are very present. Antonella relates that several guests have insisted on sleeping with her pets – "cat therapy" for some and "dog therapy" for others. Consider it a bonus included in the price of your room.

The rooms at La Gioconda are sumptuous but whimsical with lots of silk and fancy Italian showers that spray water from multiple heads arranged along the length of your body. As in many European hotels, you need to bring your own toiletries. Each room is filled with art appropriate to its overall theme (e.g. a vintage Bogie and Bacall movie poster for the room called "Casablanca"). "Romeo and Juliette" sports an interior balcony, should Juliette wish to be serenaded. We recommend Cielo Azul, the upstairs room, for privacy and quiet. A mural of a classic county scene gives the interior courtyard a pastoral feeling. In the afternoons and evenings, Antonella and many of the European guests light-up over a cup of excellent coffee in this courtyard, so if you object to smoking this may not be the place for you.

The Parque Nacional with its monument to Central America's struggle against Confederate imperialist William Walker and San José's Contemporary Art Museum, located in the old National Liquor Factory, are a ten-minute walk from La Gioconda. If you're up for a movie, Cinema Magaly is just around the block. It's one of those classic late-modern theaters with an enormous screen, lots of angles in the ceiling, and extremely comfortable seats.

Lots of hotels can arrange tours, but La Gioconda is also an office of Antonella's travel agency, Solutions (www.solutionscr.com), so you can arrange your entire trip, including air travel, with one call. It's no wonder La Gioconda, which just opened in November, 2006, is already very popular with North American and European travelers.

Grano de Oro

San José - Barrio Colón

$$-$$$$

Destination Restaurant

Photo © Alison Tinsley

Contact Information:

506-255-3322 (voice); 506-221-2782 (fax)

granoro@racsa.co.cr

www.hotelgranodeoro.com

Essentials:

40 Rooms

English, Spanish

All major credit cards accepted

Secure parking

Breakfast included, Restaurant, Bar

Room Amenities: TV, Ceiling fan, Refrigerator/minibar, In-room safe,
    Internet access at reception desk

How to get here:

Any cab driver will know the Grano de Oro. If you are coming from
the San José International Airport on your own, continue past the
Sabana Park on Highway 1, then turn left with everybody else at the
end of the park, following signs to Cartago. Go six blocks and turn
left again; the Grano de Oro's parking lot is at the end of the second
block ahead on your left (look for "HGO" on the iron gate). The hotel
is the Victorian building to the north, across the Avenida 4.

I saw them as soon as I stepped out onto our private courtyard – fish, at least two dozen goldfish, swimming in the courtyard fountain. We've stayed in many hotels with fountains and many hotels with fish, but our very own fish, in our very own fountain, was a first. We were in San José dealing with more of the endless *tramites* – meetings, paperwork, delays – that are the lot of the expatriate and, as far as we can tell, native citizens as well. It was raining. We must have looked a bit pitiful because Marco, the general manager, checked our reservation and immediately upgraded us to a nicer room. The huge bed, terrycloth robes and, to top it all, our very own fish, were just what we needed.

The Grano de Oro offers casual elegance with touches of the quaintly historical. Walls of photos from the 1890s and 1930s show women in factories, wharves full of bananas, serious-looking politicians, and Costa Rica's ill-fated army (abolished in 1948 after their defeat by "Don Pepe" Figueres' uprising). Occasionally, the sumptuously grandiose takes over – like the Romanesque upstairs patio with its two hot tubs, arbors and colonnade. The attention to detail and courtesy is impressive here: signs appear in the hallways, every evening, requesting quiet after 10 p.m. The rooms are arranged along short hallways joined by open-air courtyards, each with a fountain and its own garden, so each little cluster of rooms feels like its own small hotel. The magnificent, classically-furnished Vista de Oro suite, on the third floor, looks over the rooftops to Poás and Barva.

We return to the Grano de Oro every chance we get, if not to stay for the night, at least for a meal; the restaurant is one of the best in San José. The Grano de Oro has recently completed a major addition, incorporating a neighboring Victorian house to create four new rooms and a completely new, two-level dining space with an enclosed open-air patio and a two-sided, sunken bar. The new entryway and lobby are international contemporary style, with lots of glass and floor-to-ceiling bamboo screens – quite a contrast to the Victorian exterior and the Plantation interior of the original hotel. Unlike in many such architectural mélanges, though, it all fits. The new downstairs bar and dining room are dark-wood Edwardian and there is an equally elegant upstairs dining room that can be booked for private functions. The guestrooms in the new wing have soft pastel walls and, like the deluxe room of our first stay, their own private gardens with fountains. (No fish, however. Too bad.)

The Grano de Oro runs like clockwork, with the incredibly efficient Marco keeping a watchful eye on everything. This is the way all lodgings should run, with perfectly orchestrated grace. We expect the Grano de Oro will be the most famous place to stay in San José for a long time to come.

Casa de las Tias $$
San Rafael de Escazú   Downtown

Photo © Alison Tinsley

Contact Information:
506-289-5517 (voice); 506-289-7355 (fax)
casatias@kitcom.net
www.hotels.co.cr/casatias.html

Essentials:
5 Rooms
English, Spanish
All major credit cards (surcharge) and U.S. personal checks accepted
Secure parking
Breakfast included, Restaurants nearby (take a cab), Honor bar
Room Amenities: Ceiling fan, Refrigerator (shared), TV in dining room

How to get here:
The easiest way to get here is by cab. If you are driving from Juan Santamaria airport, take Highway 1 toward San José, then exit to the right onto Highway 39, the San José ring road. Get off the ring road onto Highway 27 toward Escazú and Santa Ana. Exit Highway 27 toward Escazú and proceed to "El Cruce," the Y-intersection in front of the Scotiabank in Escazú. Go straight for one block from the Y, then turn left into the 2nd of the two adjacent driveways (the first is Restaurante Cerutti's).

El Cruce (the cross) is the former heart of ferociously upscale, *gringo-fied* Escazú. It's the corner where the old road from San José divides, with half of it going straight on to neighboring Santa Ana and the other half turning south up the hill to Escazú. Escazú is actually three towns – San Rafael, right around El Cruce; San Miguel, the bigger town a few blocks up the hill; and San Antonio, just a handful of streets about a kilometer to the south. A Scotiabank, a Mas o Menos grocery store, and a cluster of upscale shops mark El Cruce, but the commercial heart, the true center of 21st century Escazú, has migrated west to the area around the huge Multiplaza shopping center and the Intercontinental hotel.

Casa de las Tias is a pleasant house at the end of a surprisingly-quiet alleyway just a couple of blocks from El Cruce. An unexpected bonus to staying here is its proximity to Bolaños airport just north of Escazú across the Rio Tiribi canyon. We were leaving the next morning on a Nature Air flight out of Bolaños and, since Casa de las Tias is just a few minutes to the airport by cab, the owners graciously allowed us to leave our car in their secure parking lot.

The guestrooms at Casa de las Tias are upstairs in what must have once been small, but comfortable, family bedrooms. Each is decorated with folk art and original drawings and paintings from a Central or South American country. Much of the artwork is by Coriolano Leudo, co-owner Pilar's Colombian grandfather. The decorations are quite eclectic, from very traditional to contemporary, including an aviator's map of Costa Rica showing safe flying altitudes and a wooden marionette who transforms herself into a flame-haired woman by leaping through a pane of glass.

It is a quick walk from Casa de las Tias up to the center of San Miguel de Escazú, which still maintains its character as a Costa Rican town. The central plaza has a lovely church, with the usual Costa Rican trees and park benches, a place where teenagers come to hang out in the afternoon and their parents come to hang out in the evening seeing their neighbors and chatting about the day's events. We had visited this plaza on our very first day in Costa Rica, completely by chance, on the morning of the second Sunday in March, the morning of the annual oxcart festival. Brilliantly painted traditional oxcarts were everywhere as were teams of oxen, farmers and their families in traditional costume, battered pick-up trucks, and vendors of every kind. Quite the introduction to our new country.

Aside from the ludicrously-expensive Restaurante Cerutti right next door, dinner pickings are pretty slim in walking distance from Casa de las Tias, so you'll probably want to take a cab to one of the many places on the road to Santa Ana. You can also do as we did and pick up supplies at one of the good delis in the Plaza Colonial just down the street and have a picnic on the front porch.

Hotel Posada Canal Grande $$
Piedades de Santa Ana   Relax/Get Away

Photo © Alison Tinsley

Contact Information:
506-282-4089 (voice); 506-282-5733 (fax)
info@hotelcanalgrande.com
www.hotelcanalgrande.com

Essentials:
12 Rooms
English, Spanish, French, Italian
All major credit cards accepted
Secure parking
Swimming pool
Breakfast included, Restaurant, Bar
Room Amenities: Refrigerator, TV, In-room safe

How to get here:
The easiest way to get here is by cab. If you are driving from Juan
Santamaria airport, take Highway 1 toward San José, then exit to the
right onto Highway 39, the San José ring road. Get off the ring road
onto Highway 27 toward Escazú and Santa Ana. Exit Highway 27
toward Santa Ana, then turn right at the T-intersection. Continue to
Piedades. Take the first right after the light; Posada Canal Grande
will be on your left.

The old road from San José to Escazú continues to Santa Ana and then to Ciudad Colón and Santiago de Puriscal. By the time you get to Piedades, half way between Santa Ana and Colón, you've left the highly developed, crowded suburbs for rural Costa Rica. The Posada Canal Grande is only 15 minutes from the international airport and 20 minutes from downtown San José, but is firmly planted in the countryside. You're more likely to be awakened by roosters crowing than by traffic.

We arrived a bit before noon, and most of our fellow guests were arrayed by the pool – some chatting, some sunning, and some sleeping blissfully in lounge chairs or the antique Indian daybed with its sheer curtains. This is clearly a place where people come to recover from trans-Atlantic jetlag or to rest up a bit after a week or so of hard adventuring. The Canal Grande is a classic colonial hacienda – the kind of place you find in Granada, Nicaragua, or Antigua, Guatemala, or central Mexico – with its residential wings embracing the garden and pool. Its style suggests careless aristocrats and slightly tarnished luxury, with fine antiques from India, Indonesia, and Central and South America arranged in a relaxed and somewhat haphazard manner throughout the public spaces. This is a perfect place for transitioning between vacation in Costa Rica and your regular life in the outside world.

The guestrooms are large and well-equipped with wickerwork bed-frames, tiled bathrooms, and peaked ceilings upstairs. Although not elegant, they're bright and comfortable. Ask for an upstairs room (# 6 to 12); they're more private and share a broad tiled balcony looking west over the Virilla river valley. On a clear day you can see the Gulf of Nicoya and the mountains above Montezuma. There is also a good view of Poás and Barva volcanoes due north across the urbanized Central Valley.

Right next door is the Canal Grande Restaurant, Italian like the hotel. If you're staying for a couple of days and are looking for local color, both Ciudad Colon and Puriscal farther up the mountain are real Costa Rican towns with few of the trappings of ex-pat influence and tourism that color Escazú. For alternative dining, it's better to head back toward San José. Santa Ana is only about five minutes away. Our favorite place there is Bacchus, contemporary Italian in a metro-chic setting.

Alajuela and Heredia

The Juan Santamaria International Airport is just across Highway 1 from the city of Alajuela. It's Costa Rica's second largest city, the capital of the State of Alajuela which extends from the Nicaraguan border down to the city itself. Right next door on the way to San José is the city of Heredia, a university town that is also a state capital. Both cities have nice central plazas, but are basically working towns without a whole lot for a visitor to see. The most famous building in Heredia is El Fortin, a 19th century fortification designed with gun slits that open the wrong way so as to easily allow hostile fire into the building. Oops! Major design flaw.

There are several perfectly comfortable, pretty generic, American-style hotels within a short cab ride of the airport. The nicest in our opinion is the Hotel Bougainvillea, between Heredia and San José. It looks the same on the inside as any airport hotel in the U.S., but has a large and lovely garden outside. Hotel Bougainvillea is a favorite with birding tours, and is a good near-the-airport choice if you want air conditioning, satellite TV and free shuttle access to San José.

Many other hotels within a short ride of the airport also have shuttles or will at least pay for your cab. If you're arriving at Juan Santamaria, insist on one of the legitimate orange airport taxis; you pay for the trip in advance at a kiosk inside the airport. Riding with an unmarked pirate cab is an excellent way to get ripped off.

The roads between and around Alajuela and Heredia resemble an overturned plate of spaghetti, none of them have names or road numbers and there are precious few directional signs to anywhere. There are lots of little towns, but no signs announcing their names. If you're staying in this vicinity (and you probably will be at least for your first night) get a cab to your hotel. Most rental car companies are happy to deliver your car to any area hotel the next morning. If you are planning a day of touring around the Central Valley, consider putting off the rental car for a day and hiring a driver/guide. Most hotels can set you up with one for little if anything more than the cost of a day's car rental plus gas. Many drivers are multilingual, so ask for one who speaks your language.

Alajuela is the gateway to Poás Volcano, one of two in Costa Rica that can be accessed easily by car (the other is Irazú, east of San José). The easiest approach is via the road that passes straight through Alajuela from the airport; the other routes are harder to identify and it's easy to get lost among the countless unmarked turns and identical-looking coffee-farming villages. The other must-visit in the Alajuela area is Zoo Ave, a rescue, rehabilitation, and education center for Costa Rica's bird life that features endangered *titis* (squirrel monkeys) and other mammals as well. It's on the road from Alajuela to La Garita; the easiest way to get there is to take the La Garita exit from Highway 1 (look for the signs to Jacó) and backtrack to the right towards Alajuela. Zoo Ave will be on your left in about one km.

Pura Vida Hotel $$

Alajuela - Tuetal   Relax/Get-Away, Destination Restaurant

Photo © Pura Vida Hotel

Contact Information:
506-430-2929 (voice); 506-430-2630 (voice/fax)
info@puravidahotel.com
www.puravidahotel.com

Essentials:
2 Rooms, 4 Casitas
English, Spanish, French, Chinese
All major credit cards accepted
Secure parking
Breakfast included, Dinner available by arrangement (guests only)
Room Amenities: Ceiling fan, Coffee maker, Refrigerator (except
    Orchid and Volcano), In-room safe, Private outdoor space (except
    Orchid and Volcano)

How to get here:
Take a cab – Pura Vida pays (tell the cab driver Pura Vida in *Tuetal*).
From Juan Santamaria Airport, get on Highway 1 going west away
from San José and then exit immediately to Alajuela. Drive on this
road straight through the center of town. As you leave Alajuela, you
will pass the courthouse on your right, then cross a bridge; take the
next left after this and then bear right at the Y. The Pura Vida is one
km farther, on your left.

Berni and Nhi's Pura Vida Hotel is our stopover of choice when we're leaving Costa Rica at an absurd time in the morning or getting in after dark. It's ten minutes from the airport, cabs will arrive from around the corner at 4 a.m. if you need them to, and yet it's far enough out of Alajuela to feel like the countryside. In fact, the Pura Vida, like many of the hotels around here, is on what was once a small coffee farm. When you walk through the gate here, you know you're in a different country. It's the perfect place to start – or finish – a trip to Costa Rica.

The Pura Vida manages to combine the intimate atmosphere of a family B&B – this is, after all, Berni and Nhi's (and their three magnificent German shepherds') house – with the privacy of your own comfortable, well-equipped casita in the garden. This being a former coffee farm, the garden is nearly vertical, with the four casitas arrayed on different terraces on the way down. You'll get some exercise climbing up to breakfast from Katydid, the two-bedroom casita that is our favorite, but the steep, densely-planted garden makes for plenty of privacy. Think of the steps up to the main house as practice for hiking around in Monteverde or the Osa Peninsula.

Make sure you arrange in advance for dinner at the Pura Vida. Alajuela isn't known for great restaurants, and even if it were, it would be a hard job to compete with Nhi's delicate fusion of tropical and Chinese-Vietnamese cooking. If you're lucky you may be treated to hand-made spring rolls, Kung-Pao chicken with serious Thai chiles, and an almost indescribable melted dark chocolate soufflé for dessert. Or maybe you'll have traditional Costa Rican holiday tamales made with a pillowy fine-grained corn flour completely unlike tamales you've had elsewhere. Whatever appears, you're bound to be delighted. You may find yourself staying a few extra nights just to get more chances for dinner.

Offer to share a glass of wine from the well-stocked fridge and Berni may read you some choice bits from his forthcoming book, *My Sister Thinks We Live in a Mud Hut*, an exposé of the trials of moving from sunny Southern California to Costa Rica and starting a business. Ask him about his adventures with ICE – the Costa Rican electric and phone company – or with local electricians and plumbers. You may still be sitting there at midnight listening to Warren Zevon wondering how on Earth anyone could negotiate the bureaucratic and cultural mazes of Central America, and at the same time plotting your own move to the land of former coffee farms, runaway real-estate deals, and next-to impassable highways. Forewarned is forearmed!

Orquideas Inn $$-$$$
North of Alajuela   Kid-friendly, Happening Place

Photo © Orquideas Inn

Contact Information:
506-433-9346 (voice); 506-433-9740 (fax)
info@orquideasinn.com
www.orquideasinn.com

Essentials:
19 Rooms, 6 Suites, 1 Dome
English, Spanish
All major credit cards accepted
Secure parking
Swimming pool
Breakfast included, Restaurant, Bar
Room Amenities: AC, TV, Ceiling fan, Coffee maker, In-room safe,
    Internet access (main lodge)

How to get here:
From Juan Santamaria Airport, get on Highway 1 going west away
from San José and continue west to the exit for La Garita, Atenas, and
Jacó. Turn right at the top of the ramp; continue until you get to a T-
intersection with a modern-looking church and the La Princessa
Marina restaurant in front of you, then turn left. Cross a bridge and
then turn hard right at the next main road. The Orquideas is on this
corner to your right.

The sign said "Marilyn Monroe Bar" so we trotted down the stairs to see what *that* could be like. They aren't kidding – the walls and ceiling of this fine little haven are a continuous collage of Marilyn memorabilia: movie posters, promo shots, fashion shots, first-day-of-issue postage stamps, playful nudes, and some intimate, informal photographs that could have been taken by a family member, but probably weren't. There are even a few bottles of Marilyn-label wine from a California vintner. Erich, the manager, explains that the former owner of this grand colonial-style house, now the main public area of the Orquideas Inn, assembled the collection for his Harvard classmate and occasional houseguest, John F. Kennedy. Today it's inhabited by a different kind of houseguest: in a *nicho* high on one wall stand a brass urn and an ornate, gold-plated Continental Airlines beer mug above a somewhat faded photograph of a man in a pilot's uniform. The urn contains the ashes of the pilot, who moved into the hotel after he retired. They say his ghost roamed the place at night until the barkeep started leaving his favorite stool down at the far end of the bar where he always sat.

We can see why the old pilot might have liked the Orquideas. Right outside the bar is a sparking blue-tiled pool surrounded by walls of bright yellow, deep bright blue, and an orangey-red like the inside of a guayaba. The whole hotel picks up the color scheme. Every room in the buildings down the hill among the little waterways and big old-growth trees is a different combination of bright hues. The airy new building on the hilltop above is composed of softer pastels. Red, green, and blue macaws and chestnut toucans reside in aviaries among the trees (the Orquideas participates in a bird rescue and captive-breeding program). Orchids hang in the foliage around the secluded outdoor hot tub; several friendly dogs, all adopted strays, lounge around, greeting whoever passes.

The rooms here range from colorful and well-appointed up to grand suites with carved doors and rosewood floors. Down the hill by the restaurant and pool it feels like the jungle, with the sound of running water, the chattering of macaws, and lots of shade. Up the hill is an open vista; the rooms look out onto Poás, Barva, and Irazú volcanoes. Up here is the new spa, a big circular *rancho* used mainly for weddings and dances, and even a small conference center. If you prefer contemporary to colonial styling and want a view, stay up on the hill, but our favorite at Orquideas is the dome – a private two-story geodesic casita with a kitchen, sunken bathtub, and upstairs sleeping loft. It's completely private, down in the jungle, near the well-hidden hot tub.

The Orquideas Inn is only minutes from the San José airport, but once you're here you're definitely out of town. Pull up a stool and order a tequila. A hundred Marilyns smile upon you.

Xandari $$$-$$$$
Alajuela   Honeymoons, Hiking, Spa, Art/Architecture

Photo © Alison Tinsley

Contact Information:
506-443-2020 (voice); 506-442-4847 (fax)
reservations@xandari.com
www.xandari.com

Essentials:
22 Villas
English, Spanish
All major credit cards accepted
Secure parking
2 swimming pools, Spa
Breakfast included, Restaurant, Bar
Room Amenities: Ceiling fan, Coffee maker, Refrigerator/minibar, In-
    room safe, Private outdoor space, Free WiFi (main lodge)

How to get here:
From Juan Santamaria Airport, get on Highway 1 going west away
from San José, then exit immediately to Alajuela. Drive straight
through town; as you leave town, you will on the road to Poás
Volcano. Three km after the last traffic light, you will cross a bridge.
Turn left after the bridge, following the Xandari sign. When you
reach the village of Tacacori, turn right, then bear right at the Y.
Xandari will be on your right.

What if Adam had been an architect with a liking for Luis Barragán and I. M. Pei, Eve was a multi-media contemporary artist, and they'd been given the job of decorating the Garden of Eden and building some really cool houses? The result would have been something like Xandari, built and decorated by architect-and-artist team Sherrill and Charlene Broudy. Perched on a high ridge overlooking the Central Valley half a kilometer below, Xandari is a colorful fantasy of curving walls, flowering trees, and Charlene's light-hearted sculptures. The 22 villas are bright and roomy with private courtyards and patios, high arched ceilings, stained-glass windows, and lots of art. Every one has a surprise – in ours (#5) a brightly painted bamboo pole extended floor to ceiling in the bathroom infusing the entire space with a riot of color.

The grounds here are as spectacular as the buildings and trails wind through the gardens, orchards, and steep jungle below. Color is everywhere. Bird of paradise, heliconia, and tall ginger flowers are complemented by startling sculptures, many covered with ceramic, metal, or mirrored mosaics. We walked down the perfectly-maintained trail to Xandari's five waterfalls on the Tacacori River including one that leaps 70 feet over a sheer face of black rock. The sun doesn't make it down into the steep river canyon until mid-day, but when it does there are pools under the waterfalls deep enough for a refreshing plunge and a cold high-volume shower. Blue-crowned mot-mots must be the Xandari national bird; they were everywhere.

A highlight at Xandari is the spa, acclaimed as one of the best in Central America. Treatments are offered in individual, utterly-private thatched *palapas* scattered through the lush gardens, each with its own half-moon Jacuzzi hanging over the jungle below. Alison had a facial and reflexology treatment with Alejandra who worked so gently and silently that she had to tell Alison when she was finished. After her treatment, Alison was so relaxed she could hardly move. We sat watching the lights of Escazú and Santa Ana twinkling below us and the planes coming and going from Juan Santamaria airport. Xandari is so high and nestled in the hills so skillfully that not a sound comes from the airport below; the big jets seem to take off and land like ballerinas, in complete silence.

You are only a few minutes from Alajuela here, but there is no reason to go anywhere else for dinner. We were unsure what to try for dessert after our excellent cuts of mahi-mahi, Alison's served with mild red and green sauces and mine with a ferocious wasabi, so Randall our waiter surprised us appearing with a chocolate mousse pie topped with a light froth of cappuccino in cream. Perfect! Xandari was created by Sherrill and Charlene to express a certain sense of relaxed, pleasurable engagement, the aim as well as the experience of their aesthetics. We were there.

Finca Rosa Blanca

$$$-$$$$

Santa Barbara de Heredia

Relax/Get away, Art/Architecture,
Destination Restaurant

Photo © Finca Rosa Blanca

Contact Information:
506-269-9392 (voice); 506-269-9555 (fax)
info@fincarosablanca.com
www.fincarosablanca.com

Essentials:
3 Rooms, 4 Suites, Two 2-BR Villas
English, Spanish
All major credit cards accepted
Secure parking
Swimming pool
Breakfast included, Restaurant, Bar
Room Amenities: Ceiling fan, Coffee maker, Refrigerator/minibar, In-
room safe, Bathtub, Free WiFi, Private outdoor space

How to get here:
Arrange with Finca Rosa Blanca to pick you up at the airport.
Otherwise, download the directions from Finca Rosa Blanca's website
and follow them. You'll need a navigator. If you get confused, ask
someone where the Café Britt center is in Santa Barbara; the road to
Finca Rosa Blanca is right across the street.

Soft morning light pours in through the narrow arched doorway that leads out to our balcony. Floor-length white cotton curtains frame the door. Alison meditates on the balcony; I just gaze out at the terraced green hills and the white clouds and still-grey mountains in the distance. There's a fresh but almost imperceptible breeze and a hint of brown on the trees that says early fall. It's the kind of scene that the Impressionists painted, an early fall morning in Provence. Except the tree in the foreground is a *cecropia*, and the low bushes growing on the terraces are coffee, heavy in this season with red berries. This is Costa Rica, the "Cafetal" room at Finca Rosa Blanca, a few kilometers above Heredia. And an impressionist *has* painted the scene; it covers the entire wall behind me, in a soft-edged pointillist style. All I have to do to switch from reality to imagination is turn my head.

Finca Rosa Blanca is set on a south-facing ridge surrounded by flower gardens, citrus and banana orchards, massive *higueron* fig trees and, past them, acres of coffee cascading down the rolling hillsides. Everything about this place is soft, from the ancient fused grey trunks of the *higuerons*, to the lazy curves of the free-form swimming pool, to the contours of the house itself. The white stucco walls of the house seem to melt into the ground and the three-story tower with its 360-degree windows looks like a lighthouse designed by Gaudi with Don Quixote's flat-brimmed helmet for a roof. The windows take on fanciful curves with shapes like leaves or petals. Even the steel stair railings and the pillars supporting the balconies writhe down to the ground like lianas. Step in the front door and you are on the mezzanine of an open circular space surrounded by glowing, blond and soft-brown wood – the inside of an enormous hollow tree. Dinner's in the making in the kitchen below and a cup of coffee or a glass of wine awaits you. You cannot help but feel welcome.

Every room at Finca Rosa Blanca is different, and every one is a work of whimsical art. For those in the mood, the two-story master suite is the crown jewel, its bedroom the round top floor of the lighthouse tower. You ascend by a spiral staircase with flower petals for steps and toucan heads carved into the ends of the banister. The rooms are all decorated by Oscar Salazar's colorful murals, tile mosaics, owner Glenn Jampol's or various friends' paintings, and local crafts. Downstairs in the circular sitting room, the indoor garden behind the *banco* blends with a painted jungle; even the kiva fireplace, often roaring with a real wood fire, is covered with a hillside of flowers and coffee. Here you can relax with fellow guests sipping red wine, talking about recent adventures, and eagerly awaiting tonight's closing work of art, the fabulous dinner you are about to be served.

Atenas – Grecia Area

West of Alajuela, Highway 1 descends to cross the Colorado River on a spectacular high bridge then ascends again to San Ramón and the final mountain passes between the Central Valley and the Pacific coastal plains. The tangled ridges and deep valleys of the Rios Colorado and Grande are rich agricultural lands with sugar cane growing at lower elevations and coffee and vegetables on the higher slopes. Early in the colonial period these hills were the frontier, an area where the indigenous Huetares Indians held out against Spanish encroachments from the Central Valley to the east and Puntarenas to the west. Fragments of colonial-era walls still stand overlooking the Rio Grande gorge at La Garita, once the guarded western gate between the wild lands and the populated Central Valley.

The little town of Atenas sits on a ridge high above the Rio Grande, not quite half way between San José and Puntarenas. Highway 3, which follows the path of the old ox-cart road that carried coffee from Central Valley plantations to Puntarenas for the long voyage around Cape Horn, passes through Atenas. A monument on the highway celebrates the *boyeros*, the ox-cart drivers who made the long trek on foot. Today Highway 3 is the fastest way from the San José area to the long string of Central Pacific beaches from Jacó down to Manuel Antonio, and legions of city-dwellers pass this way every weekend. For those in the know, Highway 3 is the preferred route to Nicoya and the northern Pacific as well as it bypasses the agonizingly slow, perpetually foggy stretch of Highway 1 between San Ramón and Esparza. A new highway is scheduled to go from Santa Ana to the central Pacific, but it's been on the books for about 12 years now.

On the northern side of Highway 1, the slightly larger town of Grecia is the center for the farming communities on the western slopes of the *Cordillera Central*. Grecia is the gateway to the furniture-making town of Sarchí and the string of small traditional towns, each sporting an unusual 19th century church that extends up the mountain to Zarcero. West of Grecia is Palmares, site of annual festivals every January and February that draw thousands of people, mostly young, for outdoor concerts, horse events, and fireworks.

Expats from many countries live in the hills, valleys, and towns between San Ramón and Alajuela, but you'd never know it; unlike in the beach towns or Escazú, *extranjeros* around here blend in with the local population. If you're in these parts and looking for company, your best bets for finding compatriots are the local cafés. In Atenas, try Kay's Gringo Postres (i.e. desserts), Alida, home of the best pizza in the area, or La Trilla, our favorite *restaurante tipico*.

We have a special fondness for Atenas. It's small, it's friendly, and according to *National Geographic* magazine, Atenas has "the best climate in the world," never cold and never very hot with afternoon rain in the rainy season and sunny days the rest of the year. It says so on the side of every Atenas bus, and everyone in Costa Rica seems to know it. Besides, we live here. You can check us out on VRBO (# 117923).

Photo © Kelly McGinley

Colinas del Sol $

Atenas　　　　　　　　　　　　　　　　Relax/Get Away

Photo © Alison Tinsley

Contact Information:

506-446-4244 (voice); 506-446-7582 (fax)

infohcs@hotelcolinasdelsol.com

www.hotelcolinasdelsol.com

Essentials:

8 Rooms

English, Spanish, German, French

All major credit cards accepted

Secure parking

Swimming pool

Restaurant, Bar

Room Amenities: Ceiling fan, Kitchenette with refrigerator, Cooktop, Coffee maker, Toaster, and Kitchen gear

How to get here:

Coming from the San José area on Highway 3, turn left into Atenas at the Farmacia and drive six blocks to the corner in front of the school. Turn left for one block, then right for one block, then left. Follow this road 600 meters; Colinas de Sol will be on your left.

Sunny Colinas del Sol is about a mile east of the center of Atenas on the back road down to Rio Grande, the road that will one day connect Atenas to the long-promised new, fast highway from San José to the central Pacific coast. If you've been price shopping around the Central Valley, then Jürgen's room rates at Colinas will seem like a real find. Where else this centrally located can you find a nice room with its own kitchenette plus a nice pool and gardens for so few *colones*? It's no surprise that most of the guests here come back year after year, or that some change their travel plans the day they arrive. One couple booked at Colinas for a week and ended up staying for almost three months!

The four duplex cabins at Colinas del Sol stair-step down the hill in front of the pool with dense plantings in between for privacy. The rooms aren't fancy, but are large and well-furnished and have half-cathedral ceilings so they stay cool. Each has a full-wall picture window looking out into the garden and its own porch with table, chairs, and hammock. Best of all, every room has a well-equipped kitchenette with all the tools you need for basic cooking. Not up for kitchen work on vacation? The restaurant at Colinas serves all three meals in an open-air dining area looking out over the Rio Grande valley. The food is simple but wholesome and the ambience is great.

It's a quick walk or quicker cab ride into central Atenas, with its markets, *tipico* restaurants, and local color. Busses leave downtown Atenas hourly for Alajuela or San José; the fare is about one dollar. You can catch the San José to Jacó bus at the stop across from the Farmacia to get to the beach. You can also arrange for tours with a multi-lingual guide to almost anywhere from Colinas del Sol. Actually, Colinas del Sol is a great place to just park yourself for your time in Costa Rica. Atenas is smack-dab in the center of the country and relatively easy to access from almost everywhere. English-speaking taxi drivers can also take you anywhere in the country; we recommend Walter Taxi Tours at 873-4266.

Jürgen has built several houses on the six-hectare Colinas del Sol property which he manages as rentals for their owners when they're away. It's an ideal situation. Your own Costa Rican retreat, but when you're ready to go home you just lock-and-leave. Watch out – Atenas is just about a perfect place to live. Let your guard down for even a minute and Jürgen is likely to be building your house in Costa Rica next.

Ana's Place

Atenas

$-$$

Downtown

Photo © Alison Tinsley

Contact Information:
506-446-5019 (voice); 506-446-6975 (fax)
info@anasplace.com
www.anasplace.com

Essentials:
8 Rooms, 2 Suites with kitchenettes, One 2-BR apartment
English, Spanish
All major credit cards accepted
Secure parking
Swimming pool, Massage pavilion
Breakfast included, Dinner can be arranged
Room Amenities: Ceiling fan, Guest kitchen (by pool; shared), Private
    outdoor space (Garden rooms, Suites, Apartment)

How to get here:

Coming from the San José area on Highway 3, turn left into Atenas at
the Farmacia and drive four blocks to the corner behind the church.
Turn left and drive three blocks. Ana's Place is behind the gate on
your right.

It's Sunday morning and we're enjoying a lazy brunch of eggs benedict in Ana's garden surrounded by conversations in soft Canadian English and occasional squawks from the three resident macaws. Ana's is only three blocks from the central plaza in Atenas, but Atenas is small enough and Ana's old family property is big enough that the feeling in the garden is of a stately country inn. Sunday bunch at Ana's is a good time to meet people; we know North American ex-pats who come here every week for a Sunday-morning get-together. For us, it's a special-occasion place where we take friends visiting from the U.S.

Ana's Place is the closest lodging to central Atenas and also the oldest; it's been here almost 20 years. Ana started with four colorful rooms in her house, then added two duplex cabins in the garden, and finally the two-story house with two suites downstairs and a two-bedroom apartment with a wonderful balcony upstairs. Ana's place is very popular for long-term stays. Many of her guests come for several weeks and one couple rented her apartment for two years. Atenas is a good central location for tours north and east to the farming and craft towns and the volcanoes, or west to the central Pacific beaches. But we also see guests from Ana's at the town market or walking the back roads around Atenas with their birding binoculars. Whenever we're there, we see plenty of folks just relaxing in the garden, talking to the macaws or reading their books.

Our favorite room in Ana's main house is Quetzal, which overlooks the garden and is somewhat quieter than the rooms in the front of the house. Colobri and Rohaila, the two smaller main-house rooms, share a bathroom. The Monkey-Jaguar duplex in the garden has lots of privacy and is perfect for families; Jaguar has a queen bed while Monkey has two singles. Each of the rooms has its own theme and color so check the web if you're partial to vivid or tranquil, elegant or whimsical. All the rooms share a well-equipped guest kitchen in the garden's central *rancho* by the pool.

If you're planning a longer stay and want to be able to cook, the suites have kitchenettes and the apartment has a full kitchen. There are plenty of places to get groceries within a short walk, and you'll be only two blocks from the fabulous Atenas Friday market where every kind of fresh fruit and vegetable as well as some meats and prepared foods are on offer. So move in. Ana's Place can be home.

El Cafetal $$
Santa Eulalia   Relax/Get Away

Photo © El Cafetal

Contact Information:
506-446-5785 (voice); 506-446-7361 (fax)
cafetal@cafetal.com
www.cafetal.com

Essentials:
14 Rooms, 1 Casita
English, Spanish
All major credit cards accepted
Secure parking
Swimming pool, Massage pavilion
Breakfast included, Restaurant, Bar
Room Amenities: Ceiling fan

How to get here:

Coming from the San José area, take the Grecia exit off Highway 1
just before the Rio Colorado bridge. Take the first left off the Grecia
road and follow this narrow paved road under the Highway 1 bridge,
down to the river, across the one-lane bridge, and back up the other
side. Turn left over the bridge at the "Y Griega" bar. El Cafetal is at
the top of the next hill on your right.

A *cafetal* is a coffee field and you're surrounded by them in Santa Eulalia among the narrow ridges and deep canyons of the Rio Grande and its many tributaries. We didn't know what a coffee plant looked like when we arrived here on the third day of our first trip to Costa Rica. We'd been cooped up near Escazú, fighting the traffic and having some real second thoughts about our choice of vacation spots. When we got off the *Interamericana* (Highway 1) and dropped down into the Rio Colorado canyon, we thought, "this is more like it!" Then we walked through El Cafetal's high front entryway and saw the sweeping view from the back garden. We knew that we'd arrived. This was the real Costa Rica, what we'd come all this way to see.

El Cafetal sits high on a ridge over one of the little rivers feeding the Rio Grande, looking over the *cafetals* and citrus and mango plantations that patchwork the hills and valleys of Santa Eulalia. There is coffee growing on the property – you'll be served the Inn's own "La Negrita" brand of dark roast – as well as oranges, bananas, and avocados. Trails wander through the plantings down to the river. We followed one our first morning and wandered a mile or so up the river itself, splashing through the shallow rapids in our hiking sandals. Howler monkeys had greeted the dawn. We'd seen a toucan. We'd swung in the hammocks under the arbor of brilliant magenta bougainvilleas. The perpetually-snarled traffic in Escazú was a distant memory.

Since our first visit, El Cafetal has added an open-air restaurant, Rincon Llanero, and four bungalows down by the clover-leaf pool. The new rooms are larger and a bit fancier, but our favorites are still the corner rooms in the main house with their floor-to-ceiling half-cylinder windows looking out over the valley, private balconies and 180° views. Ask for # 16 or the slightly larger #18. You won't be disappointed.

Breakfast at El Cafetal is a feast with fresh juices from the property's fruit trees and an interesting variety of vegetable dishes in addition to the usual Costa Rican fare. The breakfast tables are each on their own little terraces in the garden, so you have your meal in the dappled sunshine surrounded by the morning birds. We left El Cafetal for the Pacific utterly refreshed and very happy with our decision to come to Costa Rica. Best of all, Alison had a fabulous massage from El Cafetal's local masseuse, Norma Bolaños, who we still call whenever we're feeling creaky. Let them know when you're coming to El Cafetal, and they'll arrange an hour of bliss with Norma in the garden. Don't hit the road again without it.

Posada Mimosa $$
Grecia - Rincon de Salas   Kid-friendly

Photo © Alison Tinsley

Contact Information:
506-494-2295 (voice); 506-494-5868 (voice/fax)
mimosa@mimosa.co.cr
www.mimosa.co.cr

Essentials:
4 Rooms, 2 Suites, 1 Cabin, 2 Houses
English, Spanish, German
All major credit cards accepted
Secure parking
Swimming pool
Breakfast included, Dinner can be arranged
Room Amenities: Ceiling fan, Refrigerator (by pool; shared), Full
     kitchen (Suites and Houses)

How to get here:
From Juan Santamaria Airport, get on Highway 1 going west away
from San José. About 15 minutes from the airport, exit towards
Grecia; the exit is just before the deep Colorado River canyon.
Continue about two km; across from the factory turn right. If you see
the San Cipriano church, you've gone too far. Follow this road three
km then turn right following a sign to Posada Mimosa. The driveway
is on your left. Ring the bell at the painted gate.

The first time we drove up to Posada Mimosa, we were a bit concerned. We'd been on the road all afternoon from Arenal, it was getting late, and there were big *"Perro Bravo"* (aggressive dog) signs on the first gate down by the road and again by the brightly-painted main gate up the arbor-shaded driveway. We rang the bell, the gate opened, and we proceeded cautiously. Then we saw them: Hansi, Suzy, Fritzi, and Max, tails all wagging – the Dachshund welcoming committee. They escorted us to the office, showed us to our room, and then guided us down to the pool where our host, Martin, was waiting with a bottle of wine and – how nice! – three glasses. We talked about living in Costa Rica, watched a fine sunset, and even saw some toucans. It was our first trip down from the States, and we were really liking this country.

Everyone in Costa Rica has a story, and Martin and Tessa tell theirs in *Potholes to Paradise*, Tessa's book about moving to Costa Rica and building Posada Mimosa. The area around Grecia is still traditional central valley – small towns, twisting roads, acre upon acre of coffee or sugarcane, hardy cattle grazing slopes too steep to plant. Except for the furniture town of Sarchí, it's not very touristy, and you have to learn Spanish and get along with the locals. A sense of humor helps. We learned something about Martin's the next morning when he showed us his exercise trail with an array of weight-lifting machines constructed of ropes, strong sticks, wire baskets of rocks, and convenient overhanging tree limbs. Local ingredients and ingenuity: the basic tools of pioneers everywhere.

Posada Mimosa spreads out down a broad hill, the main house with its brilliant gardens at the top, the pool in the middle, and guest cabins and a few private homes below. We stayed in the main house in one of the three rooms on the deep south-facing verandah. What a place to just sit in your rocker, watch the hummingbirds, and smell the flowers! The rooms have windows and doors on both sides, antique furniture, and black-and-white family pictures on the walls. Grandma's house in the tropics. Walk down to the pool and the scene changes; you're looking out at the mountains south and west of Escazú across the valley. Martin will point out the "sleeping lady," with her ridge of wavy hair stretching out to the east. The guest cabins on the slope below have kitchens and anywhere from one to three bedrooms and often rent by the month. Our favorite is the "small cabin" with its great mountain view, private deck, and "paintings" made from dried Owl and Morpho butterflies by Richard Whitten, the tireless insect collector and conservationist whose Jewels of the Rainforest museum awaits you up in Monteverde.

Be prepared to be enchanted. Posada Mimosa is where we decided to get serious and make another trip to Costa Rica to look for real estate.

Vista del Valle Plantation Inn $$-$$$

Rosario   Honeymoons, Hiking, Horseback riding

Photo © Vista del Valle

Contact Information:
506-450-0800 (voice); 506-451-1165 (fax)
frontdesk@vistadelvalle.com
www.vistadelvalle.com

Essentials:
10 Cabins, 6 Condos, 2 Houses
English, Spanish
All major credit cards accepted
Secure parking
Swimming pool, River access
Breakfast included, Restaurant (with room service), Bar
Room Amenities: Ceiling fan, Free WiFi, Private outdoor space. Ilan-
    Ilan casita is wheelchair accessible, Mango Manor, Exotic Woods,
    and El Nido have kitchenettes, Condos can be rented with or
    without full kitchens

How to get here:

From the San José area, take Highway 1 west toward San Ramón,
then take the first exit after the Rio Colorado bridge. Continue west
about 200 meters along the frontage road, then turn left following
signs to Vista del Valle. The hotel gateway will be on your left in
about one km.

Do you want to be half an hour from the San José airport but feel like you're *really* in the country and have luxurious digs and a great restaurant to boot? Vista del Valle, on the other side of the Colorado River only about ten minutes from San Ramón and the road to Arenal, is the place for you. Keep your schedule flexible; you won't want to stay here just one night.

Vista del Valle hangs over the edge of the Rio Grande canyon within shouting distance of the confluence of the Rio Grande with the Colorado. These are fast rivers off the encircling mountains and there's some serious white water down there. The canyon and the slopes to the west are part of the more than 3,700 acre Rio Grande Canyon Nature Preserve. You can walk down into the canyon straight from Vista del Valle, but be advised: it's steep. Especially coming back up.

We visited Vista del Valle in foaling season, and the resident walking-horse herd had just been enriched by frolicsome new colts. Horse tours are a Vista del Valle specialty with the most special being an evening full-moon ride up over the mountains for a late picnic, usually with local riders from the village of Rosario and the countryside around. Hard to beat for traditional festive ambiance.

Vista del Valle offers ten artfully-constructed cabins, two of which are duplexes with shared central kitchens. All are tucked into the garden on the upper slopes above the river and have private decks or porches with great views. Our favorites are the honeymoon cabins, Mona Lisa and Ilan-Ilan, which are more secluded than the others and have spectacular views. In addition to the cabins, Vista del Valle manages six contemporary-styled duplex condos with separate living room and kitchen buildings. You can rent one or both bedrooms, with or without the living room and kitchen. If even the condos aren't large enough for your taste and budget, there are two houses for rent when their owners aren't there.

We shared lunch in Vista del Valle's spacious new open-air restaurant which overhangs the canyon for a lovely view to the west, with Johanna who built this place with her husband Mike. Like many of the better hotels in Costa Rica, Vista del Valle is not just a lodging; it's a social and environmental project. The 25 hectare property itself is mostly forest reserve contiguous with the Rio Grande Preserve. Most of the staff is from Rosario and many have learned their trades here. Mike is a former Peace Corps volunteer and trainer, and he and Johanna have food and micro-credit projects in neighboring Nicaragua. So when you're staying here, you're contributing to many people's lives, as well as to the local environment. Sustainability at its best.

Cartago area

Cartago, named for the ancient trading city of Carthage in North Africa, was founded by Spanish colonists in 1563, forty years after the founding of Granada in neighboring Nicaragua. The "*costa rica*" (rich coast) of the conquistadors who followed Columbus had proved to be not all that *rica* after all, with fierce inhabitants, inhospitable coastal terrain, and nothing in the way of exploitable minerals. The Cartago colony subsisted on small-scale agriculture in the fertile valleys south of Volcán Irazú high above

the malarial coast. The independent, entrepreneurial nature of Costa Ricans today is often attributed to its founding as a nation by small-scale farmers, a cultural beginning more similar to that of New England than to the rest of Spanish Central America.

The Cartago area still feels like the heartland, but there's nothing "colonial" about this city, at least nothing still standing. Cartago's first cathedral, destroyed twice by earthquakes, is a spectacular ruin, but most of the old city has simply been built over. Eclipsed by San José in the early 1800s, Cartago experienced the coffee boom as a provincial city, not as the capital. Industrialization and 20th century population growth were focused elsewhere. Cartago remains a small city of churches and colleges surrounded by small towns and agriculture, its horizons dominated by Irazú to the north and the peaks of the Talamancas to the south. When you arrive here, it's clear that you've left the noise and bustle of San José behind.

An hour east of Cartago on the old road to Limón is the railroad town of Turrialba which has the frontier feeling of a mining town in the Colorado Rockies in the U.S. (at least it does for Chris, who has a weakness for old mining towns).

Just north of Turrialba higher up the slope of Volcán Turrialba is Guayabo, the largest Pre-Columbian city thus far discovered in Costa Rica, already populated in 1,000 BC. It was abandoned before the Spanish came; as is usual for ancient cities in Central America, no one knows precisely why.

Adventurous travelers come to Turrialba to raft the Reventazón River which drains much of the rainy northern slopes of the Talamancas including the Lake Cachi basin. Some rafting companies maintain their own riverside lodges; the Turrialtico, just east of Turrialba on the road to Limón, is a favorite of rafters arranging their own lodging.

Lake Cachí itself is fed by the Rio Grande de Orosi, centerpiece of the beautiful Orosi Valley. Orosi is the perfect traditional Costa Rican coffee town with its 18th century adobe church, town square, and near-vertical

terraced plantations. It is also the northern gateway to the enormous Tapantí National Park which extends over the northern slopes of the Cerro de la Muerte (the Mountain of Death, so named for early travelers from the Pacific coast who succumbed to the cold there). With extreme luck you can see jaguars here, just like those early Spaniards did when they cleared their little farms in this wilderness 450 years ago.

Orosi Lodge $
Orosi   Hiking

Photo © Orosi Lodge

Contact Information:
506-533-3578 (voice/fax)
info@orosilodge.com
www.orosilodge.com

Essentials:
6 Rooms
English, Spanish, German
All major credit cards accepted
Off-street parking
Public hot springs next door
Breakfast included, Café serves coffee and pastries until 7 p.m.
Room Amenities: Ceiling fan, Coffee maker, Refrigerator/minibar,
    Internet access in café

How to get here:
Follow the main road from Paraiso down the mountain into Orosi.
Turn right two blocks after the central plaza, following signs to the
balneario (hot springs and baths). The Orosi Lodge is at the end of this
road on your left, just before the entrance to the hot springs.

We checked into the Orosi Lodge before lunch and Andy gave us pointers for our exploratory drive around the valley. The Orosi - Cachí valley is surely one of the prettiest spots in Costa Rica – not grand, not stunning, just pretty in the settled, well-tended way little valleys are when they have been looked after lovingly by generations of inhabitants. It was January – early dry season – and flowers bloomed everywhere. We crossed the Rio Grande and followed the river through forests interspersed with planted fields. Orosi – Cachí is the valley of coffee and trout. We sampled both at the Casona restaurant, just south of the town of Cachí, with its dining patio hanging over a scenic bend in the lake. Brilliant orange poró trees bloomed all around us.

After lunch we continued around the lake to Ujarras where the grateful villagers built a magnificent church in the 1680s to thank the Virgin for her aid in defeating a raid by English pirates. The church is now a ruin, but its thick stone walls still stand thanks to the innovative mid-wall buttresses that were invented here and then used throughout the Americas. We've seen churches like this in New Mexico and Arizona; seeing this one with its happy little stream, beautiful bright-orange *poró* trees, and flocks of noisy parrots brought back memories, but also a real sense of history. What a contrast between this lush tropical valley and the mountainous deserts of our northern home! Who were the frontier architects who had carried a style of buttress from Ujarras to Santa Fe? It had taken us two weeks to drive that distance. How long had it taken them?

We returned to Orosi in time for afternoon espresso at the Orosi Lodge café where we stocked up on organic Turrialba coffee and some local artwork for our guestroom in Atenas and consulted with Andy about early-morning hikes in the surrounding countryside. Anything you might want to do in the area, from river trips or horseback rides to an evening in the hot springs at the fancy Rio Perlas resort outside of town, you can set it up here. Andy and Connie have been in Orosi for years and seem to know everyone in town. And you don't want to miss Connie's fabulous apple cake; pick some up before the café closes at 7:00 so you'll have it on hand after dinner at one of Orosi's little *sodas*.

Rooms at the Orosi Lodge are simply furnished but very comfortable with European-style individual comforters on the beds and a generous supply of coffee and tea for the morning. The three rooms upstairs have a nice view from the balcony and the advantage of no one walking around on the floor above you during the night. The town hot springs is right next door, and the central plaza with its famous adobe church is only three blocks away. The jukebox downstairs plays classic rock and roll interspersed with Latin swing and calypso. A perfect place to just make yourself at home.

Casa Turire $$-$$$$
East of Turrialba   Honeymoons, Hiking, Horseback riding

Photo © Alison Tinsley

Contact Information:
506-531-1111 (voice); 506-531-1075 (fax)
turire@racsa.co.cr
www.hotelcasaturire.com

Essentials:
12 Rooms, 4 Suites
English, Spanish, French, German
All major credit cards accepted
Secure parking
Swimming pool, Lakeside
Breakfast included, Restaurant, Bar
Room Amenities: TV, Ceiling fan, Coffee maker, Refrigerator/minibar,
    In-room safe, Bathtub, Private outdoor space, Internet access in
    reception

How to get here:
Follow the old highway toward Limón (Highway 10) from Cartago
through Turrialba. A few minutes out of Turrialba, you will pass
CATIE, an agricultural research center, then cross a bridge. After the
bridge, turn right toward La Suiza. Turn right again at the sign for
Tucurrique; the driveway to Casa Turire will be on your right.

Lake Angostura was perfectly calm, and we swept across it in Casa Turire's sea kayaks. Besides the ducks, Alison and I had the water to ourselves. Quite a nice break from always-windy Lake Arenal or the crowds at the beach. Yellow flycatchers rose and dove from the trees along the shore; around one bend solemn black vultures held a silent committee meeting, wings outstretched, drying in the early sun. We made a passage around the lake in about 45 minutes then racked our kayaks and headed up to breakfast on Casa Turire's elegant poolside patio. What a transition – here four or five languages were being spoken, German and Costa Rican kids shared the pool, and formally-attired waiters served coffee.

Casa Turire is a grand plantation-style house set on expansive grounds surrounding Lake Angostura which covers the narrow valley that once held Turire's private golf course. There are touches of every kind of architecture here, from the grand verandah of a classic country house to the airy cathedral-ceiling interior and the Italian art deco flourishes around counters and over doorways in the dining room, but everything fits. The atmosphere is comfortable, welcoming, and self-assured without even a hint of pretension. And there's something for everyone – a dark-wood sitting room if you'd like a cigar, a private gazebo with a swing surrounded by hibiscus if you're feeling romantic, horses if you care for a romp through the countryside and, of course, the kayaks if you don't mind getting a bit wet.

Rooms at Casa Turire are ample and well-equipped and most have pleasant balconies overlooking the lake. There is a grand two-floor master suite that could be in an early 20th century New York hotel. It has a balcony covering one whole end of the building, overlooking the entryway fountain, the stately palm-lined driveway and the fields beyond. But the real stars here are the two junior suites on the third floor with high balconies looking down onto the lake. If you're planning a honeymoon, ask for one of these.

Casa Turire's property is still a working farm. Just down the drive is the main barn housing the riding horses together with goats, cattle, geese, and even a few Asian flat-horned buffalo. Gardens here grow the organic vegetables and greens you'll enjoy at dinner. Turn left at the barn and you enter a path that takes you around the lake; a gentle walk of a couple of hours perfect for a picnic. Or arrange a horse and guide for a longer tour past the sugarcane fields up into the surrounding hills.

After your day's adventures, it's time for drinks on the verandah or by the pool followed by a dinner even more elegant than breakfast. The menu is continental with a Costa Rican touch, artfully prepared, graciously served, and very tasty. Don't skip dessert!

Rincon de la Vieja to Tenorio

Inland from the coast, the high plains of northwest Guanacaste remind us of the mountains of southeastern New Mexico around High Rolls, Cloudcroft and Lincoln County. Billy the Kid country. The hills are dry and brown in "summer" – January through May – and green and lush in the rainy season. There are big cattle ranches and beautiful narrow country roads with no traffic. Folks are friendly and a bit laconic. The wind can howl through the canyons with tremendous force. The difference is that here the big trees are covered with showy pink flowers in January. And the big mountains on the horizon are active volcanoes.

The northwestern volcanoes are not as high as the monsters in the center of the country – Volcán Rincon de la Vieja, at 1,806 meters, would easily fit inside 3,432 meter Irazú – but you're looking at them from almost sea level, and from there they're pretty impressive. A sequence of national parks protects the peaks but they're not contiguous like the parks in the southern mountains and so provide less of a protected corridor for wildlife. The critters are up here, though. The area is not highly populated and even outside the parks there's lots of open country for animals to roam in.

Aside from the Pacific beaches, northwest Guanacaste is not highly developed for tourism. Lodges tend to cluster around the entrances to the national parks. Rincon de la Vieja (the old woman's corner, or hideout) is the most popular. It is Costa Rica's answer to Yellowstone with boiling lakes, boiling pots of thick multi-colored mud, and spouts of hot water and steam surrounding the active Von Seebach Crater and several inactive – or to be safer, one might say "less frequently" active – craters. We've heard that the Hacienda Santa Maria, now the park headquarters, used to be a Central American hideaway for Lyndon B. Johnson. It's easy to see how the harried Texan president would have liked this place. It must have reminded him of home – the quiet of the big open ranches with their cattle and wildflowers. And, in the 1960s, the nearest telephone was miles and miles away.

Farther south past Miravalles, Tenorio National Park extends almost to Lake Arenal and is bordered by private reserves that protect southern lake view slopes. Most of the park is over the border in the State of Alajuela, and its more eastern location gives it cloudier, wetter weather. Road access is minimal, so few people visit Tenorio. To visit the famous blue waterfalls, take the dirt road toward La Carolina Lodge off Highway 6 just north of Bijagua and turn right at the fork by the little store in the village of San Miguel, following the sign to the *cataratas*.

If you're traveling in this area, you'll probably find yourself in Liberia, the capital of Guanacaste and the biggest town around. It's a good place to stop if you want to check your email; there are several internet cafes around the central plaza. For a quick lunch, try Tinaje, directly across the plaza from the church where you can sit on the porch and watch small-town life passing by. Except for the Spanish, the cell phones and the pickup trucks from Korea, Japan, and China ("Great Wall" brand), you'd think you were in the American mid-west, circa 1955.

Casa Rural Aroma de Campo $
Curubandé   Hiking, Horseback Riding

Photo © Alison Tinsley

Contact Information:
506-236-8100 (reservations); 506-665-0008 (hotel); 506-665-0011 (fax)
info@aromadecampo.com
www.aromadecampo.com

Essentials:
6 Rooms, Camping on lawn
English, Spanish, French, German, Dutch
Cash only
Secure parking
Breakfast included, Lunch and dinner available, Honor bar
Room Amenities: Ceiling fan, Internet (in office)

How to get here:
About four km north of Liberia, turn east off Highway 1 toward
Curubandé. Follow the dirt road through Curubandé. Aroma de
Campo is on the left, about two km past the town. If you continue on
this road, you will reach the Las Pailas entrance to Rincon de la Vieja
Park.

The conversation around the big, rough-hewn dinner table was a curious mixture of Spanish, English, and Dutch. We were all heading up to Rincon de la Vieja the following morning and Charlie, who owns Aroma de Campo with his wife, Maureen, pulled out maps, books, and binders full of his own pictures whenever questions came up about things to see or how to get to various places. He will guide the tour himself, especially if it involves Rincon, waterfalls, and horses. He recommended Las Pailas, the three kilometer trail through the forest to the boiling lakes and mud-pots on the western slopes below the steaming Von Seebach Crater, for the first-day's hiking.

You can stare into the acid-green mire of Poás or gaze at the smoking slopes of Arenal, but for getting up close and personal with a volcano, it's hard to match the Pailas trail at Rincon de la Vieja. Huge *higueron* fig trees tower over the rocky path, their narrow buttress roots fanning four or five meters from the main trunks before plunging under ground. Birdsong and the skittering of small creatures is everywhere. Steam billows incongruously from the green woods; as you approach, you hear the hiss of boiling water and realize that the active vents are practically beneath your feet, hidden from view by fallen limbs, undergrowth, and the ubiquitous stones. Miniature craters filled with grey, green, and yellow muck boil away; the air smells heavily of sulfur. The devil, perhaps, indulged in a few too many black beans last night? Dip your hand into the little streams that you cross; the water is warm. Around the next bend you see why as you encounter a frothing, electric blue lake fringed with bright yellow. The ground around looks crusty and fragile with purple and lurid-orange soil. Signs warn that temperatures are well over boiling. Definitely not a place to go wandering off the trail.

Back at Aroma de Campo, our fellow adventurers arrayed themselves in the hammocks and Adirondack chairs on the shaded patio. Chattering in Dutch, three children were having the time of their lives watering the thin grass with paper cups from a big plastic bucket. A diminutive dachshund made improper advances to an aloof Persian cat. Alison browsed in the trading library with its titles in English, Spanish, Dutch, German, French, and Hebrew. I contented myself with a well-earned beer.

Aroma de Campo has six rooms named for the colors that they're painted. We like the rooms designed for couples – the Purple room on the southeast corner looking toward the volcano and the dawn or the Pink room on the west side with its view of the sunset over the distant Pacific. Blue has bunk beds and Yellow has three singles, perfect for children or budget-minded backpackers. If you're there on the weekend, you may have a treat – Maureen's Thai cooking. Otherwise, meals are Costa Rican with a touch of Belgian, good with a dark beer and a conversation in several languages.

La Carolina Lodge $$
San Miguel de Bijagua   Honeymoons, Hiking, Horseback Riding

Photo © Alison Tinsley

Contact Information:
506-380-1656 (voice); 506-466-6079 (Spanish only)
info@lacarolinalodge.com
www.lacarolinalodge.com

Essentials:
4 Rooms, Two 1-BR cabins, One 2-BR cabin
English, Spanish
Cash only
Secure parking
Riverside, Hot tub
All meals included
Room Amenities: Ceiling fan, Fireplace

How to get here:
Turn east off Highway 1 onto Highway 6 just past the Corobici river
bridge north of Cañas, following sign to Upala. Follow Highway 6
north about one hour to Bijagua. About six km past Bijagua, turn
right onto the dirt road just after the Mirador bar. Follow this road to
the little town of San Miguel; take the left fork right after the bar. La
Carolina is on your right, just before the narrow bridge.

Ah, La Carolina. Easy to get to, but in the middle of nowhere. Family-style, but *muy romantico*. One of our favorite getaways in all of Costa Rica.

The first thing to do when you get to La Carolina, rain or shine, is to strip down to the minimum necessary, hold hands with your honey, and trot down to the stone pool by the rushing little Chumillo river where a wood-fired iron heater keeps the water a wonderful 100 °F – perfect soaking temperature. We've lounged in a lot of hot tubs, and this ranks as one of the best anywhere: deep enough for total immersion, wide enough to do the backstroke, with broad *bancos* for sitting all the way around, and constructed entirely out of the smooth stones of the river. If you start to cool off, toss some more wood from the pile into the smoking furnace. If you get too warm, it's over the side into the cold pool right below or into the river itself with its swift currents and waterfalls. After the long drive to get here, this is heaven. They simply don't make water fresher or better than this.

La Carolina Lodge nestles in the thick forest on the northern border of Tenorio National Park surrounded by a 170-acre working ranch and private reserve. Don and Bill, two surfing buddies from South Carolina, bought the ranch with its old *casona* (farmhouse) twelve years ago and have restored, refurbished, and reforested with respect for local tradition and a keen eye for comfort. The wonderful hot tub is just the start; in your cabin you'll find thick blankets (it can be cold up here) big fluffy bath towels, your own fireplace, and plentiful tall candles in coconut-husk candleholders. Flickering kerosene lamps light the paths at night. There are wooden shutters on the windows and wooden pegs for hanging things everywhere you might want one. The perfect mix, says Alison, of yin and yang, comfort and practicality. Frontier Feng Shui here in the mountains of Costa Rica.

The blue waterfalls of the Rio Celeste are only a few kilometers from La Carolina near the border of Tenorio Park. For a shorter walk, just head up the trail along the Chumillo River – La Carolina has a mile of river frontage – through the deep woods and over the ridges on the network of trails and farm roads through the surrounding countryside. Keep a watchful eye out for tiny, red frogs with blue legs. Or hop on one of La Carolina's horses stabled just around the corner from the main lodge, and persuade Don to show you around the *finca*.

After a day of soaking, swimming, and roaming the hills, guests gather in the rocking chairs by the roaring outdoor fireplace next to the kitchen where dinner is cooking over wood fires. You'll eat basic *Tico* fare at the long table by candlelight. Bring some wine to share with new friends. After dinner the woods are dark and quiet in the soft flickering light with night birds and rushing water. *Muy romantico*.

Arenal Volcano and Vicinity

For many visitors to Costa Rica, the first exploratory drive heads
from San José's airport over the central *cordillera* to Arenal volcano –
Costa Rica's continuously active fiery mountain – and continues past
scenic Lake Arenal to Santa Elena and the Monteverde Cloud Forest
Reserve. From here the paths diverge. Some visitors return to San
José, others head west to the Nicoya Peninsula or south to the beaches
of the central Pacific.

From San Ramón to Fortuna, Costa Rica 142 winds through rolling
hills and misty, forested mountains – a splendid introduction to the
overwhelming green of Costa Rica. Just before the high pass over the
cordillera is the little town of Los Angeles Norte and the splendid
Villa Blanca Hotel – a great place for your first night if you got into
the San Jose airport early and you don't want to stay in the city. Once
over the pass, you are deep in rural Costa Rica. Then it all changes in
Fortuna: this is a tourist town full of cafes, tour operators, and
inexpensive hostels.

Photo © Chris Fields

El Volcán Arenal towers over Fortuna, dwarfing the town and
everything in it. Arenal exploded to life in July 1968 while students
were rioting in Paris and America still reeled from the King and
Kennedy assassinations. The eruption wiped out the farming
community of Pueblo Nuevo north of the mountain, burying 15
square kilometers in black cinders and ash. Arenal has been active
more or less continuously ever since. The last big eruption was in
March 2001, but the volcano steams and hurls smoking rocks into the
air almost daily.

There's someplace to stay every few meters, it seems, from Fortuna to the Lake Arenal dam. Most offer a volcano view, but keep in mind that it's pretty cloudy up here most of the time – we didn't see past the broad base of Arenal until our third visit. If the congestion on the main road doesn't appeal but you still want a volcano view, head up to Leaves and Lizards above El Tanque – brand new, off the beaten track, quiet and very private. And the view across the valley to the mountain can't be beat.

Other than rich soil and fireworks, the volcano's gift to the area is hot springs. The famous Tabacón Resort is by far the nicest and has a great spa, but it's also pricey – $45 a person just to get past the gate. For a lower-priced and more *Tico* alternative, try Baldi; it has a restaurant, spa, two swim-up bars, and 16 pools ranging from lukewarm to a blistering 172 degrees F. Further off the beaten track are the hot springs at Aguas Zarcas on the property of the Occidental Hotel El Tucano. The springs in the river are nice but the hotel is a bit odd; they regarded us with extreme suspicion when we showed up to look around, and we never could get them to tell us their prices.

Wooden signs posted by the government warn visitors that right under the volcano is "alto riesgo" – high risk – for volcanic activity. If you feel an earthquake up here, it might be time to get out of Dodge, double quick. You never know when a visit to Arenal might include some real excitement.

Villa Blanca Cloud Forest Hotel and Spa $$$
East of Los Angeles Norte   Spa, Birding, Art/Architecture

Photo © Villa Blanca Cloud Forest Hotel and Spa

Contact Information:
506-461-0300 (voice); 506-461-0301 (fax)
information@villablanca-costarica.com
www.villablanca-costarica.com

Essentials:
34 Cabins
English, Spanish
All major credit cards accepted
Secure parking
Breakfast included, Restaurant, Bar
Room Amenities: Coffee maker, Ceiling fan, Refrigerator/minibar, In-
room safe, Free WiFi (main building)

How to get here:
Turn east (right if coming from San Ramón) off Highway 142 in Los
Angeles Norte, at the sign for Villa Blanca. Follow the dirt road
bearing left (downhill) at the Y-junction. The road ends at Villa
Blanca's gate. Note that this road is one lane and can be very foggy.

You don't have to go all the way to Monteverde to see a real cloud forest; in fact, the morning mist was so thick when we emerged from our cabin at Villa Blanca that we could barely make out the main building of the lodge which was just above us on the top of the hill. Walking through the woods in clouds this dense is otherworldly, especially when the woods are thick with exotic tropical flowers, delicate ferns taller than you are, and massive, gnarled trees dripping with mosses, bromeliads, and orchids. Even the birds are tentative on mornings like this, and the forest is, for the most part, quiet. It's as though it's waiting for the sun to finally emerge, in late morning or maybe after lunch, and turn the forest and hillsides sparkling green. Then, in the evening, the mist rolls back in turning the lights on the footpaths into soft glowing spheres and covering everything in silence.

Villa Blanca feels like a grand estate – and it was. Before its conversion into a luxury resort in 2004, this was the private retreat of former Costa Rican President Rodrigo Carazo. The gardens and forestland of the hotel border the 2,000 acre Los Angeles Cloud Forest Reserve. A lovely little chapel dedicated to President Carazo's wife Estrella sits on the property, its ceiling an amazing mosaic of hand-painted tiles made and arranged by Rebecca Fernández Zeledón, Doña Estrella's sister. Additional works by Fernández Zeledón grace the main building together with paintings by various other artists.

The cabins at Villa Blanca are comfortable and well equipped, and all have that wonderful luxury in a high-altitude location – a fireplace with plenty of split wood, firestarters, and matches. If you are reserving a standard cabin, ask for # 29 or 30; these have bathtubs. The five honeymoon cabins (# 22 – 26) have private porches shielded from view by dense garden plantings. The deluxe cabins are larger and have separate bath and shower rooms but no outdoor space to themselves.

It's hard to get too far into the woods at Villa Blanca – there is a nice one-km nature trail, but the reserve exists mainly for the animals, not for you. Longer walks require a guide ($24 per person), and even the guided trails are only a couple of miles. For longer trips, visit the horseback outfitters up the road toward Los Angeles. Or just relax. There are plenty of locations for adventurous hiking in Costa Rica; Villa Blanca is about serenity, relaxed luxury, and a sense of wonder about your surroundings. Sit in the spacious living room of the main building in front of one of the two big stone fireplaces; order a drink from the bar and watch the evening clouds descend. Dinner is waiting, and it will be beautifully presented and very tasty. Just ask for tonight's Special and don't forget dessert. Your cabin is just down the hill and the clouds, like a heavy snowfall, assure you a perfectly silent night.

Hotel La Garza $$
South of Muelle   Relax/Get-away, Horseback Riding

Photo © Alison Tinsley

Contact Information:
506-475-5222 (voice); 506-475-5015 (fax)
info@hotellagarza.com
www.hotellagarza.com

Essentials:
12 Cabins, 2 Rooms
English, Spanish,
All major credit cards accepted
Secure parking
Swimming pool
Breakfast included, Restaurant, Bar
Room Amenities: AC, Ceiling fan, Private outdoor space

How to get here:
From San Jose, drive via San Ramón and Highway 142 instead of Highway 141 to Ciudad Quesada which is a major truck route. Turn east just south of San Isidro towards San Ramón and Florencia. From Florencia, go north on Highway 35 toward Muelle; La Garza is on the west side of the road between Platanar and Muelle.

Bucolic is the word that comes to mind as you park in the clearing and gaze across the Rio Platanar to the old *casona* – the farmhouse – and its flowering gardens. Walk across the narrow suspension bridge to the farm, and you are back maybe 50 years to a rural Costa Rica before villages were overtaken by roads and everything was mechanized. OK, you'll have to ignore the TV over the bar and the farmhands studiously surveying the pool table. But La Garza is still as close as you're likely to come to the quiet atmosphere of an era that managed somehow to be tough and gracious at the same time.

La Garza farm doesn't have the bustle it must once have had, but it still devotes almost 70 hectares to dairy cattle and horses. As we practiced our yoga on our cabin's private patio one morning, we watched one of the farms *caballeros* riding out with his dog along the river, and half an hour later returning with at least two dozen horses spread out in a long line, the dog busy with the stragglers. The front desk will organize a ride for you along the river or up into the farm's 170 hectares of primary and secondary forest. Or you can fish or bird-watch or just sit and watch the river flow. Slowness seems in order here.

La Garza's six duplex cabins face the river on the bank opposite the *casona* (the side you can get to by car without fording the river). The rooms are spacious and well-furnished (if slightly rundown) and have deep wrap-around decks with chairs and hammocks. Thick plantings separate the cabins, so your outdoor space is all your own. It's a five-minute walk among the bromeliad-laden trees along the riverbank to the suspension bridge, the *casona*, and the pool/playground area beyond. The path is nicely lit at night, but there's nothing garish. Out here, you want to be able to see the stars.

Dinner is served in the *casona* in an atmosphere of rustic elegance. It is in the subtle lighting of the evening that the well-tended age of this place becomes evident. A century old is *old* for a wooden farmhouse in the tropics, and the hardwood floors gleam with use. The menu is hearty and varied, but we asked the chef what he recommended that evening and were rewarded with generous plates of roast pork and buttered vegetables, followed by a delicious peach cheesecake. Lights glimmered on a Christmas tree decorating the verandah, and one of the farm's dogs sprawled on the sidewalk across the railing from our table, eyeing us from time to time for a scrap of pork. We could easily have been family guests, long ago.

As tourism in Costa Rica takes on a faster pace and an increased focus on "must-see" destinations, places like La Garza are slipping even farther off the beaten path. You have to really look for this kind of tranquility to find it anymore.

Erupciones B&B $$

North Side of El Volcán Arenal   Kid-friendly

Photo © Alison Tinsley

Contact Information:
506-833-0038 (voice);   506-460-8000 (fax)
arenal-erupciones@hotmail.com
www.erupcionesinn.com

Essentials:
11 Rooms
English, Spanish, German
All major credit cards accepted
Secure parking
Breakfast included, Restaurants nearby
Room Amenities: TV, AC, Ceiling fan, Refrigerator/minibar

How to get here:
Follow Highway 142 northwest from La Fortuna; Erupciones is on the
south (i.e. left) side of the highway about 10 km from La Fortuna. In
other words, right under the volcano.

We were standing on the front porch of one of Erupciones Inn's deluxe rooms, looking up at El Volcán Arenal. Smoking-hot rocks bounded down the volcano's slopes, heading straight for us. It must not have been our time though. They stopped well short of the little river that runs behind Erupciones Inn's property and buffers it from the volcano's slopes. This is about as close to Arenal's north slope as you can get: the *address* for Erupciones is "Frente al Volcán Arenal." Too bad it was cloudy that night; the fireworks must have been impressive.

In contrast to its many larger neighbors, Erupciones Inn is a small, family-operated B&B. It offers three minimal but comfortable standard rooms in an orange-and-blue bungalow, six deluxe rooms with refrigerators and air conditioners, and two bright yellow junior suites. The rooms aren't fancy, but they all have big windows facing the volcano and that's what you're here to see. The deluxe rooms and junior suites are closer to the volcano, but only slightly. Every room has a porch with an unimpeded view.

Jessenia Vasquez, your host, is one of the main reasons to stay at Erupciones Inn. After just moments with her, you feel like family. She knows all the local history and, it seems, everyone in town. She can tell you where to eat, where to find a great hot spring, and fill you in on all the current gossip. Children, pets, and guests surround her and she lavishes attention on them all.

Jessenia can arrange visits to any of the nearby sites and, at least when we were there, she passed her tour commissions on to her guests. Take a hike or horseback tour to the extinct Cerro Chato volcano with its crater lake, check out the cloud-forest hanging-bridges tour just on the other side of the Rio Arenal, or take a canoe or float trip in search of wildlife with Canoa Aventura. If it's a sunny weekend, just head down the road to the Arenal Dam – on the right kinds of days the bridge turns into an uninterrupted party, with what traffic there is squeezing between parked cars, family picnics, and impromptu dancing powered by 12-volt boom boxes.

Erupciones Inn is just part of the Vasquez family business; the rest of the property is a working cattle ranch. Breakfast, served down at the family house, comes from the farm. You can walk up to the river or take a tour of the family *lecheria* where the cows are milked. Or take a horseback tour to the very base of Arenal where the land angles upward in an abrupt cone. Watch out for those smoking rocks, though!

Arenal Volcano Inn $$
North Side of El Volcán Arenal   Destination Restaurant

Photo © Alison Tinsley

Contact Information:
877-281-8515 (U.S.); 506-461-2021 (voice); 506-461-1133 (fax)
info@arenalvolcanoinn.com
www.arenalvolcanoinn.com

Essentials:
14 Rooms
English, Spanish
All major credit cards accepted
Secure parking
Swimming pool
Breakfast included, Restaurant, Bar
Room Amenities: TV, AC, Ceiling fans, Private outdoor space

How to get here:
Follow Highway 142 northwest from La Fortuna; the Arenal Volcano
Inn is on the north (i.e. right) side of Highway 142, nine km northwest
of La Fortuna.

Looking for a quiet place with all the modern conveniences for volcano viewing? Needing a base camp for river rafting or other Arenal-area adventures? Or maybe you're thinking of staying at Tabacón but don't like the price. The answer is simple and just up the road – the brand new, sparkling clean, and nicely-appointed Arenal Volcano Inn. There are a gazillion hotels in this price range or just above lining the road between Fortuna and the bridge, but they're all pretty generic. Arenal Volcano Inn has more character and charm than most.

One of the many nice features of Arenal Volcano Inn is the location of the rooms – set back from the road, amidst nice gardens, overlooking a lovely, large-enough-to-really-swim-in pool. The rooms aren't fancy, but they're light and bright with colorful walls, comfortable queen beds, and all the appliances you'd expect in a hotel room in the States. Another plus is that they are each in separate casitas (except for the four connectable "family" rooms by the pool), and each has its own volcano view patio.

And what a view it is! You're across the road and out of the defined eruption danger zone, but the volcano still looks like it's right on top of you. The casitas have been carefully placed to look directly at the monster. The view is a little west of north, but there's been plenty of lava visible from that direction recently. You can easily hear the beast rumbling away through the night.

If you tire of volcano watching or soaking in the area's hot springs, there are waterfalls and great hiking on the eastern side of Volcán Chatto, Arenal's smaller, currently-inactive sibling to the south. To get there, head south out of Fortuna toward La Tigra and turn right after the bridge, following the signs to the *cataratas*. Several tour operators will also take you there; ask at the Volcano Inn's front desk.

The Volcano Inn's Que Rico Restaurant is a pleasant surprise – spacious, reasonably priced, great volcano view and, to top it all, excellent Italian food. The Que Rico is one of the few places we've found in Costa Rica – or in the Western Hemisphere, for that matter – that makes Spaghetti Carbonara the Italian way, with *no cream sauce*. And they serve a dynamite wood-oven pizza too. This place is so popular that tour busses stop here. Wherever you're staying in the Arenal area, a visit to Que Rico will be rewarding.

Arenal Observatory Lodge $$
South Side of El Volcán Arenal   Birding, Hiking

Photo © Arenal Observatory Lodge

Contact Information:
506-290-7011 (reservations voice); 506-692-2070 (front desk voice);
    506-290-8427 (reservations fax); 506-692-2074 (front desk fax)
info@arenalobservatorylodge.com
www.arenalobservatorylodge.com

Essentials:
43 Rooms, Dormitories, One 2-BR house; 5 Wheelchair access rooms
English, Spanish
All major credit cards accepted
Secure parking
Swimming pool, Hot tub
Breakfast included, Restaurant, Bar
Room Amenities: Semi-private outdoor space

How to get here:
Follow Highway 142 northwest from La Fortuna, then turn south
(left) at the intersection for Arenal Volcano National Park, across the
road from the small police station. Continue on the dirt road past the
park to a T-intersection and turn left. Turn left again at the next
intersection and cross the bridge following signs to the Lodge. 4-WD
required in the rainy season and advisable at all times.

Volcano aficionados and serious birders won't want to miss this famous lodge with rooms originally built to house volunteer volcano-watchers from the Smithsonian Institution. The day we arrived, the volcano was splendidly on view, the smoking summit just 1.7 miles away across a narrow forested canyon. The black and barren southwestern slopes are reminders of recent major eruptions; the main lava flows have shifted to the north side in recent years (so if you want to see their fiery trails at night you should pick other lodgings), but who knows when they might return?

The Arenal Observatory Lodge occupies a huge property – 384 hectares – bordering Arenal Volcano National Park on one side and the Monteverde Reserve on the other. Most of our fellow guests were there for the birds, equipped with powerful binoculars and massive, long-lens cameras. A "preliminary" bird list of observed species handed out to guests as a starting point includes almost 300, neatly arranged by Latin family, genus, and species names. We're not birders who keep detailed lists, but we noted in a morning at least three we'd never seen before.

The atmosphere here is different from other places we've stayed; true to its scientific origins, the Lodge maintains some of the feel of a relatively luxurious field station. A seismic monitor traces away day and night in the original Observatory building, topo maps and time-lapse photos of previous eruptions line the walls, and a poster from a 2005 scientific meeting details measurements of the distances flown by some of the larger hunks of volcanically-ejected rock (up to two kilometers!). Someone's ancient collection of pickled snakes sits incongruously on a shelf, the labels so faded they're hardly readable.

The best rooms for volcano-viewing are the "Smithsonian" rooms, some down the hill from the dining hall and others adjacent to the observatory. There are five rooms designed for full access by wheelchairs and a large house overlooking Lake Arenal with nice dorm rooms and a common area. The "White Hawk Villa" – the owner's private two-bedroom lodging and a splendid example of funky, high-modernist mountain architecture – is available for less than $500 per night. The Lodge's buildings, pool, and access roads are connected by well-lit paved sidewalks; the pretty Saino Trail into the forest is also paved and wheelchair-accessible. Don't miss the wonderful Waterfall Trail which winds deep into the forest to a pounding cascade of the Rio Danta.

While bird-watching, swimming, or even sleeping here, the volcano is a constant and commanding presence. You can hear it even in the pitch dark, rumbling and coughing out irregular blasts of gasses and smoke. One of these days, it will surely erupt again. Maybe you'll be right here (just watching, we hope).

Leaves and Lizards $$
Monterrey, North of El Tanque   Hiking

Photo © Judd Pilossof

Contact Information:
888-828-9245 (U.S.); 506-478-0023 (voice); 506-333-6863 (voice)
leavesandlizards@gmail.com
www.leavesandlizards.com

Essentials:
3 Cabins
English, Spanish
Credit cards in advance; Cash only in Costa Rica
Secure parking
Breakfast included, Lunch and dinner by arrangement
Room Amenities: Coffee maker, Refrigerator/minibar, In-room safe,
    Ceiling fan, Private outdoor space, Free WiFi

How to get here:
From La Fortuna, go east on Highway 142 (the main street through
town) to El Tanque. In El Tanque, turn left (north) on Highway 4
toward Monterrey and Upala. Cross the Arenal River and continue
to Monterrey/Santo Domingo. Bear left entering Monterrey, pass the
bank, and turn left onto the dirt road at the T-intersection. Leaves
and Lizards is 500 meters past the "Super Kike" grocery store. 4-WD
strongly recommended.

For one of the best views of Arenal Volcano, consider staying in a cozy cabin on this *finca* (farm) turned B&B about 20 minutes from La Fortuna. Opened on Valentine's Day 2006 by newlyweds Steve and Debbie Legg, with a couple of dollars and a dream, Leaves and Lizards is a bit off the beaten path – and the Arenal path is pretty beaten. Driving down the three km stretch of chunky earth that leads up to this 26-acre farm might make you think twice about your choice, but then again, this is Costa Rica, and perseverance has its rewards.

Upon arriving, you quickly realize that Leaves and Lizards is unlike the fairly standardized inns that dot the Arenal landscape. The philosophy of the farm is wonderfully progressive and leans toward self-sufficiency. With just three cabins, it is also quite intimate. Leaves and Lizards prides itself on its sustainable and eco-educational practices as well as a "just visiting friends" approach to service. We were greeted with a cold drink of fresh *carambola* (star fruit) juice from one of the trees on the property and a wonderful lunch of handmade pork empanadas (courtesy of one of the farm's own pigs) prepared by the wife of a local farmer. The pigs actually work double time, as their waste is used by an on-site biodigester that produces gas for cooking. We also collected eggs from the barn's chickens for breakfast the following morning.

The cabins are constructed of all sustainable materials including farmed teak on the porches, and there are plans to reforest the hillsides that lead up to the primary forest bordering the property, eventually extending the forest in order to encourage the wonderful wildlife to come up closer to the cabins. A natural hot spring was recently discovered between the hillsides which, in a future project, will be used to feed individual thermal Jacuzzis for each of the cabins.

Arrangements can be made for many kinds of day trips from the ever popular canopy or zip-line tours to more adventurous excursions like waterfall repelling, rafting trips through 52 rapids, fishing in Lake Arenal, mountain ridge or river hiking treks (on horse or by foot) through amazing primary forests, and a horseback ride to view Arenal's burning red lava at sunset – from a safe distance of course. You can even go to a local *Tico* dairy farm, milk a cow, and learn how they make their local cheese! `

When it's time to wind down at the end of the day, sit on your cabin's porch and soak in that killer view as the mountain's explosions glow and drizzle down its sides. If you are looking for a simple down home Costa Rican farm experience in an abundantly rich forest setting with individualized service, lots to do, and a spectacular view of the volcano while bird watching and sipping a cerveza, then pack your binoculars, throw the car into 4-WD, and head up to Leaves and Lizards. (Guest author - Liz Duffy)

Lost Iguana Lodge $$$-$$$$
West Side of El Volcán Arenal   Hiking

Photo © Lost Iguana Lodge

Contact Information:
506-267-6148 (reservations voice); 506-461-0122 (front desk voice);
    506-267-7672 (reservations fax); 506-461-0121 (front desk fax)
lostiguana@mac.com
www.lostiguanaresort.com

Essentials:
21 Rooms, 17 Suites, 2 Villas
English, Spanish
All major credit cards accepted
Secure parking
Swimming pool
Breakfast included, Restaurant, Bar
Room Amenities: AC, TV, Refrigerator/minibar, Coffee maker, In-room
    safe, Private outdoor space

How to get here:
Follow Highway 142 northwest from La Fortuna, then turn north off
of Highway 142 at the Y-intersection just past Lake Arenal dam,
following signs for Lost Iguana. The Lodge is about one km up the
road, on the left.

The Lost Iguana is relatively new and feels it. The rooms here are nicely proportioned and creatively decorated with lots of color, light, and tropical Asian touches. They all have private patios or balconies with splendid if somewhat distant views of Arenal Volcano. Avoid the lower level rooms however, as they're quite noisy when you have upstairs neighbors. Unlike many lava-viewing hotels, the Lost Iguana is embedded in the jungle with challenging trails and plenty of birds, monkeys, and other critters. Even some iguanas, but nobody knows where.

We took off on the longer of the two loop trails in the late afternoon to shake ourselves out after our drive and get ourselves a bit more ready for dinner. A fellow guest, a muscular middle-aged woman from California, told us that it was muddy from recent rains but only took about 45 minutes. We wore river sandals and were glad we did as the trail was thick ooze in places. There were several stream crossings and flights of steep, rough-cut stairs climbed higher and higher up the ridge behind the hotel. The stairs cut into the hillsides were clearly an experiment on the part of the trail's creators; they were stabilized with pieces of wood, which after one rainy season were swiftly rotting away. But the views over the lake and out toward the volcano were great, and the mid-altitude jungle is wonderful, especially early in the dry season when everything is blooming. We trucked right along, never stopping for more than a minute or two, but it still took us an hour and a half. By the time we got home it was raining, and the volcano was completely shrouded in clouds. No lava likely tonight.

For a less strenuous and even more beautiful hike, head next door to the Arenal Hanging Bridges. The hotel provides a shuttle if you're feeling lazy; otherwise there's a trail. The two-mile hanging bridges trail ($15 per person for Lost Iguana guests; $20 otherwise) traverses 15 bridges of various heights and lengths, crossing deep gorges at or above canopy level. Get there early before the tour busses from Fortuna and you will have the woods to yourselves. Parakeets were nesting when we were there and their constant ruckus filled the forest. The volcano stayed hidden but the trees and bridges themselves were wonderful. Take an umbrella; this is Arenal and, as far as we can tell, it rains up here all the time.

The Lost Iguana's restaurant has a magnificent view, but only a few tables are placed to take advantage of it. Ask for table #1, 2, or 3 when you make your dinner reservation. If you're just two people, you may need to be insistent as the waiters seem determined to save those tables for larger parties even if the restaurant is empty. The menu relies heavily on tilapia and chicken; dinner was good, but hardly inspired. If you're looking for something more gourmet, you may want to head up Highway 142 to La Mansion Inn.

Lake Arenal

Past the dam, newly-paved Highway 142 skirts the entire length of lovely Lake Arenal. The Costa Rican electric company – ICE – generates power from the lake, and restricts other uses so, other than the informal marina right under the dam, you won't see much in the way of boat traffic or the usual kinds of lakeside tourist development. Some of the prettiest spots in Costa Rica are on this road, many of them occupied by small hotels or B&Bs. While many of the lodgings nearer the volcano are close together on the highway and can seem over-run with tourists on dry-season weekends, most of the lakeside lodgings are widely-separated and set back from the highway. They are oases of calm even in the high season. Fire and water, excitement and tranquility – take a couple of days and experience both sides of this strikingly beautiful area.

The biggest town on the lake is Nuevo Arenal, sometimes just called Arenal, to which the residents of the valley were moved when Lake Arenal was created in 1973. Aside from La Mansion Arenal for dinner and the adjacent Toad Hall for lunch, most area restaurants as well as shops and the gas station are in Nuevo Arenal. The road from the dam to Nuevo Arenal used to be a nightmare but was paved in late 2006 and is now a joy. But don't drive too fast – we've often seen coatis crossing the road and occasionally howler monkeys as well.

The slopes north of Lake Arenal are sparsely populated, and above Nuevo Arenal they are protected by Tenorio National Park and the adjacent private reserves. Many hotels can arrange horse tours into these mountains. For a more off-beat adventure, at least for volcanic Costa Rica, head up to the tiny hamlet of Venado, turning north on the dirt road right across from Toad Hall. Here there are limestone caverns, with stalagmites and stalactites. Nearer Tenorio, the Lake Coter Ecolodge offers hiking and a canopy tour in primary forest. This is the only place in Costa Rica where we've seen an olingo, a fairly rare arboreal relative of the coati.

Some of our maps show a road all the way around Lake Arenal, but we don't know of anyone who's done it. The main highway – still CR 142 – turns sharply west just past the northwest end of the lake and climbs the ridge to the agricultural town of Tilarán. ICE's windmills turn lazily in the constant breeze awaiting their Quixotes. From Tilarán, Highway 142 continues on to join the *Interamericana* at Cañas; go this way if you are heading to Nicoya or back towards San José. Otherwise, follow Highway 145 – paved for a little while – toward Monteverde.

Ceiba Tree Lodge $
North Side of Lake Arenal   Horseback riding

Photo © Alison Tinsley

Contact Information:
506-692-8050 (voice)
ceibaldg@racsa.co.cr
www.ceibatree-lodge.com

Essentials:
6 Rooms, Honeymoon Suite
English, Spanish, German
All major credit cards accepted
Secure parking
Breakfast included
Room Amenities: Semi-private outdoor space

How to get here:
From the Lake Arenal Dam, go northwest on Highway 142 toward
the town of Nuevo Arenal. The Ceiba Tree Lodge is on the north
(right) side of the road, nine km northwest of the dam.

Every year the Costa Rican Biodiversity Institute – INBio – selects a tree to honor on June 15, El Dia Nacional del Arbol (National Tree Day). In 2006 Costa Rica's national tree was the gigantic 400 to 500 year-old ceiba tree that overlooks Lake Arenal from the Ceiba Tree Lodge. With their towering trunks and near-perfect symmetry, ceiba trees were sacred to indigenous cultures throughout Central America and the Caribbean. For the Maya, the ceiba was the Tree of Life that held up the sky. Gazing up at the bromeliad- and orchid-hung limbs – each one the thickness of a mature tree in a typical North American forest – one can appreciate why. These are trees that support the world.

The Ceiba Tree Lodge feels a bit like a ranch. It's perched high above the lake with several horses, a couple of dogs, and a black cat named Anastasia roaming around. Five guestrooms occupy a long bungalow at the top of the driveway with a broad shared verandah overlooking the huge tree and the lake below. The rooms are large with a queen and two single beds and carved, Mayan-themed wooden doors. There are tables and chairs on the verandah for admiring the view. Up the hill is the main house where Malte, the Bavarian owner, lives. This is a beautiful, contemporary-style structure with an open-air kitchen and breakfast area and the best two guest rooms. The ground-level honeymoon suite has a raised, curtained king bed, a big bathtub, and floor-to-ceiling windows on the two sides facing the lake. Upstairs is a smaller room with a queen bed, also with windows on two sides. These rooms have style – African-print curtains, Erte-style brass table-lamps, a European-Bohemian feel.

Uphill from the Lodge are 15 hectares of forest for walking and bird-watching. It was the lake below, however, that held Malte's attention on the day that we were there. Little ripples revealed a good breeze pouring up the lake from the east. The northwest shore, where this near-constant breeze is focused by the surrounding mountains, is famous for windsurfing. Here, in the broader middle of the lake, there was not quite enough wind for chop. "Perfect for sailing" was Malte's analysis. A friend is building him a boat. If ICE ever lifts its restrictions on marinas and watercraft, we'll expect to see Malte offering a sailing school as well as the Ceiba Tree Lodge.

Mystica Resort $$

North Side of Lake Arenal   Yoga/Meditation, Relax/Get-Away

Photo © Alison Tinsley

Contact Information:
506-692-1001 (voice); 506-692-2097 (fax)
mystica@racsa.co.cr
www.mysticalodge.com

Essentials:
6 Rooms, 1 Casita, two 2-BR Houses
English, Spanish, Italian
All major credit cards accepted
Secure parking
Breakfast included, Restaurant/pizzeria serves dinner
Room Amenities: Semi-private outdoor space, Internet available in reception area

How to get here:
From Nuevo Arenal, continue northwest on Highway 142, then turn north at the Y-intersection at the northernmost tip of Lake Arenal, half way between Nuevo Arenal and Tilarán. There is a sign for Mystica at the turn. This road wraps around the western flank of Tenorio; if you follow it, you'll reach Highway 6 to Upala.

After our morning coffee, we strolled down to the meditation platform, a covered, polished wooden deck hanging over the river at the edge of Mystica's property. The *congos* (howler monkeys) howled in the trees nearby, flights of parrots chattered overhead, a half dozen toucans played follow-the-leader through the trees. The platform is right next to a huge, sinewy, bromeliad-encrusted strangler fig – a reminder, maybe, of nature's strong and inescapable grip on all of us. Unlike Alison, I don't have the self-discipline for proper meditation, but it was a joy to just sit there, with the water gurgling through my head watching the birds and squirrels in the trees and noting the almost-imperceptible breeze running down with the water, wagging a single leaf here and there as it went.

Mystica sits on a hillside above the north end of Lake Arenal, three hectares of neatly-trimmed lawns, fruit trees, and brilliant red and purple flowering shrubs bordered by forest and river. Golden-tailed Montezuma oropendulas, crested blue jays, and innumerable little songbirds play in the trees. Horses graze freely. Two veteran dogs wander the property. Dante, evidently a little younger, will accompany you for walks, with Chaka lumbering along behind.

There are six rooms in a long, straight bungalow, a little casita, and two houses – the houses of the owners, Francesco and Barbara (for rent if their owners are away). The rooms have one or two beds, curtained closet and shelf space, light-hearted artwork, and brightly painted bathrooms. Our favorite, *pato* (the duck room), has a blue bathroom with red shelves and door and a painting of a winged cat in a field of flowers, clearly a deity of playfulness. Adirondack-style armchairs wait on the deep shared porch facing the lake. The casita is pale yellow with a kitchen and its own private porch; the two houses are full-size with two bedrooms, full kitchens, and nice private verandahs. On a clear evening, you can sit on the verandah and see Arenal volcano over 30 km away to the east. Any day of the year, you can sit and watch the lake, the flowers, and the birds.

Mystica offers thin-crust pizzas from its wood-burning *horno* and homemade pastas for lunch and dinner. Purists take heart: the *carbonara* here is done with no cream sauce and the pizzas are excellent. Breakfast is a feast of fresh-squeezed juices, plenty of fruit, and delicious homemade bread with jam from the guyaba trees just down the path; eggs are also available if you want them. The dining room and adjoining bar are open and light, with fairy lights for nightime and big windows for daytime sun and the view.

A lot of places here in Costa Rica are about activities and adventures; we review a good many of them in this book. Mystica is about letting go, relaxing, and taking some time just to watch the world around you. For us, right now, that's adventure enough.

Villa Decary $$
North Side of Lake Arenal   Birding

Photo © Villa Decary

Contact Information:
506-383-3012 (voice); 506-694-4330 (fax)
info@villadecary.com
www.villadecary.com

Essentials:
5 Rooms, 3 Cabins with kitchens
English, Spanish
Cash only
Secure parking
Breakfast included, Restaurants nearby
Room Amenities: Private outdoor space

How to get here:
From the Lake Arenal Dam, go northwest on Highway 142 toward
the town of Nuevo Arenal. Villa Decary is on the north side of
Highway 142, two km east of Nuevo Arenal.

Villa Decary was our choice the first time we drove up through Arenal. It was mid-March – high summer in Costa Rica. We had been roasting on the crowded beach in Tamarindo and were desperate for cooler weather. The big trees, cool white walls, and gentle lake breezes at Villa Decary were the perfect solution. Owners Bill and Jeff keep talking about selling this place, but then they troop off to Thailand again and come back refreshed. We hope they stay here forever.

You have a choice at Villa Decary between one of the five upstairs bedrooms in the main house with their private balconies overlooking the front lawn and the lake or one of three well-separated bungalows with two beds and full kitchens on the hill above the house. All the rooms have white walls, colorful Guatemalan bedspreads, and nature-themed artwork. The bright breakfast room downstairs opens onto a wrap-around wooden deck with *bancos*; this is where main-house guests hang out, drinking coffee, watching the songbirds flitting between fruit-piled feeders and thickets of palm trees, or just relaxing in the mid-morning sun.

Villa Decary was the first place we heard the weird, whistle-gurgle "oo-E-pl-<u>WHEE</u>-pl" call of the Montezuma oropendula and saw its meter-long hanging baskets of nests dangling from the palm trees. Jeff is a serious birder and claims over 400 species can be seen and heard in the environs of Lake Arenal. You're pretty sure to hear howler monkeys here too; the troop on the west side of Villa Decary has regular shouting matches with the troop to the east. Cross the little creek and follow the 45-minute trail that loops around the back of the property. You never know what you'll see. Our first morning, it was two white horses wandering through the lower yard in the thick white mist rising off the lake. Where are we – Avalon?

Villa Decary doesn't have a restaurant, but you're only two minutes from Nuevo Arenal and Bill or Jeff can provide suggestions. We liked the pizzas at Tramonti in Nuevo Arenal and hear that Gingerbread, the new place just up the road, is also good. For fine dining, head to La Mansion (see review next page) a few km back toward the volcano; it's not a bad drive now that the road is paved. The guestrooms share an upstairs fridge, so you can also pick up imported German cheeses and beer, excellent homemade bread, and other supplies at Nuevo Arenal's famous German Bakery and have a picnic. Don't miss the apple strudel!

Mansion Inn Arenal $$$

North Side of Lake Arenal   Honeymoons, Horseback Riding
Destination Restaurant

Photo © Mansion Inn Arenal

Contact Information:
506-692-8018 (voice);   506-692-8019 (fax)
info@lamansionarenal.com
www.lamansionarenal.com

Essentials:
17 Villas
English, Spanish
All major credit cards accepted
Secure parking
Swimming pool, Spa
Breakfast included, Restaurant, Bar
Room Amenities: TV, AC, Private outdoor space, Free WiFi
    (restaurant/bar area)

How to get here:
From the Lake Arenal Dam, go northwest on Highway 142 toward
the town of Nuevo Arenal. La Mansion is on the south side, just past
Toad Hall.

La Mansion Arenal is a luxury hotel that has maintained a sense of intimacy and, even more importantly, a sense of humor. It used to be called "The Marina Club;" the old name is still on the sign by the road. Alison and I picked up paddles in the bar and strolled down to the marina – a couple of canoes drawn up on the sand, where the old road down to the submerged town of "Viejo" (old) Arenal enters the water. ICE doesn't allow marinas at Lake Arenal, and La Mansion plays by the rules. The staff jokes that La Mansion Arenal didn't have a marina when it was called The Marina Club and doesn't have a mansion now. That may be the case, but we still had a lovely canoe trip, paddling east toward the still fog-shrouded volcano and lazily home again. Flights of white egrets skimmed the quiet water; the ubiquitous howler monkeys proclaimed their territory to all and sundry; horses grazed here and there by the shore.

La Mansion Arenal shares a name and marketing information with La Mansion Inn in Manuel Antonio, but the styles of the two hotels are completely different. At La Mansion Arenal, you have a spacious, stand-alone, private two-bedroom cottage. The furniture and decorations are grand but whimsical; tropical-themed murals and painted filigree by San José artist Daria Bruni grace the walls. The restaurant, bar, and public room with its pool table occupy the former milking barn of this 26-acre property where horses that were included when the original dairy farm was purchased still frolic on the deep-green slopes. Check at the bar to arrange a horse tour up into the mountains north of the lake, to visit the caves near the little mountain town of Venado, or to go on a canopy tour. There's a nice pool overlooking the lake and a spa coming in early 2007. Or, check out that marina.

In a part of Costa Rica with lots of lodgings but not much in the way of truly fine dining, La Mansion Arenal also boasts an excellent restaurant. The menu changes every night. We were lucky enough to catch chicken with rum and pineapple sauce and pork tenderloin with a not-too-spicy wasabi sauce. Several of our fellow diners had evidently come from other hotels in the area. Breakfast features fresh fruit and build-your-own omelets and will be delivered to your cottage at no extra charge.

The general manager can make or break a luxury hotel and Joey Duncan here at La Mansion is exemplary. He's very low-key – not at all the field-marshal type – but he knows what's happening every minute and seems to both know and pitch in on every job. Whatever we needed, even if it was a bit of arcana, he could instantly provide. If you like laid-back luxury with a personal touch, include La Mansion Arenal in your Costa Rica trip.

Monteverde Area

From Tilarán a good but mostly unpaved road snakes through beautiful mountain countryside to Santa Elena and a truly wretched road continues the few kilometers to Monteverde, the most visited cloud forest area of Costa Rica. American Quakers settled this area in the 1950s, after Costa Rica disbanded its army, and started a process of buying and preserving cloud forest that continues to this day. You'll see plenty of blond, blue-eyed Costa Ricans here.

The Santa Elena – Monteverde area has plenty of lodgings for every budget and style, from backpacker hostels to fancy mountain lodges. Monteverde also boasts more than its share of excellent restaurants; we especially like Johnny's Pizzaria (don't be fooled; this is a white-tablecloth place) and the Euro-tropical fusion at Sophia's. Johnny's is on the Santa Elena-to-Monteverde road, a little way past the Sapo Dorado; for Sophia's turn right at the intersection just before the El Establo Inn.

Santa Elena and Monteverde both have eponymous cloud-forest reserves, and both are worth a visit. The Santa Elena reserve is north of Santa Elena – start back in the direction of Tilarán and turn right instead of left at the Y. Here you will find the Selvatura hanging bridges and the "Jewels of the Rainforest" Whitten Entomological Collection. You may not be a fan of insect life when you enter Jewels of the Rainforest, but you're guaranteed at least to be impressed by our six- and eight-legged cousins when you come out. For the hanging bridges, go early to beat the crowds. We like the slow pace and quiet of the bridges far more than canopy tours, and the chance of seeing birds and critters is better too.

The Monteverde reserve is famous for quetzals, and we saw a pair of them our first morning in one of the big trees right by the parking lot. What luck! There's a fine hummingbird garden by the entrance and a café that serves espresso and excellent pies. A little grey fox trotted out of the forest as we were having our coffee break and regarded us with a mixture of curiosity and suspicion. Hulking, strange-smelling interlopers! He skittered away and we finished our coffee – pretty good wildlife sighting for one cloudy morning.

Don't miss the Monteverde organic coffee cooperative just before you reach Monteverde on the road from Santa Elena or the regional crafts co-op right next door. Some interesting local artists also show in downtown Santa Elena in the little gallery across the street from the tourist office.

After a few days in Monteverde, you'll find yourself wondering why the roads around here are so bad, and why, since this place is so remote, they haven't built an airport. The answer is that the locals don't want paved roads and the hordes of tour busses that will follow them and they don't want airplanes. In short, they don't want to look like the slopes of Arenal. You probably don't want them either.

If you're headed to Nicoya when you leave Monteverde, go back to Tilarán and follow Highway 142 down to Cañas. Do *not* take the turn-off toward Juntas as a shortcut to the *Interamericana*. Unless you're into four-wheeling as an adrenaline sport, you'll regret it. If you're heading south or back to San José, go south from Santa Elena down the long ridge toward Guacimal. You have some driving ahead of you here; this road varies

from not-bad to a real bone cruncher after wet weather. At the intersection just outside Guacimal, turn left and follow the signs to Sardinal; you'll hit paved road (whew!) sooner.

Claro de Luna $
Santa Elena   Downtown

Photo © Claro de Luna

Contact Information:
506-645-5269 (voice/fax)
reservations@clarodelunahotel.com
www.clarodelunahotel.com

Essentials:
9 Rooms
English, Spanish
All major credit cards accepted
Secure parking
Breakfast included, Restaurants nearby
Room Amenities: Internet available in office

How to get here:
From Central Santa Elena go south towards Sardinal passing the
bypass to Monteverde and Insect World. At the Y-intersection, turn
sharply right and backtrack on the dirt road toward Santa Elena.
Claro de Luna is on the left.

An especially handsome mot-mot joined Alison for her morning meditation, sitting not two meters from her for a good ten minutes. Pretty friendly for a mot-mot, colorful but elusive birds who like the shadows and tend to fly off whenever they see you watching them. A stiff breeze from the north was blowing the mist down the valley and the tall pines above Claro de Luna provided the best shelter around.

Friends in Tamarindo had advised us to stay at Claro de Luna as the best budget hotel in the Monteverde area. While most places up here are lodges or cabinas, Claro de Luna is a three-story house, the top two stories an open A-frame in chalet style. With its open kitchen and dining room, wall of windows looking east, and graceful central staircase, it reminded me of an old friend's house back in Rollinsville, Colorado where a dozen or so of us would take a break from graduate school for weekends of communal meals, cross-country skiing, and occasional construction work. Claro de Luna is about three blocks south of the center of Santa Elena, a town a lot like the Colorado mountain towns of the 1970s: laid-back, lots of healthy-looking young people, a fine place for a good time but with an air of late-hippie-era, back-to-nature earnestness instead of the all-out party vibe of the beach towns.

Red impatiens petals decorated our pillows, the swan-folded towels, and even the bathmat in our room – nice touches for a budget hotel. The "deluxe" rooms downstairs are slightly larger and have pastel, sponge-painted walls, but we prefer the upstairs rooms (# 8 and 9) with their wooden walls, peaked ceilings, and high view over the valley. All the rooms have nice bathrooms with great showers and plenty of shelf space for your stuff.

Breakfast was late, a disappointment so severe we almost wrote the Claro off as a loss. Somehow the cook was locked out of the house, and couldn't even make coffee! We commiserated in Spanish, tried our room keys in all the locks without success, then she volunteered that the little *soda* (snack-bar) across the street had coffee at 6 a.m. By the time we got back she'd made it inside, and her excellent breakfast of eggs and pancakes with plenty of real maple made up for our distress. We traded travel notes with our Dutch neighbors Camiel and Marja, marveled at the rather disconcerting swarm of tiny brown bugs that had appeared out of nowhere overnight (a common and unpreventable cloud-forest happening, we later learned), and were on our way.

Some guests have complained that the walls here are thin, but there are no TVs around (always a blessing), and it's hard for humans without electronics to compete in the night-time racket department with the tree frogs. Enjoy your stay!

Monteverde Cloud Forest Lodge $$
Santa Elena   Hiking, Birding, Kid-friendly

Photo © Monteverde Cloud Forest Lodge

Contact Information:
506-645-5058 (voice); 506-645-5168 (fax)
reservations@cloudforestlodge.com
www.cloudforestlodge.com

Essentials:
20 Rooms
English, Spanish
All major credit cards accepted
Secure parking
Breakfast included, Restaurant, Bar
Room Amenities: Internet available in office

How to get here:
From Central Santa Elena, go east toward Monteverde. The Cloud
Forest Lodge is up a steep driveway on the left side just before the
Sapo Dorado. There is a tiny sign; if you reach the Sapo Dorado,
backtrack one driveway.

The Santa Elena – Monteverde area has several lodges, but for a good combination of traditional "lodgy" feel and the relative privacy of *cabinas* try the Monteverde Cloud Forest Lodge up the steep road above the Sapo Dorado. The main building has a classic, A-frame restaurant with a small bar, a corner with couches for watching TV, and a splendid view all the way down to the Gulf of Nicoya. Twenty rooms arranged in duplexes or four-plexes are arrayed on the hillside above the restaurant, some practically tucked into the forest, some with views above it. The rooms are nothing fancy but are comfortable and well laid-out; the "family" rooms have bunk beds for the kids and plenty of storage space. Floors are terracotta tile, walls and ceilings are wood, and there are nice, semi-private porches outside.

No one comes all the way to Monteverde to spend their time in a hotel room, and the Cloud Forest Lodge provides plenty for you to do. You're at the bottom of a 30-hectare (about 75 acre) forest reserve, and this is cloud forest where every tree is a complex ecosystem of epiphytes and various arboreal creatures. Broad, well-maintained trails wind through the area around the lodge or, if you're feeling really ambitious, you can climb the 15 km up to the Santa Elena Cloud Forest. The Cloud Forest Lodge also claims the "original" canopy tour, with steel cables strung between platforms at mid-canopy level. The "ziplines" are fun if you're comfortable wearing a climbing harness, but they're too fast and too loud for much wildlife viewing. We prefer suspension bridges which allow you to go at your own pace, stop when you want to and, best of all, to be quiet and hear the forest around you. Selvatura, right at the entrance to the Santa Elena reserve, has a great suspension-bridge trail; ask at the Lodge desk to arrange transportation.

As with so much in Costa Rica, the small and nearby sights rival the large and distant ones for wonders. On a quiet morning, we took the relatively-short River Trail down from the lodge, across the creek, along the border with the Cloud Forest School, and back to the road. Late in the rainy season, this was the blue trail – blue Morpho butterflies, blue hydrangeas, tiny blue asters among the tall grasses, and four to five inch acid-blue mushrooms that just screamed, *"don't eat me"*. Raucous Costa Rican brown jays squawked and jostled overhead. Last night's rain still dripped off the trees and the creek ran clear and noisy. You don't have to be in a cloud forest long to start feeling primeval, furry, maybe even a bit green around the edges. This is an environment where you could disappear without a trace, where the imagination needs but little coaxing. Stand here a few minutes in the cool mist and all those fairy tales about the deep dark woods, the talking animals, and the strange things that happen to the boastful and unwary start to make sense.

Arco Iris $-$$$
Santa Elena   Downtown

Photo © Arco Iris

Contact Information:
506-645-5067 (voice); 506-645-5022 (fax)
arcoiris@racsa.co.cr
www.arcoirislodge.com

Essentials:
20 Rooms
English, Spanish, German, French
All major credit cards accepted
Secure parking
Breakfast included, Restaurants nearby
Room Amenities: In-room safes, Internet available in office

How to get here:
Central Santa Elena is a triangle of one-way streets. The driveway to
Arco Iris is on the right side of the westward-running one-way street,
which begins just down the hill from the main tourist office and ends
at the Banco Nacional.

The first time we stayed at Arco Iris, I woke up around 5:30, listened to the birds for a while, and then wandered over to the kitchen. It was at least half an hour before breakfast started, but one of the cooks smiled at my then-pretty-pitiful Spanish, and gave me not just two cups, but a *tray* with a pot of coffee, another of milk, spoons, and even napkins. We've loved it ever since.

Arco Iris sits part way up a hill about two blocks from the center of Santa Elena, but has the spacious feel of a rural property. Several big friendly dogs and who knows how many cats roam around or sleep in the sun. There are orange trees, bananas, mimosas, and all sorts of flowers. A creek runs along one side shaded by big cloud-forest trees. Susanna, the owner, grows her own herbs and greens and her chickens provide the eggs at breakfast. Horses graze here and there. There are three duplexes, a two-story four-plex, and the other rooms are free-standing. You can have a private little one-room cabin hanging over the creek (#8) or a big two-bedroom house with a full kitchen perched up on the hill ("the house"). Or try the brand-new, split-level Honeymoon cabin with its four-poster bed and private jacuzzi. There are even cabins with bunk beds for budget-conscious backpackers or big families. Whatever you choose, you'll have a comfortable space with terracotta tile floors, blond wooden walls and ceilings, a covered porch for sitting, and plenty of nearby flowers.

Breakfast at Arco Iris is a splendid affair – a generous buffet with German-style cold cuts and cheeses as well as the usual hearty *Tico* fare, plenty of fruit, sweet breads, and even carrot cake. The new upstairs breakfast room – just completed in 2006 – has lots of windows for a great view and wonderful paintings by Costa Rican artist Gustavo Araya. The theme of the paintings is typically Central American – in one, a mother crocodile picks up her young in her cavernous mouth to carry them down to the water – but the style is hip and indigenous-contemporary; all the animals, moons and other natural objects are really painted collages, full of additional figures and stories.

You can arrange tours from here to the Monteverde or Santa Elena reserves. There's lots of local alternatives. Walk down the hill to the orchid garden or up the next hill to the serpentarium. Drop by Chunches, the eclectic little store across the street, for books or a mid-morning espresso. Maybe you'll just want to watch the bright yellow-bellied flycatchers, the hummingbirds, and the occasional toucans going about their daily business in the bushes and trees – that's what we did.

El Sol $$
South of Santa Elena   Relax/Get Away, Horseback Riding

Photo © El Sol

Contact Information:
506-645-5838/359-3282 (voice)
info@elsolnuestro.com
www.elsolnuestro.com

Essentials:
2 Cabins
English, Spanish, German, Swedish, Finnish
Cash only
Secure parking
Pool, Sauna
Breakfast included, Dinner can be arranged
Room Amenities: Full kitchen, Private outdoor space

How to get here:
Drive south of Santa Elena on the dirt road toward Guacimal for 15 minutes, then look for the Sun sign at El Sol's gate, on the left side of the road. Coming from Highway 1, El Sol is about 30 minutes above Guacimal, on the right. Close the gate after you drive through so the horses won't get out.

Friends told us we *had* to stay at El Sol – that it was a "life changing experience" for them and everyone they knew. So we made our way up, once again, toward Monteverde, with a certain amount of trepidation. You see, we like our life. Certain kinds of changes are great fun – like moving to Costa Rica – but others we could do without. Nothing horribly drastic seemed to have happened to our friends, though, so we gave it a whirl.

El Sol certainly is a *different* experience, at least if you're used to urban congestion, a 24/7 career, and the constant ringing of telephones. At El Sol, it's just you and the mountain. Wind at night, fresh sunlight at dawn, smells of clouds, trees, oiled wood, and high grass going golden early in the dry season.

El Sol sits on the western flank of the long ridge that climbs from Guacimal up to Santa Elena, the ridge whose seemingly endless curves you'll drive along coming up here from Highway 1, and going back down. There are just two cabins, one somewhat larger, well separated so that you neither see nor hear your fellow guests. Both cabins face northwest, looking across the tumbling ridges and valleys toward Tilarán almost 20 miles away. Judging from the absence of nighttime lights, not a soul must live in those 20 miles. You can sit on your porch and just stare into space. Or meditate. Or do your morning yoga with nothing on, secure in the knowledge that no one is looking.

Elisabeth, the owner, welcomed us with a hug and, after we'd had a chance to settle in, brought us a bountiful dinner of Spanish potato *torta*, fresh vegetables, homemade bread, and her own homemade sauces. She or a neighbor will prepare a dinner with advance notice, but the cabins are also very well equipped with a gas cooktop, toaster oven, refrigerator, teapot and tea, coffee maker and coffee – everything you need to prepare simple meals. You won't want to leave once you get here, and it's a long way from anywhere, so stop for supplies in Santa Elena if you're coming from the north or before you leave home.

Over breakfast, we talked with Elisabeth about life in this high, empty place, with its long distances, big views, and frequently dramatic weather. She comes from Germany and spent many years in the Canary Islands; she understands independent living and an almost monastic isolation. Some guests, she says, come for the horseback riding or hiking across the pastures and around the network of little farm roads. But most just come here for the quiet, to really get away, to just be with themselves for a while. We can see why.

Did our lives change at El Sol? Who knows? Any number of things might have happened if we hadn't come up here.

El Sapo Dorado $$

Santa Elena   Birding, Hiking

Photo © Sapo Dorado

Contact Information:
506-645-5010 (voice); 506-645-5180 (fax)
reservations@sapodorado.com
www.sapodorado.com

Essentials:
30 Suites
English, Spanish
All major credit cards accepted
Secure parking
Breakfast included, Restaurant, Bar
Room Amenities: In-room safes, Internet available in office, Fireplaces
(Mountain Suites only)

How to get here:
Go east from Central Santa Elena toward Monteverde; the Sapo
Dorado is on your left.

The "Black Guan" *sendero* (trail) heads up into the forest just past the banana trees on the east side of El Sapo Dorado between the spreading legs of a huge, twisted fig tree. It was just after sunrise. We'd forgotten to bring our coffee maker along on this trip, and we were both feeling a bit foggy. We didn't see any black guans – a turkey-sized arboreal bird – but this trail has some truly impressive *matapalos* (strangler figs). They begin life high in the crown of a cloud-forest tree as seeds deposited by bats or birds who've recently dined on figs. They grow downward, wrapping their host in an inescapable embrace. The big ones are meters in diameter, sometimes still surrounding the rotting hulk of their former host, often hollow, and big enough for several stories of spiral staircase to fit inside. A quick movement caught Alison's eye, and we watched a family of *pizotes* – the local coatimundis – passing by, the adults crashing through the branches like oversized, clumsy squirrels and the young ones scampering along the forest floor below.

El Sapo Dorado – the golden toad – is named for one of Monteverde's more famous amphibians, discovered in 1964 but not seen since 1996, possibly an early victim of global climate change. A guide in Monteverde Reserve once told us that he had set the last golden toad in captivity free. Who knows? We hope the little critters are still out there, singing and reproducing in some quiet hollow of these perennially-wet mountains.

The hotel offers three kinds of rooms, all in duplexes set well apart from each other in lovely gardens. The rooms have blond wood interiors, plenty of storage space, and excellent lighting. The two-bedroom "family" suites are on the hillside looking south. The "sunset" rooms have two beds, a fridge, and a view of the Gulf of Nicoya on clear mornings. Our favorites are the "mountain" rooms, also with two beds, but with a fireplace and supply of wood. A wonderful thing about Monteverde is that it's often cool enough for a fire. Bring a knife – kindling is in short supply.

El Sapo Dorado is famous for its restaurant which offers a variety of vegan and vegetarian dishes in addition to the Costa Rican standards of beef, chicken, pork chops, and sea bass. The food here is good but pricey, and we find Sophia's to be more creative and exciting. Breakfast is way overpriced at the Sapo – bring your own coffee maker, and stop by one of Santa Elena's several bakeries for supplies the day before.

It's perfectly quiet here at night, great for a good night's sleep with the windows open, but be prepared for the morning chorus. At least 100 parrots were flocking in the trees on the ridgeline above the hotel on our last visit, and we listened with amusement to a vigorous shouting match between the invading parrots and the resident brown jays. The last squawk we heard, the jays had won.

Poás and Barva

El Volcán Poás is the closest volcano to Juan Santamaria International Airport. It has a lovely paved road leading to the very top, and its still-active crater sports a bubbling blue-green pool of sulfuric acid. What more could you ask for in a top-notch destination? Weekenders flock here on Saturdays and Sundays, hoping that the clouds will part. That's the rub – you have to get lucky to find a clear day on the top of Poás. Early mornings are best, so aim to get here when the park opens at 8 a.m. You'll beat the tour busses by coming early, too.

As Poás looms over bustling Alajuela, its dormant neighbor to the south, wooded Barva graces the skyline above sleepier Heredia. Barva is the western anchor of Braulio Carillo National Park, created when Highway 32 was built to more efficiently link San José with Limón. The summit of Barva is deep in the park and accessible only with a strenuous hike. You won't find many tourists up there.

There are several routes to Poás, but by far the easiest goes straight north from the center of Alajuela to the town of Fraijanes and from there to the crossroads at Poasito. Bear left at the intersection in Poasito to go to the volcano. Turning right

takes you to the mountain town of Varablanca, the crossroads for the narrow pass that drops over the mountains to the eastern slopes and the Caribbean plain.

The western slopes of both Poás and Barva are covered by coffee plantations at lower elevations and by grey and black shade-cloth as you venture higher. This is strawberry country; you'll find vendors on every roadside holding plastic bags or wooden flats filled with ripe *fresas*. Prices are good but wash the berries before eating as many of the farmers use pesticides.

There are lots of lodgings on the western slopes of Poás and Barva, but our favorites are around Varablanca. This small town feels remote but is only about 45 minutes from Alajuela and a bit over an hour from San José. Volcán Poás National Park is half an hour from here to the north, and less than two hours to the east is Puerto Viejo de Sarapiquí, gateway to the rivers and rainforests of the northeastern plains. Even Arenal is only a couple of hours from Varablanca if you don't hit heavy traffic.

Another reason to stay near Varablanca is Restaurante Colbert, one of the best French restaurants in Costa Rica, about half a kilometer out

of town on the way to Heredia. Colbert is a hidden treasure, one of those places even many locals don't know about. They make their own pastries, serve local cheeses and produce, and smoke hams over a wood-burning stove in the middle of the dining room. The home-made pâtés are wonderful, and the appetizer plate is almost a meal for two. If they're offering the *cabrito* (baby goat) cooked in beer when you arrive, don't turn it down!

Photo © Kelly McGinley

Poas Volcano Lodge $-$$

Varablanca   Relax/Get away, Hiking, Horseback Riding

Photo © Poas Volcano Lodge

Contact Information:
506-482-2194 (voice); 506-482-2513 (fax)
info@poasvolcanolodge.com
www.poasvolcanolodge.com

Essentials:
6 Rooms, 5 Suites
English, Spanish, French
All major credit cards accepted
Secure parking
Horseback tours available
Breakfast included, Lunch and dinner available
Room Amenities: Ceiling fan, Coffee maker (suites), Internet available
    (in game room)

How to get here:

From Alajuela, follow signs to Poás, then turn right in Poasito toward
Varablanca. Poas Volcano Lodge is between Poasito and Varablanca,
on the east side of the road about ½ km north of Varablanca.

Our first morning at Poas Volcano Lodge, I woke with a start from a terrible dream of snowstorms. Outside, the wind was howling and rain and clouds flew by in horizontal sheets. We contemplated making a fire – the Master Suite's fireplace was well provided with dry wood – but when Chris stepped out onto the patio, he reported that it wasn't really cold, just sweater weather. It felt like a summer morning in the Colorado Rockies of his youth. We snuggled back under the quilt of our massive four-poster bed and watched the clouds whip by through the clerestory windows. A perfect morning for a leisurely bath in the free-form bathtub, I thought. But I knew it wasn't going to happen; Chris was going to insist we hike one of the three beautifully laid-out trails.

Poas Volcano Lodge was built in the early 1970s as the family farmhouse for the 300-acre El Cortijo dairy farm and is surrounded by lush fields full of healthy, happy-looking cows. Michael, the courtly owner of the Lodge, built the main house using the rough stone and massive hand-hewn wooden beams of rural architecture in his native England. Huge windows and clerestories provide views and light and two full-size fireplaces warm the public rooms in the evenings. Every detail has been thought of – the sunken, cushioned *bancos* facing the upstairs fireplace, the piano and pool-table in the family room downstairs, and rubber boots (neatly arranged by metric sizes) and walking sticks provided for hikers. As well as the luxurious Master Suite, the Lodge offers four standard rooms and four junior suites. They are all charmingly decorated, but the standards are a bit small for two people (and they don't have an in-room coffee maker) so, if you're traveling with a companion, opt for a junior suite.

By the time we'd made coffee there were a few shafts of sunlight so we set off on the Yellow Trail which runs down through pastures to a sizeable stand of old-growth cloud forest covering the ridges and canyons of the creeks feeding the La Paz river. The trail was advertised as a one-hour walk but took almost twice that due to our constant stops to admire the huge trees covered with orchids, bromeliads, mosses, hanging lianas, and countless other epiphytes. At 1,850 meters (about 6,000 feet), the climbs up and down the canyons through the steep-sided pastures and over the dozen or so yellow-painted stiles at every fence crossing take some work. We earned our excellent breakfasts of ham & eggs, fruit, homemade muesli, and toast with delicious local strawberry preserves.

Poas Volcano Lodge also offers a wonderful dinner; we recommend it highly. Sitting by the fire before and after, sharing a glass of wine with fellow guests, you too may decide that this is one of your favorite places in all of Costa Rica.

Peace Lodge $$$$
East of Varablanca   Honeymoons, Hiking, Kid-friendly, Wildlife

Photo © Peace Lodge

Contact Information:
954-727-3997 (US); 506-225-0643 (voice); 506-234-8782 (fax)
peacelodgereservations@waterfallgardens.com
www.waterfallgardens.com

Essentials:
16 Rooms, One 2-BR villa
English, Spanish
All major credit cards accepted
Secure parking
Swimming pool, Waterfalls, Hummingbird and butterfly houses,
    Snake and frog exhibits
Breakfast included, Restaurants, Bars
Room Amenities: AC, Ceiling fan, Coffee maker, Refrigerator/minibar,
    Private outdoor space with hot tub

How to get here:
From Varablanca, go east on Highway 9 (also called Highway 126)
following signs to Sarapiquí. Peace Lodge is five km from Varablanca
on the left.

We arrived at Peace Lodge before check-in time so, before going to our room, we wandered the roughly one km loop of the Fern Trail through a part of the Lodge's 70 acres of cloud forest, then had a relaxed lunch by the combination trout pond and deep-water infinity swimming pool. After lunch, we were escorted to one of the four standard rooms that include a waterfall shower. Imagine Walt Disney designing a lavish jungle retreat and you've kind of got the picture. The orchid-hung waterfall pouring from the 12-foot ceiling in the spacious bathroom was worth the price of admission (and the price of admission is not cheap). Our walk had left us hot and sweaty, so I immediately had to try it out. Never before have I experienced such beautifully hot water tumbling over my head and shoulders. Of course, Chris had to try it next. Afterwards, we donned the robes provided and repaired to our private balcony with our own hot tub to relax. The sun shone following afternoon rains and the resident hummingbirds were everywhere. What a way to spend our anniversary!

Peace Lodge is part of La Paz Waterfall Gardens which surround the cascades of the clear-running La Paz River. Paved trails with hanging bridges and observation platforms follow the river providing close-up viewing of five spectacular waterfalls. It was August when we visited, deep in the rainy season, and the forest was dense, dripping wet, and full of morning birdsong. Many of the cloud forest's elusive creatures can be seen close-up at La Paz's hummingbird, butterfly, frog, and snake enclosures. The butterfly garden specializes in Blue Morphos and Owl butterflies which we saw emerging from their cocoons, unfolding and drying their wings, and taking their first steps with their brand-new legs.

Dinner at Peace Lodge is by reservation for guests only and was excellent, from the onion soup in a bread bowl to dark-chocolate mousse in a delicate, cinnamon pastry shell. Hunter, the Lodge's striped tabby, was sitting by our door when we returned from our after-dinner nocturnal frog tour and joined us by the fire in our room.

Peace Lodge has eight standard and eight deluxe rooms plus a two-bedroom villa. All rooms have private balconies with hot tubs, luxurious bathrooms, four-poster king beds, and fireplaces. Deluxe rooms are distinguished from standards by their upper-floor locations, peaked ceilings, and larger bathrooms with jacuzzi tubs. We recommend asking for one of the four standards that have bathroom waterfalls – just for the wonderful sound of the water. Avoid the rooms that border the central pool and spa. These can be noisy if your fellow guests ignore the 10 p.m. closing time, as some did during our stay.

The Talamanca Mountains

South of Cartago, the *Cordillera* Talamanca rises up as a steep, twisted spine of mountains that runs all the way down into Panama. The *Interamericana* Highway, called Highway 2 south of San José, begins its long ascent into the mountains almost as soon as you get out of town. The high pass of the Cerro de la Muerte, the Mountain of Death, where travelers on foot from the Pacific coast used to regularly freeze to death in their bare feet and light clothing, tops out at almost 3,500 meters – over 11,000 feet – above sea level. From here the highway descends to San Isidro El General, the Rio General valley, and the Pacific coastal plain, but the mountains continue marching south and east until they become the Andes in Colombia.

The high ranges of the Talamancas are almost all protected by a series of mostly-contiguous reserves and national parks ending in the huge Parque Internacional La Amistad (International Friendship Park) that extends across the border into western Panama. Almost no one lives in the high mountains, and even the lower slopes have been settled by European-descended people only relatively recently. It's easy to meet folks whose parents were homesteaders.

Very little of the mountain wilderness has been developed for tourism, and there are relatively few places to stay in the Talamancas unless you are willing to camp. The densest cluster of lodges is in the narrow valley of San Gerardo de Dota where Efrain Chacón started a fishing lodge on his farm in the early 1970s and quetzal watchers followed the trout fishermen. The drive into this valley, where the Savegre River begins its tumble to the Pacific, is always worth it just for the fabulous views – the good chance of seeing quetzals is a bonus.

The highest peak in Costa Rica, 3,820-meter Cerro Chirripó, rises just northeast of San Isidro El General (also called Perez Zeledón), the largest town in the area. Chirripó National Park covers most of the mountain and serves as a corridor between Tapantí National Park to the north and Amistad to the south. Several lodges cluster in the valley of the Chirripó River which joins the Talari to form Rio El General. Access to the park is from the little mountain town of San Gerardo de Rivas, not to be confused – though some do, to their chagrin – with San Gerardo de Dota, a good two hours to the north.

Far to the south almost to the border with Panama is the farming town of San Vito founded by Italians in the mid-19th century. It is the gateway to the southern part of the Amistad Park. We've not made it down to San Vito yet, but we have friends who like it so well they're building a house there. The Wilson Gardens and nearby Amistad Lodge are reported to be very nice and great for seeing birds and mammals as well as plants.

Be careful driving in the Talamancas and don't even think about driving them at night. There are lots of trucks on Highway 2, sometimes barely inching along and sometimes without much in the way of lights. There are shockingly tight curves, steep descents (especially from the high pass to El General), and the fog can be so thick you can't see the road surface in front of you. Typical of Costa Rica, there are no places to pull over, so when conditions are especially bad, traffic just stops. Drive with care!

El Toucanet Lodge $

Copey de Dota   Hiking, Birding

Photo © Alison Tinsley

Contact Information:
506-541-3054 (voice/fax)
toucanet@racsa.co.cr
www.eltoucanet.com

Essentials:
6 Rooms
English, Spanish
All major credit cards accepted
Secure parking
Birding tours available
Breakfast, lunch and dinner available (extra charges for each)
Room Amenities: Ceiling fan, Private outdoor space

How to get here:
Driving south from Cartago, turn west off Highway 2 onto the dirt road across from the yellow church at kilometer 58, seven km past Empalme. Following the dirt road you will reach a small village with a church and soccer field. Bear right at the soccer field. Copey is seven km from Highway 2; when you reach it cross the bridge, then turn left following a sign to El Toucanet. The lodge will be on your right.

The sound of running water permeates everything. El Toucanet Lodge sits right above the rushing Rio Pedregoso which drains the northwestern basin of 3,156 meter Vueltas Peak on the western edge of the Talamanca Range. The water tumbles down its rocky gorge in continuous series of little waterfalls, its music a constant presence day and night.

Most people come to El Toucanet in the northwest corner of the Los Santos Forest Reserve to see Resplendent Quetzals, trogons, and toucanets. We saw lots of hummingbirds but no quetzals; what we did find is that this is paradise for hikers. Little-used farmers' roads snake up the river gorges or switchback over the surrounding ridges. The rocky slopes have been cleared here and there, but most of the land is covered with high-altitude deciduous forest. Bromeliads and thick coats of lichen cover the branches; ferns and yuccas compete with rhododendrons for space in the understory. The air has the strong, deep smell of wet trees in the bright sun, with patches of heavy flower fragrances. At almost 2,000 meters, it's fresh and brisk in the crystal-blue morning, cool in the rainy afternoon, and downright nippy at night. It's like the woods of the northern Appalachians, but with a soft scent of tropical vegetation and crisp air from the Rockies.

El Toucanet offers six simple-but-comfortable rooms, each with a private deck overlooking the river, and a family cabin. Two additional cabins, each with a fireplace and private jacuzzi, were under construction in late 2006. Meals are served in the crescent-shaped dining room with its wall of windows to let in light and the sound of the river or on the deck outside. A big fireplace, couches, bookshelves, and small bar occupy one end of the room. Dinner is served on request. We were lucky enough to have local fresh trout, with just a slice of lemon tucked inside. Delicious!

Your host Gary, who owns El Toucanet with his wife Edna, will take you out in search of quetzals at 7 a.m. and bring you back in time for breakfast. You can hike from here up to the striking scrubby wetland of the Vueltas *paramó*, the northernmost example of a landscape and ecosystem more common in the Andes. Gary tells us you can even walk to Manuel Antonio on back roads and jeep trails. It takes two or three days and you'll need a guide. We consider this, and decide that in this country we'd want a few horses as well.

El Toucanet at night is perfectly quiet except for the night birds and the constant song of the river. The sky is blacker and the stars brighter than anywhere we've stayed previously in Costa Rica. It's November; Andromeda and her distant galaxy are straight overhead. It's time for Alison's fleece boots.

Dantica $$
San Gerardo de Dota   Hiking, Birding

Photo © Dantica

Contact Information:
506-740-1067/740-1069 (voice); 506-740-1071 (fax)
info@dantica.com
www.dantica.com

Essentials:
One 1-BR cabin, Two 2-BR cabins
English, Spanish, Dutch
All major credit cards accepted
Secure parking
Birding tours available, Gallery
Breakfast included, Restaurants nearby
Room Amenities: Ceiling fan, Coffee maker, Refrigerator/minibar, TV,
    Private outdoor space, Internet in office. Cabin #1 has a full
    kitchen

How to get here:
Driving south from Cartago, turn west off Highway 2 at kilometer 80
onto the road to San Gerardo de Dota. Follow this road four km
downhill. Dantica will be on your right.

The deep valley of San Gerardo de Dota is famous for its quetzals, and one flew across the road right in front of us as we were driving down from Dantica. Barely avoiding strangling herself with the seatbelt, Alison jumped out of her seat and scrambled for her camera as I stopped the car. The quetzal sat proudly on a high limb of an oak tree that branched over the road, fluttering his long tail at us daring Alison to get a decent shot from below. After a few minutes of turning this way and that sparkling in the noonday sun, he tired of the game and disappeared into the trees. We were stunned. They really are beautiful, almost beyond imagining. Even the very best photographs don't come close.

Dantica is San Gerardo de Dota's brand-new lodge, built by Colombian designer, Maria, and Dutch biologist-turned-art-collector, Joost. It is a perfect marriage of traditional and contemporary – plain white walls with antique wooden doors and shutters on the side facing the road, floor-to-ceiling single-pane glass walls looking out over the valley on the other side. A network of trails leads steeply downhill through Dantica's ten hectares of primary forest to the fast-running little river below. From your private deck or from the glass-walled bedrooms, you look out over the forest canopy across the canyon to the hills beyond. Mornings and evenings the canyon fills with mist and birdsong. Joost has planted hundreds of almond trees on the property to attract the quetzals.

A bonus of staying at Dantica is Joost and Maria's gallery of Central and South American folk and fine art. Here you can find paintings, wood and fabric art from many countries, colorful baskets, reproductions of pre-Colombian jewelry, even toys for children. Several pieces are gifts from artists and could easily be in museums. There are lots of folk-art souvenir shops in Costa Rica, nearly all of them the same. We've found very few galleries with a wide selection of truly interesting art and no others with the international coverage that Dantica offers. It's worth the drive down to Dantica just to browse. We certainly couldn't pass it up; Alison selected a pair of gold earrings from an ancient design from a burial mound in Colombia. I found a lightweight traditional Colombian hat.

Dantica does not serve meals other than breakfast, although a guests-only dinner service is planned for the near future. In the evening we hiked with our fellow guests a half-kilometer up the road to Miriam who serves generous home-made dinners on her enclosed patio. The special that night was fresh local trout, beautifully prepared and accompanied by vegetables and salad, white rice and black beans – country cooking at its best. The valley below was filled with cloud. Above, the stars were bright in a crystal-clear sky. A full moon was rising over the mountain behind us and the air was cool and sharp with the deep smell of thousands of trees.

Rio Chirripó B&B $$
San Gerardo de Rivas   Hiking, Yoga/Meditation

Photo © Alison Tinsley

Contact Information:
506-742-5109 (voice)
riochirripo@yahoo.com
www.riochirripo.com

Essentials:
8 Rooms, 2 Casitas, 1 House
English, Spanish
Cash only
Secure parking
Riverfront, Swimming pool, Yoga facilities
Breakfast and dinner served on request, Restaurants nearby
Room Amenities: Free WiFi, Semi-private or private outdoor space

How to get here:
In San Isidro El General, turn east off Highway 2 after the Maxi
Bodega, just past the bridge. The paved road ends in Rivas. Turn
right onto the dirt road that heads up the hill at the eastern edge of
town. Follow this road toward San Gerardo de Rivas and Chirripó
National Park. Rio Chirripó B&B will be on your right, just past the
village of Canaán.

Frank Faiella meets us at the gate, makes us coffee, and can't wait to show us the moss-covered network of stone walls, grottos, and huge boulders down below the swimming pool just above the swirling waters of the Rio Chirripó. It looks like an ancient city built by dwarves – the old-world kind out of Tolkein or German legend. The striking pagoda of the new meditation and yoga center towers above us on the ridge.

We can't help thinking of this as "Frank's Place" – in part because Frank periodically changes the name, but mainly because staying here is so much like staying with old friends. The Rio Chirripó B&B is Frank's ongoing architectural fantasy merging the dense high-altitude forest, the house-sized boulders and the pounding river with human structures in an eclectic but intriguing blend of styles. The old stone walls and barely-visible altars were the work of a previous owner, a great labor for who knows what purpose. Now they counterpoint the yoga center and maybe a new cabin or two will fit in as well. The huge, umbrella-shaped *rancho* with its rounded, half-high walls, circle of *bancos* with bright Guatemalan pillows, and blue-chimneyed fireplace looks like Santa Fe, New Mexico. The enormous kitchen with colorful tile walls and countertops came from Mexico, and the dining room with its arches could be Moroccan. *Nichos* are everywhere, housing Buddhas or saints; the Virgin of Guadalupe smiles benignly onto the dining tables. Every surface sports painted filigree, the work of an American artist who arrived one day by motorcycle just when Frank and his building-buddy Mick were wondering how to decorate the place.

The Rio Chirripó has eight rooms, simple in a Zen way, arranged in two 2-story casitas with each pair of rooms sharing a porch or balcony overlooking the river. The beds have colorful Guatemalan spreads, there are rocking chairs on the porch, and the view over the river is great. There are two private one-bedroom *casitas,* one just below the pool and the other in the rock garden, and the airy yoga center with its wall of floor-to-ceiling windows can be used for sleeping in a pinch. Many of Rio Chirripó's guests come for yoga and meditation retreats, but we came for the mountain air, the rock, and the rivers. You are just a few kilometers from the gates of both Chirripó National Park and adjacent Cloud Bridge Reserve. Cerro Chirripó itself, with its ragged ridge of bare rock, dominates the eastern sky. Rustic hot springs are just a 30-minute walk up the road toward the little town of Herradura, and the crashing confluence of the Chirripó and Talari rivers on their way to form the General and the mighty Terraba beyond is right below your feet.

Sarapiquí to Tortuguero

Northeastern Costa Rica is a broad flat triangle bounded by a line of volcanoes to the south and west, the Rio San Juan and Nicaragua to the north, and the Caribbean to the east. This is plantation country, and flying over it you see miles of neat green squares of pineapples, bananas, and papayas interspersed with small farms and cattle ranches. Through them snake countless rivers that drain the much-wetter eastern slopes of the *cordilleras* (mountain ranges). On the mountain slopes, here and there along the major rivers and in a wide swath along the coast is deep, dark green rain forest.

Visitors flock to the Pacific and the southern Caribbean for beaches. They come to the northeast, however, to run the rivers, fish, and explore the Caribbean rainforest. You won't find sprawling big-name resorts here or multi-story blocks of condos. The pace is slow, genuinely Costa Rican, and most places are as dedicated to conservation as they are to tourism. You need to spend a few days here to unwind, pay attention, and appreciate the intense greenness of it all.

The historical hub of the northeast is Puerto Viejo de Sarapiquí, Costa Rica's main port to the Caribbean in colonial times. Boats left here to run down the broad Rio Sarapiquí to its confluence with the San Juan and from there to the sea. The trip from Puerto Viejo de Sarapiquí to Barra de Colorado, the main mouth of the San Juan, takes about eight hours. The area around Barra is a vast swamp and estuary system riddled with channels and lagoons and is protected as a wildlife refuge. Barra itself is the major Costa Rican base for Caribbean sport fishing, and several operators there offer charter boats with captains. You can continue from Barra by river and canal to Tortuguero and from there by intracoastal canal all the way to Limón.

The area around Puerto Viejo de Sarapiquí is dedicated to fast-water sports and rainforest exploration. A handful of lodges and B&Bs line Highway 4 between La Virgen and Puerto Viejo de Sarapiquí and past Puerto Viejo de Sarapiquí around the eastern end of the La Selva private reserve and Braulio Carillo National Park. Many of the lodges own or are associated with private reserves or river-running outfitters.

Costa Rica Highway 4 links Puerto Viejo de Sarapiquí with Guápiles to the south and Aguas Zarcas to the west, but the best way to get here from San José and the Central Valley is over the saddle between Poás and Barva volcanoes. This route passes through the mountain town of Varablanca and down steep, twisty Highway 9 (also called 126) to San Miguel and La Virgen. The narrow ridge-top road makes for beautiful views and deters the big trucks that clog the main highways.

Tortuguero, headquarters for Tortuguero National Park and the only real town on the northern Caribbean coast, is the other major destination in the northeast. As its name suggests, the Tortuguero beaches are a major nesting site for green sea turtles; August and September are the best months to see them. The only way to get to Tortuguero other than by boat is to fly. It's half an hour from San José direct, and the views going over the mountains are awesome. For an in-flight challenge, try counting the waterfalls!

La Quinta $-$$
East of Puerto Viejo de Sarapiquí   Birding, Wildlife, Kid-friendly

Photo © Alison Tinsley

Contact Information:
506-761-1300 (voice); 506-761-1395 (fax)
quinta@racsa.co.cr
www.laquintasarapiqui.com

Essentials:
31 Rooms
English, Spanish
All major credit cards accepted
Secure parking
Swimming pool, Spa
Breakfast included, Restaurant, Bar
Room Amenities: AC (extra charge), Ceiling fan, In-room safe, Internet
    access in office, TV lounge

How to get here:
From Puerto Viejo de Sarapiquí, follow Highway 4 east toward La
Virgen. The road to La Quinta is on the north side of Highway 4,
between Bajos de Chilimate and La Virgen. Follow signs to La
Quinta or to Finca Corsicana, the neighboring pineapple plantation.

La Quinta is a bit like family camp – there's something here for everyone in an enclosed park-like atmosphere. Iridescent blue Morpho butterflies, Owl butterflies with their staring yellow eyes, and brilliant Monarchs flutter in the house-sized butterfly enclosure. Red poison-dart frogs with blue legs emerge sleepily from the leaf litter in the frog garden. A pair of caimans lounge, eyes barely above the water, in one of the ponds. Every tree, bush, and flower is labeled and birds are everywhere. The covered walkways between cabins are lined with posters – maps, local tour announcements, bird, snake, and mammal identification charts. You half expect the staff to double as counselors or maybe to lead songs around the campfire at night.

La Quinta is a Costa Rican family operation, and everything about it has a warm, homey atmosphere. The cabins are mostly duplexes and are arranged in the garden with plenty of room for privacy but without anything being very far away. Hearty *tipico* meals are served at long tables in the open-air restaurant overlooking the gardens; it and the intimate little bar right next door provide a welcome hang-out for the hot part of the day. Several tables of guests were still relaxing over coffee when we arrived late in the morning. The lazy Sardinal River rolls around the border of the property on its way to join the larger and wilder Sarapiquí on the other side of the highway.

Like most lodges around here, La Quinta was once a farm. Leonardo and Beatriz began reforesting and planting gardens over ten years ago. As on most Costa Rican *fincas*, there are many older, mature trees. One has at least two dozen pendulous nests of Montezuma oropendulas. A small museum illustrates the local rural heritage with collections of antique furniture, farm implements, and household goods; it also houses interesting collections of pottery, local insects, and costumes for indigenous dances that mock the Spanish and make light of the long-ago conquest.

This is still farming country. A large pineapple plantation is right next door, and most of the food served at La Quinta comes from the local area. La Quinta's own gardens of orchids, bromeliads, fruit trees, and tropical flowers are tended every day by friendly *jardineros* who are happy to describe their work and show you around. If you're coming from the city – and these days, who isn't – a little immersion in the agricultural lifestyle can be refreshing to say nothing of showing the kids something about where food comes from. And there's that lazy summer-camp atmosphere, a memory of your own childhood full of activities but also full of time. Splash around some in the river, or try your luck fishing for the voracious introduced tilapia. The great thing about La Quinta is, unlike the summer camp you went to when you were a kid, it has a spa attached and a bar and your own comfy bed at the end of the day.

Centro Neotropico SarapiquíS $$
La Virgen de Sarapiquí   Hiking, Birding, Wildlife

Photo © Alison Tinsley

Contact Information:
506-761-1004 (voice); 506-761-1415 (fax)
magistra@racsa.co.cr
www.sarapiquis.org

Essentials:
32 Rooms
English, Spanish
All major credit cards accepted
Secure parking
Museum, Archeological site, Riverfront
Restaurant, Bar
Room Amenities: Ceiling fan, Internet access (in office)

How to get here:
From Puerto Viejo de Sarapiquí, follow Highway 4 east toward La
Virgen. The Centro Neotropico is on the south side of Highway 4,
between Bajos de Chilimate and La Virgen. Look for a sign showing
an indigenous mask; the gate is across the road.

Although it has plenty of trees and birds and wildlife, borders a beautiful river, and it shares facilities with the 890 acre Tirimbina Reserve right next door, Centro Neotropico SarapiquíS is not your ordinary jungle ecolodge. The emphasis here is on the way people fit into the tropical rainforest landscape. Six hundred years ago, this site was an indigenous village. Jean Pierre, a human ecologist and director of the foundation that manages Centro Neotropico SarapiquíS, feels that an experience of the rainforest is incomplete without an appreciation of the role of its human inhabitants. This is what the Centro Neotropico provides.

A dozen of the more than 50 pre-Columbian tombs discovered here have been excavated, and parts of the village have been reconstructed by archeologists from the Museo Nacional de Costa Rica. While most of the original artifacts are in the National Museum, the Centro Neotropico has an on-site museum of indigenous history, musical instruments, and shamanic implements. The lodge itself and the round, thatched *ranchos* that house the guestrooms are based on indigenous designs characteristic of this part of Costa Rica.

The on-going archeological projects, the museum, the formal – if somewhat unkempt – botanical garden, and the young Tirimbina biologists and guides living next door all give the Centro Neotropico a somewhat serious, almost academic air. Judging from the big binoculars and spotting scopes and the rapt attention paid to lengthy demonstrations of ancient pottery techniques, most of our fellow guests were older and were on tours with strong natural history components. Centro Neotropico is a place people visit to learn something, not just to see the jungle.

The Tirimbina Reserve is, however, an impressive and beautiful jungle. You reach it across a 260 meter suspension bridge – reputedly the longest in Costa Rica – across two separate channels of the broad, rocky-bottomed Rio Sarapiquí. Well marked trails loop for miles through the forest. You can descend to river level by a spiral staircase from the main bridge and follow a trail to swimming holes. There's even a chocolate tour to identify native varieties of cocoa then sample their products at the end.

The rooms at Centro Neotropico are sparsely furnished but comfortable and open onto the shaded round verandahs of the four *ranchos*. You are clearly intended to spend most of your time outside. Even well after dark, couples and groups sat on the verandahs talking quietly and enjoying the evening. Meals are all buffet-style with *tipico* cuisine and reserved seating, though we saw lots of table swapping as people got to know each other. The dining room is open and surrounded by bird feeders full of fruit. You don't have to go far here to be part of nature. It's no surprise that this spot was chosen so many years ago as the ideal site for a village.

Tortuga Lodge $$

Tortuguero Birding, Wildlife, Fishing

Photo © Alison Tinsley

Contact Information:
506-257-0766 (Costa Rica Expeditions voice); 506-257-1665 (fax)
ecotur@expeditions.co.cr
www.costaricaexpeditions.com/lodging/tortugalodge

Essentials:
27 Rooms
English, Spanish
All major credit cards accepted
Secure boat parking
Swimming pool, Spa
Breakfast included, Restaurant, Bar
Room Amenities: Ceiling fan, Safe (at reception), Private outdoor space

How to get here:
If you fly to Tortuguero (call Tortuga Lodge first, as they may be
flying a charter shuttle with empty seats), Tortuga Lodge is right
across the river and will send a boat for you. Otherwise, arrange a
boat from Caño Blanco. It is easiest to do this through Tortuga
Lodge, but other boat tour operators are also available.

Our guide Fernando smiled as he cut the motor back and slanted our long boat toward the trees on the left bank. It took me a minute to see it – a five-foot caiman lounging on the bank at about shoulder level. Alison was still peering at the bank not seeing the reptile that was now less than two meters away. Then she saw it, just as Fernando cut the motor completely. The side of the boat touched the bank and the four of us just sat there until Alison started taking pictures . . . fast . . . before the critter caught on and jumped into her lap. The caiman blinked but didn't move a muscle. It must have been well fed and sleepy, because nothing with that many teeth has any point in being scared. After a few minutes we decided we'd pressed our luck enough and backed off. The caiman stayed put, but when we came back that way half an hour later he was gone.

The river is why you go to Tortuguero, and the folks at Tortuga Lodge know it like the backs of their hands. They've been running these channels and backwaters for over thirty years since Tortuga started as a fishing lodge. Captain Eddie Brown, the "Tarpon King," will still take you fishing either on the freshwater rivers and canals or in the ocean beyond. But most visitors come to look for wildlife in the vast Tortuguero National Park. Fernando showed us river otters; spider, howler, and *carablanca* monkeys; crocodiles, and more herons, egrets, and other waterbirds than we could count.

For a rustic jungle lodge, Tortuga is very comfortable. Rooms are large and furnished with big closets, all-around screened windows, well-positioned reading lights, and great solar-heated showers. There are hammocks on the balconies and under the thatched palapa by the pool. It was cool enough in mid-February – "summer" in Costa Rica – that we didn't even need the ceiling fan. Try for rooms #3, 7, or 11 – upstairs with wrap-around balconies and windows no one else walks by.

Meals at Tortuga are served family-style with long tables for groups in the main hall and smaller tables for couples or families on the verandah hanging over the river. Tortuga sources almost all of its ingredients locally and clearly takes pride in its kitchen. Every meal was a multi-course affair, served with grace and a leisurely European pace. Delicious from first to last. To top things off, there's a full bar with that wonderful rarity in Costa Rica, good single-malt scotch.

As befits its fragile setting, Tortuga Lodge has implemented a significant sustainability program with recycling, alternative energy, land conservation, and organic gardening components. As the north Caribbean coast develops and the pressure for road access to Tortuguero increases, we hope their commitment to conservation will spread to the entire community.

South Caribbean

Ask any long-term ex-pat where they like to go for time off and
they're likely to name one of the beach towns south of Limón,
especially if they're Europeans. The South Caribbean beaches are
beautiful, the ocean is wild and frothy, the food is good, and the
people are, well, Costa Rican and then some. Even more Pura Vida
than the rest of the country, if that's possible. Reading the
guidebooks, you'd expect the Caribbean to be wild and boisterous
with crazy Rasta parties until all hours on every corner and dope
smoke so thick you can't see through it. But it's not like that. Sure,
there are some stoners wandering around, and you'll hear "Jah live!"
and "One love!" as greetings. But on balance it's just a little Blacker, a
little more laid back, with a touch more melody in the voices and a
touch more spice in the cooking. A nice place. Try it.

There are essentially two
destinations in the South
Caribbean: Cahuita with its
National Park, and the string of
beach towns from Puerto Viejo
south to Manzanillo bordering
the Gandoca – Manzanillo
Nature Reserve. The Caribbean
has never been as popular as the
Pacific coast, and rampant
tourist development has so far
been kept at bay. There are no
monster resorts, no huge shopping areas, no traffic jams unless you
count bicycles. From Puerto Viejo south, bicycling is the way to get
around. You can rent them for about $5 a day at many hotels and any
number of other places. Some guidebooks say the road is paved from
Cahuita to Manzanillo, and it is – in patches here and there – most
with potholes even worse than in the unpaved parts. Rent a bike; it
beats driving. There's no fuel south of Cahuita anyway.

The Caribbean coast is a good place for wildlife, and has got to be the
slothiest place in Costa Rica. Forget
Manuel Antonio; we counted five (5!)
sloths in one morning walk on one
road in no more than 200 meters.
And we weren't even looking hard.
Howler monkeys abound wherever
the forest hasn't been cleared and if
you come at the right time of year, are
patient, and have abundant luck, you
may see sea turtles, manatees, or
estuarine dolphins.

Guidebooks rave about the spicy Afro-Caribbean cooking, but the best food we've found in the South Caribbean is Italian. Corleone's is the new spot for thin-crust pizza in Cahuita. Avoid the highly-recommended Miss Edith's – bland, barely edible food at exorbitant prices, served with a sneer to boot. Try Cha-Cha-Cha or Casa Creole if it's open; contrary to what some guidebooks report, it appears to have nothing to do with the somewhat run-down Magellan Hotel next door. Down Puerto Viejo way try Amimodo, the Gato Ce Cova, or the stunning Pecora Negra.

Photo © Kelly McGinley

The laid-back Caribbean pace has, unfortunately, impacted the management of some of the more popular hotels; we were unable to motivate responses from some places even after repeated emails and phone calls. But there are plenty of places to stay down here and, unlike on much of the west coast, most appeal to the budget traveler. Don't expect much in the way of frills. Most places have ceiling fans for cooling and funky demand heaters on the showerheads that may or may not produce hot water if you're brave enough to fiddle with them. If you absolutely must have air conditioning and your own satellite TV, try the new Bougainvillea Resort in Cocles. The rooms are a bit cramped, but it has a nice pool and some big trees out back. On the other hand, if you absolutely must have air conditioning, the Caribbean coast may not really be your best destination. If you want it snappy with all the mod cons, head for northern Nicoya.

El Encanto $-$$$
Cahuita   Downtown, Relax/Get away

Photo © El Encanto

Contact Information:
506-755-0113 (voice); 506-755-0432 (fax)
info@elencantobedandbreakfast.com
www.elencantobedandbreakfast.com

Essentials:
3 Rooms, 3 Bungalows, 1 Apartment with kitchen
English, Spanish, French
All major credit cards accepted
Secure parking
Swimming pool, Massage services, Beach Access
Breakfast included, Restaurants nearby
Room Amenities: Ceiling fan, TV (Apartment), Kitchen (Apartment)

How to get here:
Follow Highway 36 south from Limón. At the middle entrance to
Cahuita, across from the bus stop, turn east toward the beach. Turn
right onto the beachfront road. El Encanto will be on your right.
You'll need to ring the bell at the main gate, then park inside the gate
just down the road.

El Encanto is an enclosed bit of elegance in otherwise pretty funky Cahuita. It's just a couple of blocks from downtown but part, you might think, of a different world altogether. It could be the country house of a retired, well-traveled collector set in a sunny garden decorated with Buddhas and various Hindu deities. An English house in colonial India, maybe? There's a sense that things should be proper here. You don't want to talk too loudly.

You have your choice at El Encanto of upstairs rooms in the main house, slightly more private bungalows in the garden or, if you're planning on a longer stay and want to do some cooking, an apartment. Groups or families can rent the entire main house. The rooms are tastefully but not fancifully appointed and feature interesting art including large wooden panels over the beds carved in relief with scenes of Hindu deities and demons engaged in various allegorical pursuits. As with the carefully manicured gardens, there is no sense of the rustic here; the atmosphere is refined and reserved, not laid-back and certainly not South-Caribbean Rasta. For that, you'll have to venture outside the walls.

El Encanto is across the beachfront road from Playa Negra and a few minutes walk from downtown Cahuita. Cahuita is not refined; Cahuita is lazy and dusty (if it's not raining) during the day and exuberantly tropical once the sun sets. Cahuita is colorful and a little bit loud. Unless you've brought a picnic, you'll be heading into Cahuita for dinner. We've heard good things about Cha-Cha-Cha, but ask around. You'll also be passing through town to get to the entrance to Cahuita National Park at the end of the beachfront road. The crowded beach near the park entrance is good for swimming or just hanging out and absorbing the lilting local *patois*, likely mingled with several other languages.

Back at El Encanto, you can daydream and watch the birds in the quiet garden, climb up to the second-floor meditation room for some time to yourself, or have a massage, all the while contemplating the contrasts between this protected, well-regulated little space and the wildness – of nature or culture – blooming outside. What a difference a wall and an attitude make! Surely observing such divides up close is one reason to travel, and El Encanto, with Cahuita and the jungle right next door is a perfect place to take out your little notebook, adjust your spectacles, and imagine yourself to be reporting from a far, distant country, on an exotic coast only recently visited, where the people speak a strange language and savage noises come out of the jungle at night.

La Diosa
$-$$

Cahuita

Oceanfront, Yoga/Meditation

Photo © La Diosa

Contact Information:
877-623-3198 (U.S.); 506-755-0055 (voice); 506-755-0321 (fax)
reservation@hotelladiosa.net
www.hotelladiosa.net

Essentials:
4 Rooms, 3 Duplex cabins
English, Spanish, German
All major credit cards accepted
Secure parking
Swimming pool, Beach access, Yoga/meditation center
Breakfast included, Restaurants nearby
Room Amenities: Ceiling fans, AC (7 of 10 rooms), Bathtubs, Semi-
    private outdoor space, Free WiFi

How to get here:
Follow Highway 36 south from Limón. At the north entrance to
Cahuita, turn east toward the beach, following signs to La Diosa or
Casa Creole. Turn left onto the beachfront road. El Encanto will be
on your right.

La Diosa is on the shore, and what a shore it is! The ground drops down in a huge green bowl behind the swimming pool, then rises back up in crags of sharp coral before dropping a meter or two into the surf. The shelf of coral is cracked and splintered and riven with deep gashes that the water washes into and out of with every wave. The 1991 earthquake hammered this coastline, wrenching Cahuita's famous reef a meter or more above its previous position and exposing a good bit of it above the waves. Pioneer trees are already growing in the hard rock and little washes of sand are recreating a beach, but the ground still feels wounded and raw. Some people love the dramatic fury of this sight – others hate it. We were fascinated by it.

Marcelo and Jacqueline have built an oasis of calm in this violently-altered landscape, and appropriately dedicated it to the goddesses of the earth. Fruit trees and tall palms grow around their home, the main floor of which is an open, wood-floored meditation and yoga room with Buddhas and goddess figures everywhere. Four guestrooms face the house on one side; the other six are in three duplexes on the other side of the house facing the pool. A wall protects the property from the road and inside the atmosphere is tranquil and quiet – a place for guests, as well as the trees and the sandy beach, to rest and re-establish themselves. Artfully-constructed bridges span the deep bowl left by the earthquake, where the wet ground sprouts thick undergrowth. Paths lead to benches set into the exposed coral. You can sit above the surf and gaze out to sea undisturbed for hours.

Our favorite rooms here are in the two-bedroom cabins behind the main house. The simply furnished rooms are ample with space for families or couples traveling together. The cabins have a raised-floor design and plenty of windows but, as this is Cahuita, you may want to request air-conditioning. Each cabin has a front porch with chairs and a hammock for lazy afternoons.

La Diosa is about five kilometers north of downtown Cahuita, so if you are staying here you'll want to have a car or rent a bike to get around. The Casa Creole restaurant right across the street is reputedly the best in the area so check to see if it will be open when you're there. Otherwise you'll need to head into Cahuita itself for lunch or dinner or to visit the Cahuita National Park on the south side of town.

Marcelo and Jacqueline are in the process of developing their next project, The Goddess Garden – a larger garden, meditation, and yoga center just down the road from La Diosa. It promises to be a nice space as well as a showcase for local flora.

Cabinas Casa Verde $

Puerto Viejo   Downtown

Photo © Casa Verde

Contact Information:
506-750-0015 (voice); 506-750-0047 (fax)
casaverde@racsa.co.cr
www.cabinascasaverde.com

Essentials:
17 Rooms
English, Spanish, German
All major credit cards accepted (extra charge)
Secure parking
Swimming pool, Beach access
Breakfast included, Restaurants nearby, Bar
Room Amenities: Ceiling fan, Semi-private outdoor space, TV (9 newer
    rooms), Refrigerator (9 newer rooms)

How to get here:
Drive south through Puerto Viejo on the main road then turn right
just when you see the beach. Go one block and turn left. Cabinas
Casa Verde will be on your right. If you miss the first turn and find
yourself passing the beach, take your next right, then right again.
Casa Verde will be on your left.

A lot of hotels on this part of the coast have their resident sloths, but how many can boast that their lazy creature has lived on site its entire life? René's been keeping an eye on his sloth ever since it showed up as a mere youth, four years ago. It's not too hard a surveillance job, since the little guy mostly hangs out in one of the gardens maybe two feet from where you're standing. He was fast asleep when we were there . . . what a surprise.

If you want to be right downtown in Puerto Viejo, try Casa Verde first. Where else can you get a nice room for just $25 (with shared bath), set in a lovely garden with a spacious pool, a bar, and plenty of space to hang out? You're a block from the main drag, two blocks from the beach, and a quick paddle out to the Salsa Brava wave just offshore. This is the middle of things, the classic Puerto Viejo place to stay.

René has been building Casa Verde, piece by piece, ever since the 1991 earthquake rearranged the local real estate. In the past seventeen years, the trees have had a chance to grow and the gardens here are impressively thick. Many of the cabins have semi-private porches with just flowers for walls. During the gradual building process, a great deal of eclectic art has also blossomed at Casa Verde. Every wall (inside and out), ceiling, and odd nook in the garden sports some kind of creativity, whether an interesting network of twigs and vines, a tile mosaic fountain, a seashell chandelier, or a painting in a bewildering array of styles and attitudes. Plenty of swanky places have less interesting art collections than this.

Casa Verde serves breakfast as well as snacks and drinks in the bar, but for dinner you'll want to head into town. We've heard good things about Chile Rojo, about a block and a half away on the main drag. If you're a bit more adventurous, hike out to Amimodo, right on the point where the Salsa Brava kicks up. I had the very best *pargo entero* (whole red snapper) of my career so far, and I consider myself an expert when it comes to *pargo*. The difference at Amimodo is that they treat the noble snapper as a delicacy, and they understand herbs, spices, and baby zucchini. Wonderful! And you can't complain about the view from your table there either.

Costa de Papito $-$$
Playa Cocles   Surfing, Spa, Happening Place

Photo © Costa de Papito

Contact Information:
506-750-0704 (voice); 506-750-0080 (fax)
costapapito@yahoo.com
www.lacostadepapito.com

Essentials:
13 Bungalows
English, Spanish
All major credit cards accepted
Secure parking
Swimming pool under construction (Feb 07), Spa, Beach access
Breakfast available, Restaurant (dinner only), Bar
Room Amenities: Ceiling fan, Semi-private outdoor space, Internet
     access in restaurant

How to get here:
Follow the coast road southeast from Puerto Viejo toward Manzanillo
(where it ends). La Costa de Papito is across the road from the east
end of the beach, just past Playa Cocles.

Three young Americans were hanging around on the porch of their bungalow in "Happy Town" – the cluster of bungalows across Costa de Papito's little creek – inexpertly cracking coconuts, harvesting what they could of the coconut water, and carving off the thin layers of coconut meat with their diving knives. They'd been over to the Salsa Brava wave that morning, found it disappointing, and spent the rest of the day on the shore breaks at the beach across the street. It was their first day on Playa Cocles, and they were clearly loving it. We asked where they'd come from; "Nosara, yesterday" was the casual reply. It's at least an eight-hour drive without stopping, much of it over awful, truck-clogged roads. They'd probably picked their way down through the potholes from Limón well after dark.

The Costa de Papito is the cool hip place in Cocles, aggressively inexpensive and well-appointed, with a somewhat self-consciously offbeat feel. "For the noble savage," proclaims its motto. Décor in the public room includes posters advertising anti-deforestation rallies and, over the guest-access computers, framed front pages from La Nacion reporting "Don Pepe" Figueras' Costa Rican revolution in 1948 and the triumph of the Sandinistas over Nicaraguan dictator Samoza in 1979. On the wall outside in a collage with period photographs is the most detailed economic history of the south Caribbean coast we've yet seen.

Papito's bungalows are roomy and stylish with zebra-print sheets, filmy mosquito nets over the beds, and colorful tile mosaics in the showers and framing the mirrors. Each has a poster of Bob Marley by the door; some have red, green, and yellow painted ceilings. The wrap-around decks have tables and chairs and hammocks, most of which are shielded from view by the abundant gardens. A swimming pool is under construction. There are plenty of birds to watch plus monkeys and sloths. Surf – relax –surf – relax. What could be better?

If you *are* looking for something even better than hanging out watching the monkeys and nursing a beer, how about "ultimate total body chocolate decadence" at the Pure Jungle Spa just steps from your bungalow? Spa director Jiyoung uses lots of local dark chocolate from the Bri-Bri Indigenous Reserve, as well as local coconuts and tropical fruits in her treatments, facials, and pedicures. Or you can opt for a massage in one of the open-air, thatch-roofed treatment rooms, like Alison did. There's a great bonus – a slab of crumbly dark chocolate wrapped in a banana leaf as you walk out the door. It's worth stopping by the spa just for that.

In the evenings Chef Danilo whips up fish curries and other fusion cuisine in Papito's restaurant (closed Sundays), or you can stroll or bike into Puerto Viejo for even more choices. After dinner it's stories by the bar or a stroll on the beach or just goodnight. *Pura Vida*!

Aguas Claras $$-$$$
Playa Cocles   Oceanfront, Relax/Get Away, Wildlife

Photo © Aguas Claras

Contact Information:
506-750-0131 (voice); 506-750-0368 (fax)
aguasclaras@racsa.co.cr
www.aguasclaras-cr.com

Essentials:
5 Cottages
English, Spanish
All major credit cards accepted
Secure parking
Beach Access
Breakfast available, Restaurant (lunch only)
Room Amenities: Ceiling fans, Semi-private outdoor space, Internet
  access in restaurant

How to get here:
Follow the coast road southeast from Puerto Viejo toward
Manzanillo. Aguas Claras is on the beach side of the road, between
Playa Cocles and Playa Chiquita.

If you're planning on moving into the Playa Cocles area for a few days, you can't do much better than the colorful Caribbean-Victorian casitas at Aguas Claras. They are raised up on stilts in the traditional way and so hidden by mature gardens and the surrounding jungle of the Gandoca – Manzanillo reserve that only the smallest one, the one-bedroom Blue Cottage, is even visible from the road. The kitchens and living rooms are open-air to take maximum advantage of the coastal breezes. And the beach is just a short walk from your door through the trees.

With the many jungle-themed lodgings in the South Caribbean, the vaguely British-Colonial architecture and ambiance at Aguas Claras is refreshing. These cottages are actually elegant, in a low-key, slow-moving way. It's not just the bright exterior colors and the fanciful gingerbread; the interior décor has also been carefully thought out and even the pictures on the walls fit the style. You expect to see D. H. Lawrence lounging on the verandah with a gin-and-tonic in hand, a bamboo cane, and wire-frame spectacles. It's much too refined here for Hemingway.

Aguas Claras is famous as a setting in the award-winning 2004 Esteban Ramirez film *Caribe*, which celebrates the on-going struggle of the South-Caribbean communities to keep off-shore oil exploration from destroying their beaches, reefs, and tourism-based economy. You'll find mementos of this campaign for sale in the gift shop, including *Caribe* DVDs, T-shirts and bumper stickers supporting Adela, a Costa Rican coordinating group for alternative energy projects and legal action to protect the coastal environment (www.grupoadela.org).

The café at Aguas Claras, Miss Holly's, serves breakfast every day and lunch until three p.m. every day but Tuesdays. The menu is *Tico* Caribbean, and the verandah atmosphere is delightful. You can sit here with your corn muffins and eggs and good black coffee watching the resident sloths going about their slow business in the trees right off the porch. Inspiring, no?

As an added bonus of staying at Aguas Claras, you're just down the road from two great Italian restaurants, the informal Gato Ce Cova by the main beachfront road and the posher Pecora Negra at the end of the dirt driveway next to the Gato. The Gato is the place for lively conversation as well as a good meal and is open late. For that special dinner with your honey, head for the Pecora Negra.

Playa Chiquita Lodge $
Playa Chiquita   Oceanfront, Wildlife

Photo © Playa Chiquita Lodge

Contact Information:
506-750-0062 (voice); 506-750-0408 (fax)
info@playachiquitalodge.com
www.playachiquitalodge.com

Essentials:
12 Cabins
English, Spanish, German, French
All major credit cards accepted
Off-street parking
Beach access
Breakfast included, Restaurants nearby
Room Amenities: Ceiling fans, Semi-private outdoor space, Free WiFi

How to get here:
Follow the coast road southeast from Puerto Viejo toward
Manzanillo. Playa Chiquita Lodge is on the beach side of the road in
Playa Chiquita, five km south of Puerto Viejo.

We rolled into Playa Chiquita in the late morning, and the owners, Wanda and Wolf, were sitting in the breakfast area relaxing from the morning's work. Our friend Kelly was feeling a bit queasy and Wanda had just the solution – *pipa fria*, fresh coconut water. "The freshest water in the world," she said. "It's what we give the kids." She rustled up a fresh *pipa*, gave it to Kelly with a straw, and in no time she was feeling better. How's that for hospitable hosts? Nice rooms, good conversation, and cures for tummy aches to boot.

Playa Chiquita Lodge nestles in the jungle between the coast road and the beach, its central palapa and colorful duplexes set among gardens and huge trees. We watched an extended family of howler monkeys on an afternoon prowl high above us, many of the adults accompanied by young that were probably only a few weeks past riding on their mother's backs. The young ones were already making daring leaps from one tree to the next at least 50 feet off the ground. One of our fellow guests, an Italian on vacation from his home in the Talamancas, explained to us that howlers are a sign of good energy and will only stay around if the human inhabitants are friendly and allow them their space. One family he knew had offended their local howlers by subdividing their land, and the monkeys tore their house apart while they were gone one weekend. Don't cross those guys; they'll get you.

Playa Chiquita Lodge is, as you might expect, just a quick walk through the jungle to Playa Chiquita in its little protected cove bordered by rocky points. We went out for our morning beach walk early and headed south towards Punta Uva. We shared the beach with a family of horses having their own beach walk, consuming nuts from the beachfront almond trees as they went. At high tide the water laps almost at the base of the trees; there's no expanse of sand in this part of the Caribbean. The beach points north, toward Cuba – looking out to sea, we were gazing toward Havana. The waves that bash ashore here have come a long way.

Ask the right questions and you can learn a lot about the local culture and politics from Wolf and Wanda. Wolf was one of the coastal landowners who worked with the government to create the Gandoca-Manzanillo refuge which protects the beachfront forest from Cocles all the way to Panama as well as a substantial parcel of inland rainforest south of Manzanillo. Because a lot of people live within its boundaries, Gandoca-Manzanillo is an experiment in blending economic and ecological priorities with an emphasis on sustainability. Wanda is one of the organizers of the South Caribbean Music and Arts Festival, an annual cultural project that combines music, art, and theater. Both are activists for culturally and ecologically sensitive tourism.

Shawandha Lodge $$
Playa Chiquita   Honeymoons, Wildlife

Photo © Alison Tinsley

Contact Information:
506-750-0018 (voice); 506-750-0037 (fax)
shawandha@racsa.co.cr
www.shawandhalodge.com

Essentials:
13 Bungalows
English, Spanish, French, Italian
All major credit cards accepted
Off-street parking
Beach access
Breakfast included, Restaurant (dinner only), Bar
Room Amenities: Ceiling fan, In-room safe, Private outdoor space,
    Internet access in office

How to get here:
Follow the coast road southeast from Puerto Viejo toward
Manzanillo. Shawandha is across the road from the beach in Playa
Chiquita, five km south of Puerto Viejo.

Shawandha's well-regarded restaurant was closed the night we were there (a Wednesday, alas), so we rented bicycles and headed back up the dirt road to the little "gourmet" grocery store for wine and picnic provisions. Ignacio at the front desk provided us with candles, and soon we were sitting on our bungalow's front deck feasting on salami and cheese sandwiches, Argentine Malbec red wine, and dark chocolate by flickering candlelight. A bat flitted around, probably consuming mosquitoes because none bothered us. We burned some incense to add to the ambiance; there's a supply in every bungalow, another of Shawandha's delightful extras.

Shawandha Lodge is the low-key luxury option on the southern Caribbean coast, offering spare-but-spaciously-elegant bungalows tucked among huge old trees, trailing vines, and clusters of heliconias and other flowering under-story plants. Most of the bungalows are designed for couples and have big king beds but a few feature queens with an added single for families. All have ample front porches – some more hidden than others – with couches and hammocks for picnics or outdoor lounging. But the real surprise is the bathrooms: semicircular, step-down spaces with tile mosaic floors and colorful mosaic walls, most made by French tile artist Filou. Our shower featured a Mayan lightening god armed with a spear-thrower and a cluster of crystal-tipped spears. Bolts of light radiated from his body. Above the sink was a mosaic mask of a Native American singer that reminded us of petroglyphs on canyon walls near our old home in Galisteo, New Mexico. Several of the bungalows have Mayan or Aztec themes, the inside art complemented by relief carvings by co-owner Maho Díaz on the exterior concrete walls. Other bungalows are African, with bold angular shapes in mosaic and African-style textiles on the walls.

The public spaces at Shawandha are designed for relaxed, intimate conversation, in comfortable sitting areas like those in the lobbies of grand urban hotels. All are outside covered by thatched palapa roofs and separated by gardens featuring bright flowers and pre-Columbian stone carvings. Turn around, and you discover tall tree trunks carved with strange totems from some jungle culture or a stone face peering placidly out of dense foliage. Hummingbirds zip here and there. Toucans croak and chatter above you, out of sight in the tall trees.

Playa Chiquita is about 100 meters away, across the road and down a shady trail through the trees. Behind you, the forest climbs slowly up into the eastern Talamancas. There are no clocks here but the howler monkeys will wake you, sometimes as early as four a.m. Dawn is gentle here deep in the trees. Whatever's happening in the rest of the south Caribbean, here at Shawandha you're in your own little world.

Tamarindo and Northern Nicoya

Talk to any two ex-pats in Costa Rica and chances are good that at least one of them started out in Tamarindo, just a speck of a beach town on the northwest elbow of the Nicoya Peninsula, so small it's hard to find on many highway maps. This is where the great ex-pat migration started back in the 1970s, and it's still the first place many tourists hear about and the first place they head for. It was our first stop on our first exploratory driving trip. It was March, blazing hot, and crowds of energetic young people on Spring Break caroused in the bars and played in the surf. We took one look around and got out of there. We like Tamarindo and environs better in the fall and early winter – late rainy season in Costa Rica – when it's cooler and there are no crowds.

They call the area from Tamarindo to up around the Gulf of Papagayo the "Gold Coast", and you'll see why as you drive in through the forest billboards for real-estate companies, condo developments, and swanky golf-course gated communities. The state of Guanacaste has embraced Pacific-coast tourism and the second-home business with entrepreneurial zeal, and sometimes it seems like everything in sight is for sale. The international airport at Liberia delivers vacationers and house-hunters right to the front doors of the developers. Old-timers moan about it, but all the development must be good for somebody's business. High-end shops and new restaurants are everywhere. Judging from the number of people we've run into who've moved *from* Tamarindo, though, we expect the turnover must be pretty high.

There are some monster resorts on the Gold Coast and some places where the condos are so thick you can barely see the water. Playa Hermosa (the northernmost one of that name, up above Playa del Coco) is such a place. We recommend avoiding these areas unless you're researching impacts of rampant overdevelopment or want to feel like you're in Miami. But there are also spots like Ocotal where the development blends in better and the scene on the beach could be from 1970. Playa Grande still has a funky, surf-camp feel even with its *se vende* (for sale) signs and second homes. South of Playa Langosta, Tamarindo's hyper-upscale southern suburb, there are still uninhabited beaches with basically no roads. But development is coming; you can feel it in the air and see it on every roadside. If you're looking for someplace truly isolated, head farther south.

We have to admit, though, that we find the combination of style and seediness, the multi-million dollar walled mansions on the muddy, pitted dirt roads, the fast-buck speculators hanging out with the old hippies and the spring-break crowd, to be intriguing and even charming in an offbeat way. Tamarindo is a microcosm of the unfolding collision between the overcharged techno-culture of the First World and the attitudes, very-alive environment, and climate of the tropics. It will be sad, though, if it spreads to all of Nicoya. Around Tamarindo it's already happened. It's not for everybody, but it can be fun.

Rancho Armadillo $$$
Playa del Coco   Birding, Wildlife, Kid-friendly

Photo © Rancho Armadillo

Contact Information:
506-670-0108 (voice); 506-670-0441 (fax)
info@ranchoarmadillo.com
www.ranchoarmadillo.com

Essentials:
5 Rooms, Two 2-BR Suites
English, Spanish
All major credit cards accepted
Off-street parking
Swimming pool
Breakfast included, Guest-accessible kitchen (dinners on request), Bar
Room Amenities: TV, AC, Ceiling fan, Refrigerator, Coffee maker, Free
    WiFi

How to get here:
From Liberia, follow Highway 21 west and then CR 151 toward
Playas del Coco. Turn south (left) off of CR 151 immediately before
the start of the boulevard. This dirt road ends at Rancho Armadillo.

For a welcome alternative to the well-polished all-inclusive resorts and endless upscale condo projects of northern Guanacaste, head to Rancho Armadillo up the mountain just outside Playa del Coco.

The cabins of Rancho Armadillo have a nautical feel, although they're much more spacious than a boat would be. The wood paneling, heavy doors and stained-glass porthole windows of the original rooms were created by the captain of a private yacht sailing from L.A. to Houston. Somehow, he stumbled upon Rancho Armadillo, fell in love with the property, and called the yacht's owner to tell him he needed to send a new captain. Rick, the current owner, has added gardens, hidden sculptures, tiled pathways and several additional rooms.

Rancho Armadillo now offers five rooms and two suites in three buildings that climb up the steep hill. All the rooms are spacious and well equipped, not luxurious but very comfortable. Our favorites are the "Shark," which is the honeymoon suite (don't ask!), and the "Cacique" high up at the top of the property, just above the pool.

The property covers 25 acres, so there's a lot of wild land in addition to the lawns and gardens. Rick has tallied 76 species of birds over the years, as well as miniature grey foxes, coyotes, coatis, and the tiny Costa Rican white-tailed deer. We watched a family of howler monkeys for a while then wandered down the lawn to visit a Laughing Falcon that nests in the same spot every year. Rick warned Alison just before she stepped on a fast-moving snake – contiguous red and yellow screamed CORAL snake to our North American eyes, but it turned out to be more ambiguous down here where false corals mimic their venomous cousins.

The big breakfast palapa has a serious, professional-quality kitchen that Rick opens to guests, and the view from the tables and the bar is great. Rick is a former chef and, if you ask, he will cook what you catch in the ocean or provide from other sources. The swimming pool and library are next door at the top of the property or you can follow the stepping stones with their colorful tile mosaics of local birds and flowers through the sculpture gardens. Rick keeps adding more attractions; a combined orchideum and hummingbird garden was in progress when we were there. The air is clear, there's no traffic, and the view down to the beach is fabulous. Best of all, this is the real Costa Rica, not an import from somewhere else – a refreshing change on this too-developed part of the coast.

Hotel Villa Casa Blanca $$
Playa Ocotal   Wildlife

Photo © Hotel Villa Casa Blanca

Contact Information:
506-670-0518 (voice); 506-670-0448 (fax)
vcblanca@racsa.co.cr
www.hotelvillacasablanca.com

Essentials:
12 Rooms
English, Spanish
All major credit cards accepted
Off-street parking
Swimming pool
Breakfast included, Bar, Restaurants nearby
Room Amenities: AC, Ceiling fan, Refrigerator, In-room safe, Free
    WiFi; Suites have bathtubs

How to get here:
From Liberia, follow Highway 21 west and then CR 151 toward
Playas del Coco. Turn left off CR 151 in downtown Playas del Coco
and follow signs to Playa Ocotal. This road winds through several
turns for three km. The road forks immediately before you reach
Ocotal beach; follow the left fork through the gate and tell the guard
you are going to Villa Casa Blanca. The hotel is straight up the hill.

At the top of the stairs by the big beer cooler a dark scurrying motion and then a long bushy black tail caught my eye. We were relaxing on Hotel Villa Casa Blanca's upstairs porch just after sunset. At first I thought it was a black squirrel, but then he strolled right past us . . . a little *zorillo*, a skunk, probably the small black hooded skunk common in Guanacaste. Our host Juan Manuel explained that the little fellow made his rounds every night with hardly a whiff of skunkly *olor*. After the squawking parrots, absurdly-crested magpie jays, black and green iguanas, playful squirrels, and howler monkeys we had already seen and heard, we could hardly be surprised at a family of skunks.

Hotel Villa Casa Blanca (could they think of any more nouns to put in their name?) feels like a small rural hotel in some little European town a century ago. Twin sweeping stairways, four-poster beds, ornate mirrors, layers of drapery from sheer curtains to fancy valences on the heavy-framed windows, even a classic green awning all around the roof of the ample upstairs porch, add to its old-fashioned charm. It's cozy, like grandma's house. But it has iguanas and a swim-up bar. My grandma sure didn't have these. As a bonus, it looks right down the hill to Playa Ocotal.

Tiny, secluded Playa Ocotal is only three km from bustling Playas del Coco, but it feels like your own private beach. Sure, there are some fancy houses up in the hills and some construction here and there, but down at Father Rooster's, with an Imperial beer and one of their huge one-lb (that's right, one *pound*) *hamberguesas* for a snack, you'd think you were in a 60s surfer movie in one of the lazy, downtime scenes on the little side beach away from the waves. Boats for fishing and diving and ridiculous pontoon party boats bob offshore. Palms sway. Iguanas poke around, looking for whatever iguanas look for. Nothing is happening here; some say that's heaven.

The best rooms for couples at Villa Casa Blanca are #11 and #14 (the Honeymoon suite), both upstairs with big beds, bathtubs, and great views of the playa. We had #10, which also has a nice view; #1 and #2 connect to form a family suite. Coffee was ready at 6 a.m. in time for a nice walk before the *tipico* breakfast served from 7:30 – 9:30. The staff was lovely, the rooms were spotless and the price was definitely right.

Hotel Las Tortugas $$
Playa Grande   Oceanfront, Surfing, Wildlife

Photo © Hotel Las Tortugas

Contact Information:
506-653-0423 (voice); 506-653-0458 (fax)
surfegg@cool.co.cr
www.lastortugashotel.com

Essentials:
10 Rooms, Dormitory facilities, Rental houses
English, Spanish
All major credit cards accepted
Off-street parking
Swimming pool, Hot tub
Breakfast included, Restaurant, Bar
Room Amenities: TV, AC, Ceiling fan

How to get here:
From Liberia, follow Highway 21 west and south, then CR 155
toward Tamarindo. In Huacas, turn off Highway 155 and follow
signs to Playa Grande and Brasilito. Just out of town there is a Y-
junction; take the left (southern) branch toward Matapalo and Playa
Grande. In the town of Matapalo, the road to Playa Grande turns
sharply left. Once in the "town" of Playa Grande, bear right at the Y-
junction, following signs to Las Tortugas or the MINAE turtle
museum.

Walking up the front stairs here is walking back in time. Well-tanned guys with tattoos, wet shorts, and no shirts hang around, smoking and drinking beer, reggae tumbles out of the stereo, Brittany at the front desk is a volunteer here to teach English and study the turtles. The tide table and the surf report are posted by the open front door; a blackboard says there's fresh-caught tuna for lunch. No one is moving fast except Brittany who is organizing a spare room for a couple of backpackers who just turned up. Las Tortugas is full – it almost always is.

We sat down for lunch, ordered our drinks and the owner, Louis, appeared, dripping wet, surfboard in hand. He's been here forever, first to surf, then as a conservationist and leader of the campaign to protect Playa Grande as a nesting beach of the leatherback turtle (*la baula* in Costa Rica). Las Baulas National Park created in 1990 is the result of that effort. Hotel Las Tortugas was originally conceived as a scientific station to observe the night-nesting, light-sensitive giant turtles which can weigh up to a ton. Most of the rooms started out as group quarters for scientists and students; windows and other sources of night-time illumination are below tree level or face away from the beach. The hotel still serves as a nature and information center for the park, although tours for the public are now managed and led from the MINAE (Costa Rican Environment Ministry) park office just up the street. But the crowd here, even at the start of turtle-nesting season, is mainly after the surf. Playa Grande is three and a half miles of west-facing, light-sand beach with what Louis calls the most consistent beach break on the Costa Rican Pacific. The same people turn up year after year, often with their families. Louis actually asks us how we heard of Las Tortugas, explaining that they don't advertise and rely mainly on returning guests and personal referrals.

Las Tortugas has ten rooms in the pyramid-like main building. Three of them are downstairs, multi-bedroom suites originally designed for nocturnal turtle-watchers. Although necessarily quite dark so as not to disturb the turtles with ambient light at night, the rooms are well-equipped and decorated with hand-laid tile and shell mosaics. On the other side of the pool are dorms with room for up to 30 students or others who don't mind group living and plan to spend most of their time outside. If you want a view, reserve the "lighthouse room" at the top of the main building over the bar or ask Louis about his apartments. They're just up the hill, inexpensive, and spacious. We liked apartment #7 in the Lighthouse Building, the top two floors of a round tower with all-around windows and Louis' signature round bed (he has to *make* the sheets). The even-bigger apartment #4 is in the octagonal Octopus Building. There's a funky feeling to all of Louis' rooms – but the kind of good funky that's reminiscent of '70s surfer movies.

Bula Bula $$
Playa Grande   Wildlife, Happening Place

Photo © Alison Tinsley

Contact Information:
877-658-2880 (U.S.); 506-653-0975 (voice); 506-653-0978 (fax)
frontdesk@hotelbulabula.com
www.hotelbulabula.com

Essentials:
10 Rooms
English, Spanish
All major credit cards accepted
Off-street parking
Swimming pool
Breakfast included, Restaurant, Bar
Room Amenities: TV, AC, Ceiling fan, Refrigerator, Coffee maker

How to get here:
From Liberia, follow Highway 21 west and south, then CR 155
toward Tamarindo. In Huacas, turn off Highway 155 and follow
signs to Playa Grande and Brasilito. Just out of town there is a Y-
junction; take the left (southern) branch toward Matapalo and Playa
Grande. In the town of Matapalo, the road to Playa Grande turns
sharply left. Once in the "town" of Playa Grande, bear to the left at
the Y-junction, following signs to Bula-Bula and The Great Waltini
restaurant. Or, call to get a boat pick-up in Tamarindo – it's a ten-
minute ride.

Once upon a time there were two guys from California, successful as entrepreneurs but increasingly eager to just get away from it all. One night they were up late with their friends and everyone had a story about Costa Rica. So they did what any pair of young Californians would do – they found a realtor and arranged to see property all along the Pacific coast. Why think small – maybe they'd buy a hotel with a restaurant so Wally could cook and a funky-chic bar where Todd could hold court and tell stories. They prowled up and down the coast, scoping out competitors and thinking about marketing. Then they hit Playa Grande and fell in love: it was the middle of nowhere, but just an hour from the new airport! Bula Bula!

Bula Bula (Wally'n'Toddian for "Happy Happy") is the cool Tamarindo hotel that isn't in Tamarindo. The easiest way to get here is by boat – it's just ten minutes from Tamarindo across the estuary. Which means, of course, that you can also get back to Tamarindo in no time flat. It just *feels* isolated out here in Playa Grande – no street lights, no traffic, no late-night racket from the bars next door. Just your own little laid-back tropical getaway, a handful of fellow guests out here braving the wilderness, and the local residents who turn up for Wally's cooking and Todd's famous martinis. The TV over the bar is showing James Bond with the sound off, Bert the resident parrot is greeting everyone who passes, and someone's just handed you a massive dose of Ketel One. Paradise!

The Bula Bula has ten rooms with all the comforts of home – air conditioners, coffee makers, refrigerators, cable TVs. They're painted bright colors and out on the porch are rocking chairs straight from the Raj. You're a five-minute walk from the flat Playa Blanca beach with its big breakers in the daytime and turtles at night. And you're right on the bank of the Tamarindo Estuary, 1,200 acres of protected saltwater marshland full of crocodiles, coatimundis, and howler monkeys. Rent a canoe over at the Hotel Las Tortugas, or ask Todd to set up a tour. Bula Bula can arrange tours for almost any interest – ocean fishing or diving, ATV or horseback riding, even golf or tennis (Where are you? Some swamp in Costa Rica?).

In the evening pull up a chair for blackened fish or a steak, then just hang out at the bar. You're bound to meet some interesting folks and you'll probably hear some tall tales. Once the sun sets you and your *compadres* are in the only circle of light around. The surf crashes, howlers swing in the trees, and those big crocs prowl around just outside. This *is* the tropics – it's just like the in movies.

Luna Llena $$
Tamarindo   Downtown, Kid-friendly

Photo © Alison Tinsley

Contact Information:
506-653-0082 (voice); 506-653-0120 (fax)
lunalle@racsa.co.cr
www.hotellunallena.com

Essentials:
7 Rooms, 7 Cabins with full kitchens
English, Spanish, Italian
All major credit cards accepted
Off-street parking
Swimming pool, Swim-up bar
Breakfast included, Restaurant under construction
Room Amenities: TV, AC, Ceiling fan

How to get here:
The highway to Tamarindo (CR 155) turns into Tamarindo's main
street. In town, follow the left branch at the Y-junction just past the
Hotel Diria. Take the second right after this Y-junction, following
signs to Playa Langosta or the Barceló resort; there is a strip mall on
the corner. Turn left onto Calle Real just after the Iguana Surf Shop.
Luna Llena is about a block down on the right.

Just ask for the "yellow hotel" in Tamarindo and you'll probably get directions to Luna Llena, Pino and Simona's delightfully playful version of Oz. Most hotels have rooms and some have cabins, but at Luna Llena your "bungalow" is a little round tower with a spiral stairway climbing up to a round master bedroom with a 360-degree view. Everything is brightly painted with a full palette of colors and every kind of fanciful design – dancing fish, birds, flowers, clouds – an old-fashioned children's coloring book on every wall. The colors look so fresh that we suspect Simona races in and repaints everything whenever someone checks out.

Luna Llena also has regular rooms, but the tower-bungalows are the place to be. Each has a kitchen and your hosts are Italians so they are *nice* kitchens with the appliances and tools you'll need to actually cook real meals. There are comfy sitting areas and beds downstairs for the kids. Luna Llena is a very kid-friendly place; the whole property is walled, the towers are set protectively around the perimeter, and the enclosed gardens and pool are meant to be played in. There are resident cats and dogs. So move in and just hang out for awhile. Let the kids run around; you can cool off in the pool and tank up at the swim-up bar.

You're not on the beach at Luna Llena, but you're only about three blocks away. This is the part of inland Tamarindo that we call "Little Italy" because so many of the hotels are owned and managed by Italians. There's some development going on here, but it's not as manic as down on the main strip and you don't have to contend with all-night traffic or beach parties. On slow days when the folks who live here are relaxing, doing some clean-up, repainting, or just hanging around, you can almost feel the old Tamarindo before the boom when this was a sleepy beach town that attracted surfers and assorted alternative types – mainly from the U.S., France, and Italy – to an existence far removed from the "real world" and the various hassles of their native countries. Luna Llena is a masterpiece of that old spirit . . . a fairy tale, a place from a parallel universe, a more whimsical, gentler version of the world.

A bonus of staying back here away from the main street action is that two of Tamarindo's best restaurants are around the corner. Everyone talks about Pachanga, but we've never managed to find it open (it closes on Tuesdays, and we must have a jinx). We can vouch for Dragonfly with its fusion of Costa Rican and Pacific Rim. Luna Llena will soon be opening their own restaurant, so we're eager to see how they'll join in the mix. Real Italian, we hope.

Villa Alegre $$$
Playa Langosta   Oceanfront, Kid-friendly

Photo © Villa Alegre

Contact Information:
506-653-0270 (voice); 506-653-0287 (fax)
vialegre@racsa.co.cr
www.villaalegrecostarica.com

Essentials:
4 Rooms, 1 Casita, Two 2-BR Villas
English, Spanish
All major credit cards accepted
Secure parking
Swimming pool
Breakfast included, Restaurants nearby
Room Amenities: AC, Free WiFi, Villas have full kitchens with coffee
    makers and private outdoor space

How to get here:
The highway to Tamarindo (CR 155) turns into Tamarindo's main
street. In town, follow the left branch at the Y-junction just past the
Hotel Diria. Take the second right after this Y-junction, following
signs to Playa Langosta or the Barceló resort; there is a strip mall on
the corner. Follow this dirt road past Capitan Suizo then go right at
the Y-junction. Continue past Cala Luna; Villa Alegre is on your
right.

Barry, our genial host, greeted us upon our arrival at Villa Alegre and welcomed us as though to his own home – which it is. The big living room is comfortable and informal with picture windows, a wall of books, and a fridge full of beer and soft drinks. Step outside onto the deep verandah and you are greeted by a sparkling pool, an open, conical-roofed palapa with an outdoor kitchen, and the green of the coastal Guanacaste jungle. This house is designed to be shared and Barry and Suzye Lawson welcome you like family.

A short walk downhill past the pool brings you to a different world – empty, west-facing Playa Langosto with its soft, water-soaked sand and hard black rock. High tide here comes right up to the gnarled, wind-twisted trees. You can walk from Villa Alegre to central Tamarindo if the tide is out. Aside from weekend crowds at the Barceló Resort at its southern end, the beach here is quiet except for the surf.

Villa Alegre offers four main-house rooms, a casita (the only room with a full ocean view), and two villas each named for a country and decorated with folk art and souvenirs of Barry and Suzye's travels. The main-house rooms face away from the public spaces providing privacy and quiet. Our favorite room is Mexico with its huge outdoor bathroom. If you want a private patio opt for El Caribe. Japan and Russia, the villas, are beautifully decorated with full kitchens, big master bedrooms, private patios, and either jungle (Japan) or jungle and ocean (Russia) views. The USA room in the main house and the Russia villa are handicapped accessible.

Villa Alegre is equipped for families, and even small children are welcome. There's a shuffleboard court, a horseshoe pit, and a list of tours and activities the Lawsons can organize for you.

Barry cooks an impressive breakfast and promises a different breakfast every day. Everyone eats together at 8:30, so if you want something light before your early-morning walk, purchase it in town the night before. The villas have their own coffee makers, but the rooms do not. Barry graciously prepared the coffee maker for us the night before so we could fuel ourselves for our 5:30 a.m. beach walk. Tamarindo is full of restaurants for lunch and dinner; three are within an easy walk of Villa Alegre. We particularly like the restaurant at Cala Luna for lunch.

Sueno del Mar $$$-$$$$
Playa Langosta   Oceanfront, Honeymoons, Adults Only

Photo © Sueno del Mar

Contact Information:
506-653-0284 (voice); 506-653-0558 (fax)
innkeeper@sueno-del-mar.com
www.sueno-del-mar.com

Essentials:
3 Rooms, Honeymoon suite, 2 Casitas
English, Spanish
All major credit cards accepted
On-street parking
Swimming pool
Breakfast included, Restaurants nearby
Room Amenities: AC, Ceiling fan, In-room safe, Casitas have full
    kitchens with coffee makers

How to get here:
The highway to Tamarindo (CR 155) turns into Tamarindo's main
street. In town, follow the left branch at the Y-junction just past the
Hotel Diria. Take the second right after this Y-junction, following
signs to Playa Langosta or the Barceló resort; there is a strip mall on
the corner. Follow this dirt road past Capitan Suizo then go right at
the Y-junction. Continue past Cala Luna then turn right. Sueno del
Mar will be on your left.

Had a honeymoon lately? We figured we were due for one so we checked into the Honeymoon Suite at lovely Sueno del Mar. It's just the spot for a romantic interlude by the sea. The suite is big enough to live in and comes with an elevated king bed, rocking chairs, a two-person hammock, sarongs to wear however you like and complementary champagne. A wall of windows looks down onto the ocean and two more look into the treetops on either side. Décor is tropical bungalow with a bit of the Kasbah for romance. There's a private outdoor shower (for two, of course) and private stairs down to the beach. And you're right over the kitchen, so you can smell breakfast cooking as you relax, sip your coffee, and soak in that early-morning ocean view.

Sueno del Mar is small and intimate and Tui, the innkeeper, gets our vote for most welcoming, what-can-I-do-to-make-your-day-perfect hostess in Costa Rica. Besides the splendid honeymoon suite, there are two split-level two-bedroom casitas with kitchenettes and three nicely-appointed rooms with queen beds. The real star here, though, is the public space – a beautiful enclosed sitting area by the big open kitchen, the open-air breakfast area with tables and *bancos,* and the gardens and pool. And then of course there's the beach! Sueno del Mar is one of the few beachside places where the transition from hotel to beach is truly flawless. The only indication of a boundary is a little shell-encrusted foot-washing pool built into the pathway. Hammocks are tucked into the gnarled beachside trees, chaises and Adirondack chairs are perfectly placed for watching the surf, and the weathered black rocks poking out into the waves are full of holes and channels that convert every 12 hours, like magic, to tide-pools filled with creatures.

Breakfast here is a treat. You start with warm, very sweet cornbread (that's what smelled so tempting earlier). Then comes fresh-squeezed fruit juice, a variety of fresh fruit, and finally omelets (made with mushrooms our morning) with homemade toast. By 8 a.m. everyone's up; the breakfast area is perfectly designed for meeting your neighbors, comparing travel notes, and planning your day. Sueno del Mar doesn't serve dinner, but Taboo – maybe the best restaurant in the whole Tamarindo area – is just two blocks down the road to the south. Nicholas the owner/chef hails from Paris, and his attention to detail shows it. If it's anywhere near the high season, you'll want to make a reservation; just ask Tui to call when you check in.

If by some tragedy Sueno del Mar is fully occupied when you call, Tui can set you up in a nearby apartment or house – just ask. But first try for that honeymoon suite. We're scheduling regular honeymoons from here on out.

Central Nicoya

The Central Nicoya coast faces west from Playa Junquillal down to Punta Guiones then turns like an elbow and faces more or less south from Punta Guiones to Punta Coyote. It's one beautiful beach after another, the stretches of white or black sand separated by rocky headlands, rivers, or patches of mangrove forest. Highway 160 wanders down the coast unpaved except in odd patches, sometimes

one lane and sometimes two, joining the little towns and fording any number of streams and rivers. The road is poorly marked and indistinguishable in many places from the tiny unpaved side-roads that lead here or there and then vanish. Most of it is likely to be impassable in the rainy season or after any heavy rain, so ask first and make sure your vehicle has 4WD and a good, high clearance.

Photo © Berni Jubb

The main Central Nicoya destinations are Nosara and Sámara, and they couldn't be more different. "Nosara" for travelers really means the beach community at Playa Guiones and next-door Playa Pelada, a

cluster of hotels, surf shops, restaurants and real-estate offices surrounded by a mostly part-time ex-pat community. Through luck or wisdom, development here has spared the beachfront; everything is set back on the other side of a barrier of low trees and dune brush. It looks like what a beach is supposed to look like.

Photo © Berni Jubb

Surfing is the major Nosara occupation, but yoga and other wellness activities are a close second, anchored by the long-running Nosara Yoga Institute (www.nosarayoga.com). There are some great restaurants. We like the Café de Paris and have heard good things about La Luna and Almost Paradise as well. Nosara is about 45 minutes north of the paved road (CR 150) from Nicoya to Sámara. The first turnoff marked "Nosara" is a rough dirt road, but doesn't ford any rivers and is the most likely to be passable. You can also fly directly to Nosara on Nature Air or Sansa. The one down-side to Nosara is the incredible dust generated by the dirt roads in dry season. For this reason we actually prefer Nosara in the rainy months.

Photo © Berni Jubb

Sámara is not an ex-pat community – it's a real Costa Rican town. Unlike at Nosara, the first line of hotels, bars, and campsites is built right on the beach. You'll find surfers here, but the Sámara beach crowd is mostly kids swimming or playing beach soccer and families enjoying the sun. The atmosphere is bustling during the day and only slightly less bustling at night. For dinner, try El Dorado for great Italian seafood and wonderful desserts.

Just south of Sámara is the even-better lounging and swimming beach at Playa Carrillo. Bring your picnic and hammock and join the afternoon crowds – mainly Costa Ricans – basking in the sun or frolicking in the waves. Or just keep driving; there are fewer people the farther south you go.

Luna Azul $$

Playa Ostional   Wildlife, Relax/Get away

Photo © Luna Azul

Contact Information:
506-821-0075 (voice)
info@hotellunaazul.com
www.hotellunaazul.com

Essentials:
7 Bungalows, 1 Room
English, Spanish, French, Italian, German
All major credit cards accepted
Off-street parking
Swimming pool
Breakfast included, Restaurant, Bar
Room Amenities: AC ($10 extra charge), Ceiling fan, Refrigerator, In-
   room safe, Private outdoor space

How to get here:
From Nosara, go north on Highway 160 (dirt road) through Ostional.
Turn east (right) about three km past Ostional following signs to
Luna Azul. The hotel is on your left. If coming from Playa Junquillal
or Tamarindo (better in the rainy season), the turn is about three km
south of San Juanillo.

Luna Azul is closed in October.

If you're feeling crowded even in laid-back Nosara, head up the coast road to Luna Azul in the hills between the little towns of Ostional and San Juanillo. You'll have to ford a few rivers on the way, but once you're here you'll understand why people leave the big city and move to Middle Of Nowhere, Costa Rica.

The bottom line is, it's beautiful. And it's totally private. Nobody's up here but your fellow guests, Rolf and Andreas your hosts, and a handful of friendly dogs. You can see a house here and there behind you in the hills, but there's a lot of barely-penetrable jungle in between. In front of you, it's nothing but trees and then, way down below, the ocean. This is one of those places where the world outside could disappear and you'd never know it.

Luckily you have a lovely, well-equipped bungalow with a private deck overlooking the garden. Your own private escape. If you feel like company, Luna Azul's public space is open, colorful, and inviting with plenty of comfortable seating by the pool. The restaurant offers pizzas and an Italian menu, but we were there on Tuesday when it's closed and guests have to head either north or south on the coast road for dinner.

When you feel like exploring, there's plenty around here to see. The adjacent jungle is a 150 hectare private reserve. It's a quick drive down to the beach and the Rosario river estuary. The most fun drive is about 15 minutes north – two more rivers to cross – to the little town of San Juanillo. There you'll find two beaches, one that you can drive to and the other accessible only via the footpath on the east side of the soccer field. Also right by the soccer field is the delightful Buddha Bar with its surprising combination of a bar (as you might have guessed), a Buddhist sanctuary (in San Juanillo?) and excellent food. Try the curry – a great accompaniment for a cold beer.

A few minutes south of Luna Azul is the town of Ostional and the black-sand Ostional beach. Thousands of Olive Ridley sea turtles come ashore here to nest in massive group *arivadas*. The arrivals cannot be predicted to the day but usually occur between September and November, in the heart of the Pacific Coast rainy season. Check with Rolf if you are interested in turtle-watching; he's a biologist and keeps an eye on turtle activity. They are present in the waters off Playa Ostional all year. Rolf can also tell you about all the other wildlife around here, from the crocs in the estuary to the *pizotes* (coatis) in the forest.

Take a day or two and leave the bustle in Nosara behind. For sheer hide-away appeal on the Nicoya Peninsula, it's hard to beat Luna Azul.

Lagarta Lodge $$

Nosara/Playa Pelada   Hiking, Wildlife

Photo © Lagarta Lodge

Contact Information:
506-682-0035 (voice); 506-682-0135 (fax)
lagarta@racsa.co.cr
www.lagarta.com

Essentials:
6 Rooms
English, Spanish, French, German
All major credit cards accepted
Off-street parking
Swimming pool
Breakfast included, Restaurant, Bar
Room Amenities: Ceiling fan, Semi-private outdoor space, Internet (in
    restaurant)

How to get here:
Just north of Playa Guiones turn off Highway 160 following signs to
Playa Pelada, then turn right following signs to Lagarta Lodge. This
road climbs the hill with several turns but is well marked with signs
to Lagarta Lodge. The Lodge is on top of the ridge on your right.

We were sitting on Lagarta's splendid verandah overlooking the Nosara River when a large family wandered in speaking a mixture of English and Spanish. They had come to see the lodge's Nosara Biological Reserve and began rattling off questions almost before Amadeo, Lagarta's manager, could say hello. Are there crocodiles down there? How far is it? Amadeo explained that the entrance was just off the verandah, and you started with 168 steps that led down to the trails along the river 50 meters below where we sat. One young woman, not altogether steady on fairly high heels, peered over the edge and asked if they had to walk – she imagined, perhaps, that an escalator was hidden in the bushes? Finally they all decided that their grandmother, who was speaking Spanish and looked as hale as any of them, probably couldn't make it, and they trooped back to their car. We had considered the trail ourselves, but were heading up the coast road that morning instead. Next time.

Lagarta Lodge is perched atop a steep ridge that rises above the southern bank of the Rio Nosara just before it opens into the sea. The slope down to the river is thick jungle, 35 hectares of it protected as the Nosara Biological Reserve. Across the river is a thicket of protected mangroves filling the space between the Rio Nosara and the Rio Montaña to the north. Shorebirds and river birds abound as do mammals and the ubiquitous river-mouth crocodiles. Entry to the reserve is included in the room rate and a guide is only $5 per person. But you have to like steps or be content to watch the birds and the lazy crocs with binoculars from the verandah.

Lagarta's rooms are simple but comfortable with views of the river and ocean on one side and the forest on the other. The two larger family rooms are the same price as the four smaller ones. Our favorites are #1 and #2, the upstairs rooms for couples. They have big balconies with great views and the ridgetop breezes make them plenty cool without air conditioning. Farther up the ridge is a guest *palapa* with several hammocks for those lazy afternoons when your room feels a bit confining and you want a truly magnificent view. Tucked between the rooms and the restaurant is a small swimming pool with chaises and a patch of sun. If the verandah doesn't give you a sufficient sense of hanging in the air over the river below, wander down the path to the Sunset Bar on a curve of the ridge right over the river's mouth.

Lagarta's restaurant is closed on Tuesdays, but on other evenings serves a homegrown blend of continental and tropical fare – check the blackboard in the restaurant for what's on offer. You won't want to drive back up here after dinner somewhere else, and you sure can't beat the view!

Giardino Tropicale $$

Nosara/Playa Guiones   Downtown

Photo © Giardino Tropicale

Contact Information:
506-682-4000/682-0258 (voice); 506-682-0353 (fax)
info@giardinotropicale.com
www.giardinotropicale.com

Essentials:
8 Rooms, 2 Apartments
English, Spanish, French, German
All major credit cards accepted
Off-street parking
Swimming pool, Beach access
Breakfast included, Restaurant, Bar
Room Amenities: AC (extra cost), Ceiling fan, Refrigerator, Coffee
    maker, Semi-private outdoor space, Free WiFi, Apartments have
    full kitchens

How to get here:
Turn off Highway 160 toward the coast (left if coming from the south)
at the second road into Playa Guiones. Giardino Tropicale is on the
NW corner of this intersection; their parking lot is on your right after
making the turn.

Staying at Giardino Tropicale is a bit like staying with your old buddies in Nosara. Our fellow guests when we were there have been coming back every year for more than a decade to stay with Marcel and Myriam, first at Lagarta when they were the managers there and then here at the Giardino. We spent a good deal of the afternoon just hanging out in the pool talking about bus journeys in Honduras and Nicaragua, border-crossing adventures, and the trials and pleasures of life in Costa Rica. It was hot. What better place to be than the pool or under the shaded patio with a beer?

Giardino Tropicale is about three blocks from Playa Guiones beach and two or three blocks from just about everything else of interest in the area. We headed to the beach early in the morning as soon as the sun crept over the hills behind us. The tide was starting in, but the beach was almost deserted – a few walkers, a few friendly dogs, a passel of shorebirds here and there. This is one of the Nicoya beaches with hundreds of little conical shells, long and tightly-wound like unicorn's horns. The surf was running a meter to a meter-and-a-half just off shore, and soon the morning's first exploratory surfers were out testing the waves. By the time we'd made a loop and headed back for breakfast, the beach was in full swing with plenty of riders awaiting every good wave. Even some sunbathers had taken up residence. It was the kind of day you dream of in January in the frozen North.

Back at Giardino Tropicale, we learned a bit more about Nosara and the local community's ongoing struggle not to become the next Tamarindo or Jacó. Marcel is a local campaigner for sustainability, small-scale enterprise, and preservation of the coastal environment. It's due to people like him that Playa Guiones is still shielded from commercial development by its scrubby dune forest. Nosara in general, despite its plethora of real-estate offices, seems determined to stay Nosara – laid back, not crowded, a little bit hard to get to. It is still the sort of place you can disappear to for a week or so to play in the surf, prowl the estuaries, or just be quiet and relax.

If you are planning to move in for a week, reserve Giardino's junior suite in the main house; it has two bedrooms, a full kitchen, and a huge wrap-around deck overlooking the pool. The upstairs deluxe rooms (A and B) have the best cross-ventilation as well as private balconies. The Giardino Tropicale restaurant (operated by different management) is just up the hill from the rooms and serves wood-fired pizzas as well as pastas and various specialties. Half the town seems to show up there in the evenings. Your advantage is that you're staying here, and all you have to do after dinner is roll down the hill to your room.

Harmony Hotel $$$-$$$$
Nosara/Playa Guiones   Oceanfront, Yoga/meditation, Spa

Photo © Alison Tinsley

Contact Information:
506-682-4114 (voice); 506-682-4113 (fax)
reservations@harmonynosara.com
www.harmonynosara.com

Essentials:
10 Rooms, 14 Bungalows, 1 House (off site)
English, Spanish
All major credit cards accepted
Secure parking
Swimming pool, Spa
Breakfast included, Restaurant, Bar
Room Amenities: AC, Ceiling fan, Refrigerator, Coffee maker, In-room
    safe, Free WiFi, Private outdoor space (semi-private for some
    Bungalows)

How to get here:
Turn off Highway 160 toward the coast (left if coming from the south)
at the first, main road into Playa Guiones. The Harmony Hotel is on
your right; look for the two-meter high brick "beehive" towers.

The surfer's paradise of Playa Guiones is just a short walk through the scrubby dune bushes from the Harmony Hotel, but you'd never know it walking through the carefully-tended gardens and into the shaded lobby with its comfortable couches and easy chairs. Everything was quiet; the early customers at the bar and even the kids in the pool weren't making much noise. When this was the old Villa Taype, it was a surfer hotel and a local hangout. Newly made over as the Harmony, it's something different. The spa, the juice bar, the café tables scattered through the gardens on their round little lily pads of patios, the morning and evening yoga classes all suggest a retreat, a focus on wellness, a place for calm and contemplation and a certain amount of self-indulgence. But then there's the bright water of the pool right outside your front door and all those deck chairs and the constant lure of the ocean just past the trees. The *layout* is still like a beach hotel. What is this place, anyway?

We did some beach wandering, but decided to focus for the day on yoga, starting at 6 a.m. Josie's "gentle" class was challenging, but we and one of the spa staff were the only students so we could take it at our own pace. The setting is lovely – the covered platform with its wafting fabric "walls" nestles up to the jungle on one side and faces a pond with real lotus flowers on the other. We liked it so much that we came back that evening for a slow and even more challenging class before dinner. In between yoga sessions, Alison sampled the newly-opened spa. Her pedicurist was visiting from Sweden. In fact, the Swedish government had *sent* her to Costa Rica for the winter. How do we get jobs like that? In a bizarre twist, the nail polish applied to Alison's toenails was "water-based" and did not come off, not even with lots of polish remover. Do you know how *long* it takes for nails to grow out?

As evening came on we retired to the bar and another facet of Harmony Hotel emerged. The bar was full of pairs or groups of young people earnestly staring at their laptops, talking in low voices about finance and their clients' needs for more sophisticated search functionality. What was this, a Starbuck's in Palo Alto? We'll never know. Maybe they were really here for the surf. But it's a different vibe at Harmony; we didn't see people like this anywhere else.

Whatever you're coming here for, the Harmony gets two things as right as anywhere we've been. One is outdoor space – the "Cocos" rooms around the pool each have a totally private, open-air patio almost as big as the room itself with a table and chairs and a comfy hammock big enough for two. The other is the showers, indoor and out, that deliver loads of hot water through high-pressure heads for a serious full-body water massage – heavenly, especially on that private patio with the bright sun to dry you. Take off your clothes, blast off that ocean salt, and don't think for a moment about software.

Hotel Belvedere $

Sámara   Downtown

Photo © Hotel Belvedere

Contact Information:
506-656-0213 (voice); 506-656-0215 (fax)
hotelbelvedere@hotmail.com
www.belvederesamara.net.

Essentials:
20 Rooms
English, Spanish, German
All major credit cards accepted
Off-street parking
2 Swimming pools
Breakfast included, Restaurants nearby
Room Amenities: AC, TV, Refrigerator, Coffee maker, In-room safe
(extra charge)

How to get here:
As you enter Sámara, turn south off Highway 150 onto Highway 160, following the sign to Carrillo. The driveway up to Hotel Belvedere is on your left across from the El Samareño restaurant. The hotel is up the hill directly behind the Budget car rental office.

Hotel Belvedere is one of those inexpensive, unpretentious, nothing fancy but perfectly comfortable, European (in this case German) run hotels that you can still find in the untouristified parts of Costa Rica. If you're rolling into Sámara with no fixed plans, looking for some relaxed company, and you don't have to be right on the beach, the Belvedere is the place for you. Sámara, keep in mind, is tiny – the Belvedere is on the outskirts, but it's still only four blocks from the beach.

The Belvedere has two buildings, one old and one new. We like the old one best. It's a rambling structure built onto the side of a hill, with guest rooms looking down on a swimming pool that seems to hang in space over the parking area below. The very best rooms are numbers 12 – 15 on the floor above the pool with a view of the forested hills to the north. Although not in any way swanky, the rooms are clean and comfortable with that recognizable (and very welcome) German practicality. Everything in them works! Around the corner is the breakfast room and "belvedere" – a breezy covered deck looking southwest over the town and toward the ocean. You're easily high enough to watch the coastal freighters skirt the Nicoya reefs on their way up to Nicaragua.

In the hot afternoons, you'll find most of your fellow guests propped up with their novels and a beer on the belvedere or lounging in the shade down by the pool. An advantage of an older hotel is that the trees have had time to grow, and the Belvedere is full of lush vegetation even though its grounds are small. Even the solar-heated jacuzzi is nicely shaded. Unlike down in town, up here on the hill there's a nearly constant breeze.

The Belvedere doesn't serve meals other than breakfast, but all you have to do is walk across the street to El Samareño for great local food at typical *soda* prices. Try the *pargo entero* – the classic Costa Rican version of whole red snapper, fried or grilled, head, fins, tail and all. I'm a *pargo entero* connoisseur, and El Samareño's is right on up there with the best. If you need variety, every place else in Sámara is just a 10 or 15 minute walk away.

Laz Divaz B&B $$
Sámara   Oceanfront

Photo © Laz Divaz

Contact Information:
506-656-0295 (voice); 506-656-0296 (fax)
lazdivaz@hotmail.com
www.lazdivaz.com

Essentials:
3 Cabins
English, Spanish, German
Cash or PayPal
Off-street parking
Breakfast included (Marlene Dietrich and Farinelli only), Restaurants
    nearby
Room Amenities: Ceiling fan, Full kitchen (Tina Turner only)

How to get here:
As you enter Sámara, turn south off Highway 150 onto Highway 160,
following sign to Carrillo. Take the fourth right turn off this road and
go all the way down to the beach. The road bends sharply left and
runs along the beach; Laz Divaz is the second driveway on your left.

There are five divas at Laz Divaz. Three are colorful, whimsically-appointed cabins named and themed for Marlene Dietrich, Tina Turner, and 18th century Italian *castrato* singer Farinelli. The other two are Laz Divaz' owners, Berit and Sara. You'll find them on the beach south of central Sámara under the rainbow flag.

With just three cabins on a small property, staying at Laz Divaz is a bit like joining a family. It's likely to be a fun family, whoever your fellow guests are. And you're not only right on the beach, you're far enough from downtown – maybe a ten-minute walk – that the beach is not overrun with partiers from the in-town hotels. There are plenty of hammocks strung among the trees for when you tire of saltwater and sun. Laz Divaz is a kick-back kind of place.

Marlene Dietrich is the cabin closest to the beach and so has the best view from its wrap-around windows and shaded porch. Tina Turner is the farthest away but is also higher up and oriented to preserve the view. Tina also has a full kitchen so is a good choice if you're planning to stay awhile and don't feel like walking in to Sámara every night for dinner. It's also the most private. Whichever cabin you chose, it will be bright and whimsical and sparkling clean – a tropical oasis of light and pastels and pungent salt air.

It's worth talking with Berit and Sara if you want to learn a bit about culture and ecology in the Sámara area. They are among the driving forces for preservation of the *Humedal Cantarana* – the coastal wetlands north of Sámara on the road to Nosara. School children have proven to be a key ally in the struggle to protect the fragile coastal environment from over-development, and laz divaz (the two human ones) spend a fair amount of time in the local schools. You can admire some of the children's work in the Laz Divaz office. Or you may end up counting birds or planting trees as part of the family.

Laz Divaz bills itself as "straight friendly." They were certainly friendly to us!

Villas Kalimba $$
Sámara   Downtown, Kid-friendly

Photo © Alison Tinsley

Contact Information:
506-656-0929 (voice); 506-656-0930 (fax)
villaskalimba@hotmail.com
www.villaskalimba.com

Essentials:
Five 2-BR Villas, One 2-BR House (Off-site)
English, Spanish, French, Italian
All major credit cards accepted
Secure parking
Swimming pool
Breakfast included, Occasional dinner service, Honor bar
Room Amenities: TV, AC, Ceiling fans, Full kitchen, CD player

How to get here:
Follow Highway 150 (the road from Nicoya) through Sámara all the
way until it ends at the beach, then turn left. Villas Kalimba is on
your left just past the Mini-Super grocery store.

Villas Kalimba is as close as you'll get to luxury here in sort-of scruffy Sámara, and it's just a block from laid-back, dogs and kids and pick-up soccer games Sámara beach. It's also perfect for families or couples traveling together – each villa has two well-furnished bedrooms with a fully-equipped kitchen in between. A bonus here is the air conditioning which we usually eschew but in steamy Sámara we greatly appreciated. It's amazing the difference a slight elevation and cross-ventilation can make. Villas Kalimba, like many beach hotels, has neither so, yes, crank up that dial. The local grocery store is right next door; the surf shop and kayak rental are across the street. All you have to do is move in.

Even though it's right downtown, Villas Kalimba has lush tropical gardens, a high enclosing wall, and a private, intimate feel. You can hear the surf but not much else at night – at least on a weekday evening. Each villa has a shaded private patio with a dining table and chairs and hammock. Our fellow guests seemed to spend most of their time on their patios except when they ventured to the pool. The poolside *palapa* doubles as breakfast area and honor bar; the bar fridge is well stocked with Costa Rican beer and Italian wines.

Roberto, the owner, cooks Italian dinners for guests – his specialties are traditional pastas and grilled meats or fish – but only when he feels like it. It's a good idea to reserve ahead. We didn't and Roberto wasn't feeling inclined to cook, so we were own our own. This being Sámara, the beachside bars were either blasting with music suitable mainly for those much younger than we are or else dark and deserted. We took in the sunset beach-soccer – maybe two dozen players per team, but who could tell – and headed for dinner. Fortunately there are several restaurants within a few blocks. We opted for the El Dorado where I had an excellent *cioppino*. Walking back down the main drag, evening Sámara was coming to life with strolling crowds and streetside vendors hawking wood carvings, shell jewelry, beach gear, and artfully-crafted bongs. We heard some English here and there, but not much.

If you're looking for total privacy and you're not into the downtown scene, Roberto also has a lovely two-bedroom house for rent on the outskirts of Sámara – which means four blocks to the beach, not one. It has a full-size kitchen, Santa Fe style living room, its own pool, and secure parking. We met the friendly Canadians who had moved in for a couple of months. It was January and they didn't seem at all inclined to go back north anytime soon

Southern Nicoya

The southern third of the Nicoya Peninsula is divided by the sharp point of Cabo Blanco into two domains of markedly different character: the line of southwest-facing Pacific beaches from the Rio Bongo down to Malpais with their off-shore reefs and wild surf, and the southeast-facing coast from Cabuya up to Playa Naranjo with its protected coves, rocky headlands, and near-shore islands. Most visitors aim for the beaches at Malpais and neighboring Santa Teresa on the southwest side or the old fishing village of Montezuma on the southeast.

Santa Teresa and Malpais were "undiscovered" five years ago, but a couple of years of non-stop publicity has changed all that. They are the new "in" places today, and hotels and prices are going up fast. Most people come here for the surf, but there's an interesting undercurrent of Asian influence and a spiritual-wellness orientation similar to Nosara's. Lots of places here offer massage, meditation areas, or yoga. Sushi, curries, and subtler Asian touches appear on menus; Asian architectural motifs pop up unexpectedly in restaurants and hotel rooms. Many in the first wave of *extranjeros* to settle here were looking for peace and relative isolation, and it shows.

Locals call Montezuma the "hippie town" for the wave of European and American ex-pats who settled here in the `80s and `90s. The feeling in Montezuma is that Malpais and Santa Teresa aren't really towns at all. Montezuma is clearly a place where people live as well as visit, and both the funky vibe and the rusting hulks of vintage VW vans still visible in some backyards attest to its counterculture roots. The little downtown is full of boutiques, cafés, beachside seafood places, and tour operators. You see more dreads and hear more reggae here than in Malpais. There are fewer surfers as the beaches don't get the big Pacific waves. This is a place for an easygoing sort of traveling with a focus on relaxed bliss, not adrenaline.

Malpais and Montezuma are only about 30 minutes apart with the crossroads at Cóbano (stop here for gas, groceries, and an ATM) in between. The easiest ways to get to either are by air from San José to Tambor or by water via the car ferry from Puntarenas to Paquera. There's also a water taxi from Jacó to Montezuma. If you're set on driving here overland, make sure you have a strong 4-WD and be prepared for some adventure. The only "all-season" road is basically a jeep trail over the mountains from Playa Naranjo to Paquera, with plenty of rocks, deep ruts, steep climbs, and stream crossings during the rainy season. You can also drive down the coast from Sámara to Malpais on Costa Rica 160, but only in the dry season and then only if no freak rainstorms have set the rivers running. Ask about conditions on both ends of this road before starting out!

The Place $-$$
Malpais   Surfing, Happening Place, Downtown

Photo © The Place

Contact Information:
506-640-0001 (voice); 506-640-0234 (fax)
info@theplacemalpais.com
www.theplacemalpais.com

Essentials:
3 Rooms, 5 Bungalows, One 2-BR Villa
English, Spanish, French, German
All major credit cards accepted
Off-street parking
Swimming pool, Beach access
Breakfast available, Bar
Room Amenities: Ceiling fan, Villa has full kitchen

How to get here:
Follow Highway 160 from Cóbano to Playa Carmen (the intersection
of road from Cóbano with Coast road, where Highway 160 turns
north). The Place is just south of this intersection, on the left.

We're not surfers, but the beaches north of Cabo Blanco also offer acres of tide pools, some broad and deep enough for swimming and all teeming with fish, crabs, and shelled creatures of all kinds. The rock is black so on sunny days the water trapped here at low tide quickly heats to warm-bath temperatures. If it has rained recently, countless little fresh-water streams sheet down the broad beaches, or emerge unexpectedly from the sand and race to the sea. Ospreys and herons fish the pools. Some of the rock is soft and worn smooth and slick by the constant bashing of the ocean; in other places it is hard and razor-sharp. Good river sandals are a must. All of this was once ocean bottom, and if the angle is right you can read thousands of layers of history in the ragged broken edges. Here and there massive monoliths tower several stories above the surf, last holdouts of what must once have been formidable seaside cliffs. You can walk for miles to the north, but the Cabo Blanco reserve itself can only be entered legally from the other side by Cabuya.

We spent the night at The Place in one of their comfortable wooden bungalows shaped like big, square, center-pole tents. The walls are mostly louvered panels that open either as double doors or as windows to let in light and air. It was cool enough at night with two ceiling fans – and the nightly rain – that we were happy for the quilt. Each bungalow has a theme. Ours was Africa with lions, tigers, and giraffes on the bedspreads, ceramic masks for reading lights, and the skeleton of some ancient riparian creature as a rock mosaic in the poured-concrete floor. The Place offers five bungalows, three smaller rooms, and a two-bedroom, air-conditioned villa with a full kitchen and private parking.

 Aside from the villa, the lodgings here do not have private outdoor spaces, but the public spaces are ample and pleasant. The green-tile swimming pool is big enough for a few lazy laps and has a broad shallow edge where you can sun like a crocodile, half in and half out of the water. There is an open-air living room with rattan couches, coffee tables, books and a TV. A small bar serves beer and tropical drinks and is clearly a local hang-out. A weekly "movie night" attracts both guests and locals. There is also a small shop where you can pick up a new swimsuit, a sarong, or a souvenir T-shirt.

You're not right on the beach at The Place, but it's only two blocks away by road and close enough to hear the surf at night. You'll also have to head down the road for lunch or dinner; The Place only serves breakfast. There are several little *sodas* for roasted chicken or fried fish within an easy walk and taxis a block away at the main intersection in Carmen if you want to go farther.

Milarepa

$$-$$$

Santa Teresa

Oceanfront, Relax/Get away

Photo © Milarepa

Contact Information:
506-640-0023/640-0663 (voice); 506-640-0168 (fax)
reservations@milarepahotel.com
www.milarepahotel.com

Essentials:
4 Bungalows
English, Spanish
All major credit cards accepted
Off-street parking
Swimming pool
Breakfast included, Restaurant, Bar
Room Amenities: Ceiling fan, Refrigerator

How to get here:
Follow Highway 160 from Cóbano to Playa Carmen (the intersection of road from Cóbano with Coast road, where Highway 160 turns north). Milarepa is on the ocean (west) side of Highway 160, north of Santa Teresa.

Legend has it that the notorious highwayman, Milarepa, achieved enlightenment and his true vocation of poetry while living in a cave on the high, snowy slopes of the Himalayas. The beachfront gardens here at Milarepa have never seen snow, but the ancient master would surely appreciate the constant rhythm of the waves with the raucous chattering of parrots as a counterpoint. And what a mighty voice the diminutive howler monkey has!

Milarepa was designed as a retreat with just four bamboo-walled bungalows, the open-air Soma restaurant, and a simple rectangular pool arranged on a gentle slope overlooking the beach. A Buddha stares placidly from Soma's center table down the long axis of the pool, all out to a black rock standing in the surf, well above high tide. The air of tranquility is palpable. The bungalows have clean lines and simple but elegant furnishings: a king bed, a mosquito net, a chest for your belongings. There are no phones, TVs, or other distractions. Just roll up the hanging bamboo curtains, welcome in the breezes, and let the surf wash out that space between your ears.

The downside to this degree of tranquility is that it seems to have spilled over into Milarepa's management and staff. They are hard to contact and seem to have little information or motivation to help you when you do contact them. This was disconcerting and we almost didn't include the hotel in the book, but the atmosphere is so lovely that we reconsidered.

A place this calm and intimate can, unfortunately, also be spoiled by obnoxious guests. As we waited for our lunch, a loud American shouted at her children to put on their shoes in case there were bugs. *Bugs?* There must be at least 1,000 ants for every square meter in this country, not to mention everything else! Had she somehow managed not to realize that she was taking her little boys to the *tropics*, and a pretty remote and hard to find part of the tropics at that? The manager rolled her eyes, and explained to us that these guests would be here for a week. We hope in that time they gained some kind of enlightenment, and that the kids took off their shoes, splashed around in the tide pools with the crabs, and lay on their bare bellies in the grass watching the bugs.

The lesson in all this, of course, is to gather some like-minded friends and reserve all four bungalows for yourselves. Then you can enjoy Jim, the chef's, garlic-papaya soup and splendid rare-seared tuna salad with those delightful little *uchua* berries in peace and quiet. I know, achieving enlightenment is supposed to be a challenge, but this is your vacation after all.

Flor Blanca $$$$

Santa Teresa   Oceanfront, Honeymoons, Surfing, Spa,
                          Yoga/meditation, Destination Restaurant, Adults Only

Photo © Flor Blanca

Contact Information:
506-640-0232 (voice); 506-640-0226 (fax)
florblanca@expressmail.net
www.florblanca.com

Essentials:
11 Bungalows
English, Spanish
All major credit cards accepted
Secure parking
Swimming pool, Spa
Breakfast included, Restaurant, Bar
Room Amenities: AC (Bedroom), Ceiling fan, Refrigerator/minibar, In-
    room safe, Coffee maker, Free WiFi, Bathtub

How to get here:
Follow Highway 160 from Cóbano to Playa Carmen (the intersection
of road from Cóbano with Coast road, where Highway 160 turns
north). Flor Blanca is on the ocean (west) side of Highway 160, north
of Santa Teresa (just past Milarepa).

We spent an hour or so at the bar trading international-living stories with Susan and Greg who designed and built this place in 2002 and manage every aspect of its operation today; then we sat down to dinner. By course number four – a tiny cup of the richest, most explosively-flavored truffled mushroom soup we had ever experienced – we were beginning to understand why Flor Blanca's Nectar Restaurant is so well-regarded. Then came the grilled salmon, followed by a palate-cleansing sorbet of mango and Grey Goose. We finished with Dijon lamb chops and an utterly exquisite chocolate soufflé. It wasn't until after dinner that we learned just how lucky we'd been: Chef Demian Geneau was leaving the next morning to judge an international chef's competition in Madrid. Welcome to World Class.

A destination restaurant. Miles of stunningly-pristine coral-sand beach. A consistent three-meter-plus reef break right off shore. These are only the beginning of what Flor Blanca has to offer. Then there's your "room" – a tropical-contemporary house with fully open-air living room, perfectly-appointed master bedroom, and deliciously luxurious outdoor bathroom. Everything here reflects Susan's masterful design for luxury. Perfect lighting is one example, as is the absolutely-silent ceiling fan *inside* the romantic mosquito netting over the bed and the two-foot-diameter hand-punched copper shower head that dumps a monsoon of hot water over your head. Our guidebooks said Flor Blanca is the best beachside resort in Costa Rica and we'd felt our expectations rising with every axle-deep, rain-filled pothole we'd lurched through getting here. But we can tell you now: the guidebooks are right. This is it.

Alison chose a massage with Stefano (divine!) and yoga with Nancy (awesome!). I just poked around in the tide pools, roamed the beach, and sat in the shade listening to the surf break. And we talked with everybody. The Flor Blanca staff feels like an extended family; many of them have been here since opening day. The same guests return year after year, often staying for weeks at a time. Everyone is on a first-name basis. Susan explains that when something needs to happen here, it simply does, often in a surprising or quirky way. She, Nancy, and Greg are designing a new place now – Villa Samadhi – that will focus more on yoga and meditation. We'll be getting our reservations in early. Maybe today.

Tell the kid to get a job and go ahead and raid that college fund to spend a few weeks here at Flor Blanca. Greg will even send a pilot to pick you up at the airport in San José. Ride the monster breakers or just soak up the sun, the splendidly laid-back ambience, and the fabulous food. It'll be hard to call anyplace else "luxury" once you do.

Los Mangos

Montezuma

$-$$

Yoga/meditation, Downtown

Photo © Los Mangos

Contact Information:
506-642-0076 (voice); 506-642-0259 (fax)
homangos@racsa.co.cr
www.hotellosmangos.com

Essentials:
10 Rooms, 9 Bungalows
English, Spanish, German, Greek
All major credit cards accepted
Secure parking
Swimming pool, Beach access
Restaurants nearby
Room Amenities: Ceiling fan, Refrigerator/minibar (Bungalows only),
　　Semi-private outdoor space (Bungalows only)

How to get here:
In Cóbano, turn southeast (left if coming from Paquera) at the main
intersection toward Montezuma. Follow this road through
Montezuma toward Cabuya. Los Mangos is on the right side of the
road, just before the bridge.

Peaked black witch's hats poke out among the trees – the conical roofs of Los Mangos' nine bungalows. The owner, Costas, is from Athens, but the bungalows look more Black Forest than Greek with their deep porches, dark-stained wood, and cozy interiors. You half expect to see curious people with long beards and bright red hats speaking a language that sounds like the whistling of birds. Turn around, though, and you're looking straight south through the trees and flowers of the garden to the lazy surf below. These porches have hammocks – nothing particularly Germanic about that. Relax, this is Costa Rica after all, and you're a five-minute walk from the middle of Montezuma, surely one of the most laid-back places on earth.

Patin the cat – the name means "ice skate" and he appears everywhere, without obviously crossing the ground in between – accompanies us up to the rock-bordered, free-form swimming pool and the circular yoga studio above. Los Mangos is famous mainly for yoga. The ocean-view restaurant became a yoga studio years ago, and Dagmar Spremberg offers classes every morning. With its hibiscus blossoms and ocean view, it's hard to imagine a more pleasant setting. Dagmar specializes in week-long retreats and is booked months in advance with groups and guest instructors coming from California, New Mexico, New York, and other wellness-conscious places. Everyone in Montezuma seems to come here too, so you'll meet plenty of locals with your morning stretches.

Los Mangos offers ten rooms in addition to its bungalows, six with three beds and private baths and four even less expensive with shared baths. The upstairs rooms have a shared balcony with an ocean view, but all the rooms are close to the road and hence can be noisy. The bungalows are still reasonably priced and are very nice, well-appointed, and quite private. Up here in the trees, you mainly hear the birds with the surf providing a backbeat at high tide. Unless you're really strapped for cash, we definitely recommend springing for a bungalow.

There's no restaurant here, but breakfast is served at the *soda* right across the street. For dinner, one of the best places on the Pacific coast – Les Artistes – is practically next door. The menu is tropical Italian and the tables are set in the garden overlooking the surf below.

Amor de Mar

Montezuma

$-$$

Oceanfront

Photo © Amor de Mar

Contact Information:
506-642-0262 (voice/fax)
shoebox@racsa.co.cr
www.amordemar.com

Essentials:
10 Rooms, 2 Houses
English, Spanish, German
All major credit cards accepted
On-street parking
Breakfast available, Restaurants nearby
Room Amenities: Floor fan, AC (#7 only), Houses have full kitchens

How to get here:
In Cóbano, turn southeast (left if coming from Paquera) at the main intersection toward Montezuma. Follow this road through Montezuma toward Cabuya. Amor de Mar is on the ocean (left) side of the road from Montezuma to Cabuya, just after the bridge. Park in front.

All night long we heard the waterfall, even louder than the sea. At dawn we walked up the short trail to the first of the falls, a broad expanse of rain-muddied water tumbling over several meters of irregular boulders. The rocks were too slick to go farther upriver where the higher, more dramatic falls are. Besides, we were ready for coffee and breakfast.

The Amor de Mar was a tumble-down hostel when the owners, Richard and Ori, moved there with their family from Santa Fe, New Mexico in 1991 and set to work turning it into a sort-of European, sort-of California style B&B. The first thing you notice is the lawn – in fact you can see it as you cross the bridge from Montezuma – a rich green expanse running down to the black rocks and the water. It sprouts big wooden lawn chairs and a forest of hammocks. Everyone not out on the lawn is lounging under the big portal studying their birding charts, puzzling over the road map, or just napping. We hit the hammocks and listened to the waves on the incoming tide.

Most of the room numbers at Amor de Mar are changing as Ori converts the last two rooms that shared a bath into one big room with its own bath. After the renovation, the biggest room will be #4 upstairs with a grand view of the sea from a wall of windows. Our favorite is #9 (will be #8) downstairs on the corner over the river. The rooms are comfortably furnished with pristine white bedspreads and whimsical art and have excellent lighting and storage space. Avoid the rooms that back onto the road; guests in these complained of road noise. One surprising down-side to Amor de Mar was the constant drone of the portable television set the guard watched most of the afternoon. (Shouldn't he be walking around guarding?) Fortunately, there are plenty of outdoor spaces to get away from this annoyance.

The real gems at Amor de Mar are the two houses that Ori and Richard built, first for themselves and then for their children. These are fantasies of wood, glass, Santa Fe style plasterwork, and natural light. The big house has three bedrooms and a full kitchen downstairs and a huge circular bedroom with a domed roof, all-around windows, and vines climbing down the center-pole upstairs. A wrap-around upstairs deck looks over the lawn and the rocks below. The smaller house has a big kitchen and open sitting room downstairs and a grand master suite upstairs. The houses connect so a large group can use both – a real house party.

Amor de Mar has its own tide pool for lounging or even – we didn't try this – diving into. It's meters deep and refilled twice a day at high tide. The rocks are home to pelicans and thousands of crabs. Herons and kingfishers patrol the river mouth. You swing in your hammock, taking it all in. Aaahhh.

Hotel Celaje

$$

Between Montezuma and Cabuya   Oceanfront

Photo © Hotel Celaje

Contact Information:

506-642-0374 (voice/fax)

celaje@racsa.co.cr

www.celaje.com

Essentials:

7 Cabins

English, Spanish

Visa, MasterCard accepted

Secure parking

Swimming pool

Breakfast included, Restaurant, Bar

Room Amenities: Ceiling fan

How to get here:

In Cóbano, turn southeast (left if coming from Paquera) at the main intersection toward Montezuma. Follow this road through Montezuma toward Cabuya. Hotel Celaje is on the ocean (left) side of the road coming from Montezuma toward Cabuya, about one km before Cabuya.

We would never have found the Hotel Celaje, but we were poking up the dirt road to Cabuya looking for La Floresta, the studio of artist Claudia Bassauer. Claudia makes colorful paper lamps that decorate many of the hotels and restaurants and, we suspect, a lot of the private homes in and around Montezuma. Her partner, Daniel, carves stone and concrete into animals, flowers, and Escheresque abstractions.

Hotel Celaje offers seven two-story, A-frame cabins with thatched roofs and chalet-style wooden interiors. Each has a bedroom upstairs and a bathroom, storage space, and patio downstairs (kind of dangerous for those of us who get up in the middle of the night to go to the bathroom, but oh well). The bedrooms have a double and a single bed, a big window looking onto the garden and, since there's nothing else up here, plenty of room. The cabins are arranged in a wide arc around a free-form swimming pool and a little stream that runs down to the beach. Tall coconut palms stand all around. The hills that crowd down to the beach around Montezuma have receded a kilometer or more inland here, and the land is flat and lazy. Crested jays forage in the trees, but other than that the air is still.

You're right on the beach at Hotel Celaje, and it's a very different beach from Montezuma's: broad and flat with mounds of driftwood brought in by the currents eddying below Cabo Blanco. Streams pour out between the beachfront palms onto beds of well-polished rocks. Here and there a well-used little boat is drawn up on the sand. Just to your right is rocky, tree-covered Isla Cabuya with a graceful arch marking the entrance to the town cemetary. You can walk over to this gentle resting place at low tide. A bit down the road toward Montezuma is another wonder – the most enormous *matapalo* (strangler fig) we've ever seen, its tangled trunks spreading a good nine meters along the road and about five meters the other way enclosing an area the size of a small house.

Hotel Celaje is owned by Belgians and you can enjoy Leffe and Stella Artois beers at the bar under the tall thatched A-frame roof of the restaurant. The menu mixes Costa Rican standards with a variety of pastas and crepes, and there are good Italian wines. Someone has painted beach scenes and marine critters on big swathes of raw burlap above the bar, an interesting counterpoint to the red tile floor and high, high – three stories, maybe four – peak of the roof. There's something a bit 19th century about this mix of tropical and European styles, as if the two cultures had just touched and hadn't yet had time to mix. This isn't tourist Costa Rica; you're on the very edge of civilization here.

Finca Los Caballos $$

Between Cóbano and Montezuma   Hiking, Horseback riding

Photo © Finca Los Caballos

Contact Information:

506-642-0124 (voice); 506-642-0664 (fax)
naturelc@racsa.co.cr
www.naturelodge.net

Essentials:

12 Rooms
English, Spanish, German
All major credit cards accepted
Secure parking
Swimming pool
Breakfast included, Restaurant, Bar
Room Amenities: Ceiling fan, Refrigerator/minibar (Pacific rooms),
    Coffee maker (Pacific rooms), Private outdoor space

How to get here:

In Cóbano, turn southeast (left if coming from Paquera) at the main
intersection toward Montezuma. The finca is on the left side of the
road coming from Cóbano toward Montezuma, four km from
Cóbano. Look for the "Finca Los Caballos" sign, then follow the dirt
driveway up the hill.

You guessed it – this is a horse farm. There they are, at least twenty *caballos* of every size and color milling around as you drive into the property. No wonder everyone in and around Montezuma – at least the natives – seems to be on a horse! In this rugged countryside, they make a lot more sense than a car as transport.

Finca Los Caballos is up on the ridge about 200 meters above the Pacific. A rustic trail runs from the *finca* down to a little river then follows the river to the beach. There are waterfalls and, if there's been rain, fresh pools for a dip. It's about a three-hour walk on foot to the beach (you can get a cab back) and only a bit shorter on horseback. Once by the ocean you can go for miles, depending on the tide. If waterfalls and the beach don't appeal, you can head west over the rolling hills of the farm itself into the woods and fields of inland southern Nicoya. This is ranching country . . . high and open. A different world from the beach.

New owners, Christian and Luis, have transformed Finca Los Caballos from a resort devoted primarily to riding into a more up-scale retreat and nature lodge. They have added four new "superior Pacific" rooms with private balconies overlooking the beach. These rooms have more amenities and visually-private balconies or patios so they're perfect for couples. If you're staying in a Pacific room, you can have dinner delivered and dine in privacy.

The refurbished restaurant offers tropical-continental fusion cuisine served on an open-air dining area with beautiful views over the canyons. The menu favors German touches and changes daily. After dinner, this space is transformed into an intimate and comfortable poolside bar, softly lit with a big view of the sky. There is art everywhere (most of it local) from the carved stone *bancos* featuring horses, devils, and sea creatures to the fanciful lighting and original paintings in the guestrooms.

Finca Los Caballos faces east, so the sun rises over the Gulf of Nicoya to greet you – a surprise on the Pacific coast. On a clear day, you can see across to Punta Conejos and the mountains above Jacó and watch the hawks circling in the sky. Montezuma and the beach are right below you but, sitting up here, they seem miles away.

Ylang-Ylang Beach Resort $$$-$$$$
Montezuma   Oceanfront, Honeymoons, Art/Architecture

Photo © Alison Tinsley

Contact Information:
506-642-0636 (voice); 506-642-0068 (fax)
reservations@elbanano.com
www.ylangylangresort.com

Essentials:
6 Rooms, 8 Domes, 6 Tents with platforms
English, Spanish, Dutch
All major credit cards accepted
Secure parking
Swimming pool
Breakfast and dinner included, Restaurant, Bar
Room Amenities: Coffee maker, Refrigerator/minibar, In-room safe,
    Ceiling fan, Free WiFi (restaurant area)

How to get here:
In Cóbano, turn southeast (left if coming from Paquera) at the main
intersection toward Montezuma. Once in Montezuma, turn left at
the main intersection, park across the street from the Sano Banano
restaurant, and ask the receptionist to call Ylang Ylang. They will
send a car to drive you and your luggage across the beach to Ylang
Ylang.

I awoke in the middle of the night to thundering surf. Thinking the water must be right up to our doorstep, I folded back the louvered door onto our dome's covered patio to check. The incoming tide crashed against the rocks below, right where it should be. It took me a minute to figure it out – our round dome with its arched roof flaring out over the patio was like a giant hand cupped to our ears to amplify the sound of the water. The surf sounded much louder inside than out. Satisfied that no tidal wave was imminent, I went back to sleep. Alison never even noticed.

Ylang Ylang's eight concrete-shelled domes are an innovative approach to beach accommodations and give the place an early-1970's, Whole-Earth-Catalog kind of feel. Nestled as they are into the jungle, the red-roofed white domes with their triangular doors and windows look almost like odd growths, or some kind of alien conveyance. Inside, they're roomy and comfortable with king beds, good lighting, plenty of storage space, and outdoor showers (except #2, where everything's inside). Buckminster Fuller would be proud.

Aside from the domes, Ylang Ylang offers six conventional rooms with private baths and six tents on wooden platforms all sharing a single bathhouse. For those on a tighter budget, there are 11 rooms at the Sano Banano restaurant and hotel in downtown Montezuma with full use of the grounds and facilities at Ylang Ylang included in the price. But the prime spots here are the five domes right down by the little half-moon beach with its off-shore rocks to break up the surf and numerous shaded hammocks for lounging in the dappled sun.

The landscape at Ylang Ylang typifies the southeastern Nicoya coast: steep terrain, dense jungle, little protected beaches and lots of hard volcanic rock jutting out into the sea. A 20-minute walk to the east crosses red, green, straw-yellow, and black rock with deep crevasses sloshing with water and innumerable tide pools. At the next small cove, on the border of the Nicolas Wessberg Absolute Reserve, fanciful river-rock cairns and a brass plaque mark the resting place of Nicolas Wessberg and Karen Mogensen, pioneer conservationists of southern Nicoya. Walk even farther and you have another beautiful beach with no road access, secluded and quiet except for the birds and the surf.

Ylang Ylang is in Montezuma, but seems no longer of it. There's a hint of exclusivity, and some locals express open resentment about Ylang Ylang's Land Rovers driving over the town beach. But once you're here, there's no reason to leave. We can see why Ylang Ylang is popular for weddings, honeymoons, and yoga retreats: it is its own little world, close but far away. It's too bad you have to take that Land Rover when you leave and can't just slip away unseen as if you'd never had to touch down in the regular world at all.

Jacó Area

The Pacific coast from the crocodile-infested Rio Tarcoles to the oil-palm plantations around Parrita offers miles of beautiful beaches, some great surfing breaks, and one of the best stretches of highway – Costa Rica 34 from CR 3 south to Esterillos – in the entire country. The area around Carrera National Park just south of the Tarcoles bridge is one of two places in Costa Rica (the other is the Osa Peninsula) where scarlet macaws can be seen flying wild. Unlike on the northern coast, here the steep, forested, and largely uninhabited mountains come down almost to the beach. The strip of land between mountains and sea is home to the highway, the towns, and thickets of luxury condos and housing developments.

Photo © Judd Pilossof

The urban center for this area is Jacó, sometimes known by its old name, Garabito. Two generations ago this was a fishing village. Now it's a boomtown with a mix of seedy bars and quality restaurants, casinos and health spas, weekender families from San José and aging *Norteamericanos* accompanied by very young ladies in bikinis. Newcomers wonder if they're too late; old-timers offer their take on when the bubble will burst; upstanding citizens grouse about the town's loose morals, and the young and carefree take in the sun, the surf, and the still-pretty-funky atmosphere.

South of Jacó, Highway 34 speeds past beautiful south-facing beaches on its way to Manuel Antonio. Some of the best surfing is at Playa Hermosa, just south of Jacó. We're hoping this beach isn't ruined by condo developments. Half an hour farther south are three towns named Esterillos: *Oeste* (West), *Centro*, and *Este* (East). All have nice beaches. Esterillos Oeste is mainly a surf camp; for hotels and restaurants, head on down the coast to Esterillos Este. It's still a real jewel, a hideaway for weekenders from San José and ex-pats from just about everywhere.

There are more hotels in the central Pacific area than you can count and new ones open every month. Our favorites sample the spectrum, but there are pickings here for every style and budget. Punta Leone is a popular family resort with its own beaches and park. Villa Caletas with its commanding altitude and vaguely Roman-empire styling is great if you want the privacy of your own swimming pool, but a tad pretentious for our taste (and the food is expensive and not impressive). For a family-oriented option in Jacó, try Mar de Luz, with its comfortable rooms, two pools, and no bar. Just west of Playa Hermosa, several reasonably-priced small hotels and B&Bs catering mainly to surfers hug the ocean side of the highway. We've stayed here, but prefer to have hot water and a bit less wind. For family surfing lessons away from the crowds, try Puesta del Sol in Esterillos Este – three nice rooms with good ocean views are available with breakfast included.

Getting groceries between Jacó and Parilla can be a challenge. Don't forget to stop by La Petite Provence, Jacó's wonderful French deli, for picnic provisions; it's located in the Pacific Center just north of the estuary bridge on the main drag.

Poseidon Hotel $$

Jacó   Downtown, Happening Place

Photo © Chris Fields

Contact Information:
888-643-1242 (in US); 506-643-1642 (voice); 506-643-3558 (fax)
info@hotel-poseidon.com
www.hotel-poseidon.com

Essentials:
15 Rooms
English, Spanish
All major credit cards accepted
Street or public lot parking
Swimming pool, Beach ½ block away
Continental breakfast included, Restaurant, Bar, Sports bar
Room Amenities: AC, Coffee maker, Refrigerator/minibar, Internet
    access in lobby

How to get here:
Take the first (northernmost) Jacó exit from Highway 34; bear left
onto Main Street at the end of the boulevard. Cross the bridge over
the estuary, continue one block toward the center of town to Calle
Bohio, and turn right. The Poseidon will be on your right. Park in
the public parking lot across the street.

The Eagles were playing "Already Gone" when we walked into the Hotel Poseidon past couples enjoying a late breakfast, an early beer, or both. No anthem could be more appropriate. Owned by Tim and Chrissy from Aspen, the Poseidon exudes an early-70's, escape-to-Mexico ambiance. Hunter Thompson's ghost would be perfectly at home here.

Hotel Poseidon is located smack in the middle of downtown Jacó on Calle Bohio between the main drag and the beach. It has two bars and a casual open-air restaurant serving good basic beach food – fish tacos, fish burritos, French fries with the skins still on (Yum!). There's an air-conditioned sports bar with three TVs upstairs. If that's not enough, the Poseidon is just steps away from dozens more eateries and drinkeries, pool halls, dance halls, casinos, and other nightspots. The poolside bar with its pretty garden feels more tropical, but Hunter's ghost prefers the streetside bar where on any given night you'll meet a fair sample of the local denizens as they make their way between Jacó's main street and the beach.

The beach scene here in the center is livelier and more continuous than at either the north end by Canciones del Mar or the sleepy south end at Club del Mar, our other two Jacó beach favorites. The only real public beach parking is just around the corner on the Calle Bohio loop and the main beachfront entertainment establishments – the Bohio bar, the casino, and the disco – are just down the beach to the south. Even the local *Fuerza Publica* have their station here. Expect to see early-bird surfers if the famous beach break is right, mid-day loungers, and beach parties to the wee hours.

The rooms at Hotel Poseidon are reasonably priced and have everything you need – there's even milk for your early-morning coffee in the in-room fridge. The upstairs rooms behind the pool look over the wall toward the sea and are more open to the breeze than the garden-view rooms. Rooms 7, 8, and 9 are on the second floor right above the streetside bar, and right below the 3rd-floor sports bar, so you might not want these unless you really enjoy bar noise (or plan to close them down yourself). Even in a back corner, though, you probably can't expect to have a perfectly quiet, restful night here at the Poseidon. However, if you've picked the center of Jacó for lodgings, we don't expect a quiet, restful night is exactly what you had in mind.

Canciones Del Mar $$
Jacó   Downtown, Oceanfront, Surfing

Photo © Canciones del Mar

Contact Information:
506-643-3273 (voice); 506-643-3296 (fax)
info@cancionesdelmar.com
www.cancionesdelmar.com

Essentials:
11 Rooms – 10 with full kitchens
English, Spanish, Dutch
All major credit cards accepted
Secure parking
Swimming pool
Hot breakfast included, Bar, Light snacks available, Restaurants
    nearby
Room Amenities: AC, Fan, Coffee maker, Refrigerator, Microwave,
    Cooktop, TV, Private outdoor space (balcony or patio)

How to get here:
Take the first (northernmost) Jacó exit from Highway 34; bear left
onto Main Street at the end of the boulevard. Turn right on Calle Bri
Bri (a dirt alleyway) at the sign to Canciones del Mar. If you cross the
bridge, you've gone too far; backtrack one block and turn left into the
alley.

Imagine your great-aunt-Mildred died (she was 99 and had a wonderful life) and left you $10,000. You decide to spend a month on the beach in Costa Rica. If she'd left you $50k, you might go to Xandari down in Esterillos, or Makanda in Manuel Antonio. But you've only got $10k and you need to pay for airfare and that new surfboard. Your best bet is Jacó and Canciones del Mar.

Canciones del Mar is what a beachfront hotel in the tropics should be: relaxed, not fancy or prettified or pretentious – and right on the beach. When you check in here you can forget that the rest of the world exists, and you won't be reminded.

All of the eleven rooms but one – # 5, the "Jungle Room," – are suites with full kitchens, making it easy to settle in for a week or more. The Honeymoon Suite (#10) has an ocean view. We stayed in an upstairs, garden-view room with a balcony so private you can sit outside and drink your morning coffee naked if you want to.

The rooms at Canciones are simple, but well equipped. The kitchens have everything you'll need, there's a table and comfortable chairs on the balcony (or patio if you're in a downstairs room looking out on the large, free-form swimming pool), a couch in the living area, and two double beds in the bedroom. For a non-luxury hotel the attention to detail is impressive. Hibiscus blossoms are tucked into towels and various other nooks and crannies. There's enough shelf space in the bathroom to unpack your toiletries, the closet is ample and, in case it rains, every room has a large umbrella.

The gardens here are lush and inviting with lots of private spaces. Breakfast (very tasty and included in the room price) is served in a thatched *palapa* where you can also buy a cold beer or curl up in one of the comfortable upholstered chairs and read a trashy novel. You can borrow the trashy novel from the lending library in the tree house at the back of the property.

The best thing about Canciones del Mar is the wide swath of black-sand beach. Canciones is slightly north of the center of town – you can walk to any number of excellent restaurants and all sorts of shopping in a matter of minutes – so the beach is not as crowded as it is right in front of downtown Jacó. It's fringed with palm trees and the ocean crashes in with wild explosions of frothy spume. It's 6 p.m. Surfers catch the big ones, dogs frolic, horseback riders canter by in the sunset. You're relaxing in a chaise lounge sipping a piña colada. Thank-you Aunt Mildred.

Doce Lunas $$
Jacó   Relax/Get Away, Spa, Destination Restaurant

Photo © Doce Lunas

Contact Information:
506-643-2211 (voice); 506-643-3633 (fax)
docelunasresort@gmail.com
www.docelunas.com

Essentials:
20 Rooms – 1 full-handicap access
English, Spanish
All major credit cards accepted
Secure parking
Swimming pool, Spa, Massage and yoga center
Restaurant, Bar
Room Amenities: AC, TV, Coffee maker, Refrigerator/minibar, Semi-private outdoor space, Internet access in lobby

How to get here:
Continue past the main Jacó traffic light on Highway 34, then turn left (toward the mountains) onto the dirt road at the Doce Lunas sign. Follow the dirt road straight about ½ km to Doce Lunas' gate.

We had just sat down to dinner when two purring cats appeared, and in an instant the black-and-white one – "Spooky" – was in my lap. I'm a cat magnet and I never mind a furry dinner companion. Our host David recommended the pork tenderloin, which proved to be excellent, and Spooky watched while I devoured every bite. No problem – the chef beckoned, and both cats followed him back to the kitchen for their treats. We later learned that Spooky was the most famous of Doce Lunas' 13 resident felines, having recently charmed a *New York Times* travel writer. He and his cousins appeared here and there throughout our stay.

Doce Lunas is across Costa Rica 34 from the town of Jacó and, unlike Jacó's other lodging options, it has nothing to do with the beach or, for that matter, the town. No surfing regalia, funky music, or hopping singles scene here. You come to Doce Lunas to be *tranquilo*, and for that it provides everything you need – a quiet setting, a beautiful garden with some truly magnificent trees, a well-equipped spa and yoga studio up above the restaurant, and even cats, whose low-key approach to the sybarite's life we would all do well to emulate.

Besides its excellent restaurant, Doce Lunas gets our prize for the best pool on the Central Pacific coast for actual swimming. It's huge, free-form, and deep enough throughout to swim respectable laps. When you're finished, glide over to the waterfall at the deep end and let the cascade pound your neck and shoulders. Or if you're feeling catlike, forget the tiresome laps and head straight for the cascade; in a few minutes it will remove all the strain of driving here from San José. A smiling sun mosaic graces the bottom of the pool carrying on the sun-moon theme you'll find throughout Doce Lunas' public spaces with artist Felix Murillo's colorful paintings and murals.

The rooms at Doce Lunas are all at ground level and climb up the gentle slope in separate two- or three-unit buildings. All face the garden and have semi- or fully-private front patios. High clerestory windows complement the big garden-view picture windows to provide plenty of light. Most rooms have a king bed plus a single for the kids; the junior suites on the south side are somewhat larger with a sitting area and a stereo. Room # 5 is wheelchair accessible as are the paths through the garden.

Doce Lunas received its fourth star in October, 2006 and sets a new standard for Jacó. Have a massage or a chocolate wrap at the Equilibrium Spa, sign up for the special "Chef's Table" seven-course dinner, or just sit under a tree, pat a cat, and enjoy the silence. Who needs the beach?

Club del Mar $$$-$$$$
Jacó   Spa, Oceanfront, Fishing

Photo © Club del Mar

Contact Information:
506-643-3194 (voice); 506-643-3550 (fax)
hotelclubdelmar@racsa.co.cr
www.clubdelmarcostarica.com

Essentials:
8 Rooms, 1 Suite with full kitchen, 22 Villas with full kitchens
English, Spanish
All major credit cards accepted
Secure parking
Swimming pool, Spa
Restaurant, Bar, Room service
Room Amenities: AC, Coffee maker, Refrigerator/minibar, Internet
access in lobby, Private outdoor space (upstairs rooms and villas only)

How to get here:
Continue past main Jacó traffic light on Highway 34. Turn right at
the Club del Mar sign just past the Enersol station. If you start up the
hill, you've missed it.

It was five p.m. when we arrived at Club del Mar so after unpacking we headed to the spacious bar for a well-deserved piña colada. The conversation around us was all about blueprints and land deals. Jacó is booming with new hotels and luxury condos going up on every corner. Club del Mar seems to be a center – maybe one of several – for the wheeling and dealing.

Club del Mar is not your usual small hotel. Besides its eight second-floor hotel rooms, all with ocean views from private balconies, the Club offers a sumptuous third-floor penthouse and 22 fully-equipped condos, all owned by private individuals and managed by the hotel. A conference facility is available for business meetings. The atmosphere is well-groomed and professional; the décor and furnishings in the condos are very first-world. If it weren't Costa Rica, this would be the fast lane. Expect to meet gated-community ex-pats, sportfishers and business people here, not the youthful surfers and aging hippies you find elsewhere in Jacó.

Owner Philip Edwardes built the Club del Mar almost two decades ago when the population of Jacó was only about 300 people. The Club occupies the tranquil southernmost corner of Jacó's black-sand beach just north of the rocky headland that separates Jacó from Playa Hermosa to the south. The center of town is a 20 minute amble up the beach or a quick taxi ride. A complete remodel in 2000 updated the entire property. Edwardes' playful architectural touches are everywhere from the swooping spinnaker roofline of the main hotel/restaurant building to the beach-umbrella-shaped stairwells gracing each of the condos.

The best condos are # 13 – 16, two-bedroom units facing the beach and farthest from the highway. Upstairs condos offer more privacy as all the grounds are public spaces. The condos are extremely well-equipped with microwaves, televisions, full-sized refrigerators and stoves – all the comforts of home (as a matter of fact, if you don't look outside and North America is your home, you'll feel like you never left). When you do go outside, however, you'll find lush, beautifully landscaped grounds, a fabulous pool, and the beach just footsteps away. If you can afford it, stay in the two-bedroom penthouse suite with its vaguely African-colonial décor and fabulous five-panel linear ceiling fan – almost as good as your own private frond-wafter.

The Club's Sandalia's Restaurant features inspired local cuisine such as the ample filets of fresh-that-day snook smothered in tiny shrimp that we enjoyed for dinner. Prices are very reasonable and service is attentive and efficient in either English or Spanish. Everything is open-air but with broad roof overhangs to protect from sun and rain. Settle back with your piña colada, enjoy the sunset, and maybe you'll end up owning part of Jacó!

Pelican Hotel $-$$
Esterillos Este   Oceanfront

Photo © Pelican Hotel

Contact Information:
506-778-8105 (voice); 506-778-7220 (fax)
aubergepelican@racsa.co.cr
www.pelicanhotelcr.com

Essentials:
12 Rooms
English, Spanish
All major credit cards accepted
Secure parking
Swimming pool, Pool table
Restaurant, Bar
Room Amenities: AC, Fan, Private outdoor space (upstairs rooms only)

How to get here:
Take first (northernmost) Esterillos Este exit from Highway 34,
following sign for Pelican Hotel or Xandari. Cross the grass airstrip
and turn left onto the dirt road. The Pelican is just past the east end
of the airstrip, on the right side.

At the Pelican Hotel you might think it was thirty years ago, before Costa Rican tourism was a big business and it was just you, the friendly staff, and the beach. Rooms at the Pelican are a bit basic, but you're not here for the rooms. You are here for the ocean: the mighty Pacific stretching from your doorstep straight south to Antarctica. The waves here were born far away; they break like thunder. The bright blue sky can turn black and wild in a twinkling.

Guests at the Pelican are clearly expected to spend their time outside. There is the endless beach with long stretches of black sand separated by occasional rocky headlands. The Pelican provides chaises, as well as huge driftwood logs drawn up like theater seats. A wood-fired grill is available in the garden for cooking your day's catch, as are shaded picnic tables, hammocks, and a small wet bar. A full-sized pool table occupies its own covered patio next to the main bar and restaurant.

This isn't Jacó; don't expect much nightlife. Ex-pats we know come to Esterillos to get away, no kidding. There is no center of town and no evening hang-outs where you'll meet whoever's around. If you're interested in a lively scene, you're better off up the road in Playa Hermosa – that is, if you're a surfer – or in Jacó or Manuel Antonio. Esterillos offers something different: peace and quiet, or rather, peace and the constant song of the surf.

The Pelican's restaurant serves breakfast, lunch, and dinner with an emphasis on steaks and local seafood. Our marlin *ceviche* with rice-flour tortilla chips was excellent, but we found the prices a bit high by central-Pacific standards. If you want something fancier, slip on your high-heeled sandals and walk along the beach or back up the dirt road (that is, west) to Xandari for contemporary cuisine. Across Highway 34, Las Brisas offers upscale Italian. For snacks, beer, or anything else in the way of groceries, stop in Jacó on your way to Esterillos.

The best rooms at the Pelican are # 7 and 8 above the pool with queen beds, private balconies, and ocean views. If these are taken, go for # 4 or 5 upstairs over the restaurant; they also have private balconies, and you can enjoy the view from the new deck at the end of the upstairs hall. Avoid the two cheapest rooms out by the road unless you want only a place with a bed that's out of the rain.

Xandari by the Pacific $$$$

Esterillos Este   Oceanfront, Art/Architecture, Relax/Get Away

Photo © Alison Tinsley

Contact Information:
866-363-3212 (in US); 506-443-2020 (reservations voice); 506-442-4847 (reservations fax); 506-778-7070 (front desk voice); 506-778-7878 (front desk fax)
info@xanpac.com
www.xandari.com

Essentials:
16 villas by end of 2007, 13 beachfront
English, Spanish
All major credit cards accepted
Secure parking lot
2 Swimming pools, Spa in early 2008
Continental breakfast included, Restaurant, Bar
Room Amenities: AC, Coffee maker, Refrigerator/minibar, Internet
      access in lobby

How to get here:
Take first (northernmost) Esterillos Este exit from Highway 34, following signs for Xandari. Cross the grass airstrip and turn left onto the dirt road. Xandari's gate is on your right with the colorful vertical flags.

When we need a break from real life, Chris and I drive down to Xandari before lunch, eat in the open-air *palapa* restaurant, then check-in. After lunch we wander down the long, smooth beach (if it's shady – otherwise, it's very hot at mid-day) to collect sand dollars and exquisite deep pink shells. We have a long siesta in the late afternoon, watch the sunset from our private patio, then it's back to the restaurant for a delicious dinner. At night we sleep deeply, only subliminally aware of the surf crashing on the beach just meters from our villa.

The next morning we get up and make coffee in our own little kitchen (no stove, but a refrigerator, coffee maker and complimentary goodies in the mini bar) then venture out to the beach to do our yoga in the sunrise. After the complimentary breakfast, we generally take another long walk in the other direction on the beach and collect a gazillion more sand dollars and pink shells. Then I swim in the lap pool, we check out and drive home. It is a 24 hour vacation that makes me feel like I've been away for a week.

You'll want to stay at Xandari longer than 24 hours, though. Three or four days would be just right. Not only is there plenty to do at the hotel itself, but your Xandari hosts can arrange horseback rides, river rafting, jungle tours, and trips to ever-popular Manual Antonio park. Actually, a great trip to Costa Rica could include a stay at the original Xandari (above Alajuela) for several days as a base from which to explore the Central Valley and northern part of the country, then a stay at Xandari on the Pacific.

If you doubt that a spectacular boutique hotel could establish a second, equally fabulous location, Xandari on the Pacific will convince you. You'll find the same sweeping, modern architecture and the same eclectic color, phantasmagorical mosaics and vivid art that owners Sherrill and Charlene Broudy are known for from the original Xandari (he's the architect, she's the artist). The villas at Xandari are huge, cool, brightly colored spaces with elaborate tile showers, expansive leather sofas, comfy king-sized beds and very private patios. The two "Maxima" villas even come with tiny private pools.

The most dramatic difference between the two Xandaris is the location. While the original Xandari is high above San José in thick high-altitude forest, Xandari by the Pacific borders the long, flat Esterillos Este beach which seems unending when the tide is out. Both locations have two swimming pools, extensive gardens, and exquisitely designed restaurants serving healthy food, but the Pacific Xandari has a tropical paradise flair that makes even the briefest of vacations seem like a long, long time in a distant destination.

Manuel Antonio Area

Manuel Antonio is Costa Rica's most visited national park, and the strip of highway from Quepos to the park entrance – passing through the town also known as Manuel Antonio – is possibly the most tourist-intensive six kilometers in Costa Rica. Every kind of lodging is available here as are restaurants, real estate offices, guide services, and a smattering of ordinary urban services like grocery stores. Some places have been here forever, others are brand new, and we expect that turnover will increase as the competition heats up. But this is Costa Rica, and the response of most locals to an outsider's prediction is a laugh, rolled eyes, and *"quien sabe."*

After the scary one-lane bridges made of loose railroad rails (United Fruit built the railroad, and the town of Quepos to serve it, long before anyone thought of putting in a highway) and the typically-awful road conditions, one of the first things you'll notice about Manuel Antonio is the abundance of pricey places to stay. We've seen them all and stayed in many of them. Our favorites reflect our standards and biases, but you might want to explore. The newest place in town is the totally over-the-top Gaia, but even with its own forest reserve stretching down the hill behind it, it feels more like Dubai than Costa Rica. La Mansion provides traditional European ambiance, a mimosa with breakfast, and celebrity cachet; we liked it, but some of the basic amenities need an upgrade. If you're traveling with kids and want fabulous views, plenty of monkeys, and "jungle" stripped of all that annoying undergrowth, try Issimo Suites. If you're gay or lesbian and like a gays-only setting, Big Ruby's La Plantacion with its lovely garden and cascading waterfalls is the place for you. For an American-style resort with all the amenities, try Si Como No, or the more Costa-Rican feeling Costa Verde. El Parador at the very end of the Punta Quepos road combines resort amenities with a Spanish-Colonial atmosphere.

There are plenty of lower-priced options as well and a few in the middle, but prices here are going up and there's construction on every corner. Manuel Antonio is not the kind of camp-on-the-beach place it used to be. But here you are, so enjoy the beaches, have fun with the monkeys, and spend at least a little time emulating the noble sloth. Don't miss Bambu Jam, everyone's favorite place for dinner and (check the schedule when you get to town) live music. If Manuel Antonio gets too intense, head south toward Dominical or follow the Rio Savegre up to Rafiki where it's just you and the jungle.

Who knows, maybe you'll fall in love with Manuel Antonio. Half a million U.S. dollars may still get you a starter condo. Come to think of it, those pricey hotels may be a real deal.

Didi's B&B $
Manuel Antonio   Downtown

Photo © Didi's B&B

Contact Information:
506-777-0069 (voice); 506-777-2863 (fax)
didiscr@racsa.co.cr
www.didiscr.com

Essentials:
3 Rooms
English, Spanish, Italian
Visa, MasterCard accepted (cash preferred)
Private parking off highway
Swimming (well, cooling-off) pool
Breakfast included, Dinner available on request
Room Amenities: AC, TV, Fan, Private outdoor space (upstairs rooms
only), Internet available

How to get here:
Follow the road from Quepos to Manuel Antonio; DiDi's is on the left
side, just past Gaia.

Despite being on the main drag between Quepos and Manuel Antonio, it's so well hidden behind the jungle vegetation that we drove past Didi's a couple of times before we actually spotted it. Everyone told us it was fabulous, but the prices were so reasonable we were a bit skeptical.

Everyone was right.

Didi's is the kind of place that stays full due to word of mouth. It's so charming and such a bargain that people can't wait to tell you about it. After a stay there you, too, may be walking up to strangers on the street and ordering them to stay at Didi's.

The house is two stories high, constructed of what looks like rose colored adobe (but probably is concrete block). A long, wooden verandah stretches across the front where rocking chairs and little scattered tables welcome guests. The small swimming pool is just a few steps down from the verandah (not big enough to do your laps in but, hey, you're on vacation) tucked into the gardens surrounding the B&B.

The Toucan Room on the first floor opens out onto the verandah. Upstairs the blue Butterfly Room and the white and green Monkey Room (our favorite) have their own private balconies. Each of the rooms is artistically painted and each has wooden ceilings, fans and air conditioning (the room rates are $15 higher if you use the air conditioning), and expensive mattresses as good as any you'll find in upscale hotels.

Apart from the charm and price, one of the best reasons to stay at Didi's is the easy-going Italian host, Ezio. Pretty much anything you want to do is OK with him. Bring your kids? Sure. Bring the pets? No problem. Hang out in the hammock all day; Ezio will brew you a cup of *real* espresso.

And speaking of espresso, the continental breakfast at Didi's is a treat. Fresh fruit, homemade pastries and (can you guess how we feel about our coffee?) that wonderful espresso. No other meals are formally served, but if you let him know ahead of time Ezio will cook you an Italian dinner that will knock your socks off.

Be advised, Didi's is on the main road. That means road noise although it's dulled some by the gardens and doesn't continue on too late into the night. Didi's is also right next to a nightclub. We weren't there on a weekend so we don't know how loud it can get or how late it lasts. But what the heck. Why not put on your dancing shoes and go join the fun?

La Posada　　　　　　　　　　　　　　　$$

Manuel Antonio　　　　　　　Wildlife, Kid-friendly, Hiking

Photo © La Posada

Contact Information:
506-777-1446 (voice); 506-898-8251 (cell)
info@laposadajungle.com
www.laposadajungle.com

Essentials:
2 Rooms (1 with kitchenette), 4 Bungalows, 1 Apartment
English, Spanish
Cash only
Private parking off street
Swimming pool, Cold-water jacuzzi
Continental breakfast included, Pizza available at dinnertime
Room Amenities: AC, TV, Fans, Coffee maker, Microwave,
　　Refrigerator, In-room safe, Semi-private outdoor space

How to get here:
Follow the main road through Manuel Antonio toward the park; turn left across from the Manuel Antonio beach one block before the road ends. Turn right in front of Villa Bosque; cross the narrow bridge. La Posada is on the left at the end of the road, just before the park entrance.

At the very end of the road, just before it turns into Manuel Antonio National Park, you'll find friendly little La Posada. We'd heard about it from our friends Kay and Tom, owners of Kay's Gringo Postres in Atenas (when you're driving through stop and get a supply of Kay's cocoa bars to take with you to the beach). Then when we asked several of the upscale, high-dollar Manuel Antonio hotels which budget hotels they recommended, they all said La Posada. Like Didi's back up in town, La Posada is a tiny, not-too-well-kept secret.

La Posada is tucked into the jungle, a footstep away from the park and a moment from the main beach. It has four brightly painted palm-thatched bungalows: Surfer's Paradise, Parrots of Paradise, The Jungle Room and, this tells you a little bit about owner Mike Auvil's sense of humor, Fisherman's Dwarf. All the bungalows are spacious, tastefully decorated with bamboo and local art, and open onto the pool and BBQ area. In the main house, the Posada Room comes equipped with a kitchen and the Monkey Room has three beds and can accommodate up to five people.

La Posada is the kind of place we stayed in when we hitch-hiked around Europe in the '70s. Yes, we're that old, but we don't look – or act – it. It's not the least bit snazzy or pretentious. Actually, it's kind of funky. The rooms are simple but well thought out with lots of storage space, reading lights that actually shine on your book, and nice sitting areas outdoors. A hot breakfast is included in the room rate and you can get a pizza in the evenings. You have to go to the internet café down the dirt road to email your friends, there's no bar (but there are plenty of bars and restaurants over at the beach), and there's no room service.

But everyone we've talked to who has ever stayed there LOVES it. And we think we know the secret. There's a camaraderie among the people staying at La Posada. Twenty-year-olds with tattoos, young couples with kids, middle-aged adventurers – everyone who stays there knows they've found a good thing. They're enjoying hanging out in the hammocks eyeing the wildlife ambling in from the park or lolling by the pool working on their suntan. Best of all, when they get the bill they realize they can afford to stay another week!

Mango Moon
Manuel Antonio

$$-$$$$

Downtown, Wildlife

Photo © Mango Moon

Contact Information:
506-777-5323 (voice); 506-777-5128 (fax)
stay@mangomoon.net
www.mangomoon.net

Essentials:
10 Rooms (avoid the least expensive room downstairs, which has no view and practically no light)
English, Spanish
All major credit cards accepted
Private parking off street
Swimming pool, Cold-water jacuzzi
Breakfast included; Bar
Room Amenities: AC, TV, In-room safe, Refrigerator/minibar

How to get here:
Turn right off the main road in Manuel Antonio onto Punta Quepos Road (just after the Barba Rosa Restaurant), following signs to Makanda or La Mariposa. Start down the hill; Mango Moon is on the right 200 meters past La Mariposa.

We rolled into the Mango Moon at about 10 a.m. while late-rising guests were still having breakfast. Jeff didn't disappoint us: "No problem" to checking in early, sticking our bags in his *bodega*, and sure, he'd call somebody and organize a boat tour for that afternoon when the tide would be right for running up into the mangroves. We were invited to have coffee, enjoy the view from the big open breakfast area and look at the maps and bird charts conveniently posted on the walls. In almost no time, Paul Gonsalves from Manuel Antonio Expeditions arrived to collect us and another couple who were also going mangroving. We spent the afternoon on the water staring down crocodiles, spotting water birds, and feeding palm nuts by hand to *carablanca* monkeys that appeared out of the trees, obviously used to boats full of tourists with handouts.

The next morning we slipped and slid down the steep trail to the Moon's secluded little strip of beach, making it back just in time for the great weekday breakfast spread: pancakes, *pan francais, gallo pinto*, eggs, sausages, bacon, all sorts of fruit – the kind of meal that lasts all day. Which was a good thing since we spent the day hunting sloths in the national park. We spotted the first one – a big guy lounging on his back way up in a roadside tree – before we even got to the gate then saw several more on our loop past the park's beaches and up to the overlook. There were plenty of *carablancas*, as well as a little crab-eating raccoon that ambled over and sampled my toes – very gently – while I stood as still as I could given the circumstances.

The Mango Moon doesn't serve meals after breakfast so on Jeff's advice we headed over to El Avion, a bar/restaurant and general local hangout built around the reassembled hulk of one of Ollie North's clandestine CIA transports. This one was abandoned at the San José airport after its sister ship was shot down by the Sandinistas, blowing Ollie's cover and opening up the Iran-Contra scandal. Oh well, mistakes were made. Nothing like calamari and good tequila to close off an excellent day.

The Moon has a great little pool for cooling off in the long afternoons, the local *congos* (howler monkeys) show up and howl every morning right on schedule, and the view from the deck can't be beat. Jeff can arrange anything and will regale you with stories of ex-pat life into the wee hours if you'll just hang out at the bar and let him. Our only complaint is that the only way to get from your room to anywhere is to walk past everyone else's sliding glass doors, so be forewarned if you have a strong sense of personal modesty. We don't, and you probably don't either, so hey – no problemo!

Buena Vista Villas and Casas $$$$
Manuel Antonio   Downtown, Kid-friendly

Photo © Buena Vista Villas

Contact Information:
866-569-6241 (in US); 506-777-9081 (voice)
reservations@buenavistavillas.net
www.buenavistavillas.net

Essentials:
6 Villas, five 3-BR and nine 2-BR Houses
English, Spanish
All major credit cards accepted
Secure parking
3 swimming pools, Houses have private hot tubs
Private beach
Breakfast included delivered to villa or house, Poolside bars
Room Amenities: AC, TV, DVD player, Fully equipped kitchens, In-room safe, Private outdoor spaces

How to get here:
Turn right off the main road in central Manuel Antonio at the gate into Tulemar Resort, and follow signs to Buena Vista Villas or Casas. Parking lots are near assigned lodgings.

Every now and then we think we'd like a house down on the coast. Someplace high enough up for great views and a constant breeze, but with a secluded, private beach nearby for morning walks and kayaking, and plenty of jungle for bird and monkey watching. Oh, and we want a pool, a bar, secure parking, and plenty of restaurant options. Most important, it has to be lock-and-leave; we like the coast, but it's way too hot and touristy to live there all the time.

Big mortgage, you're thinking? Not at all. At least, not ours. We just call up Buena Vista and stay in someone else's beautiful lock-and-leave beach house. Whoever has been kind enough to buy these places has equipped them with everything we could conceivably need including quality sheets and kitchen gear, a fully-stocked spice rack and a nifty non-stick electric grill out on the balcony. If we had kids, we'd even appreciate the miniature Sarchí-style rocking chairs. Why stay in a hotel when you can have a whole beach house with all the mod cons plus an obliging staff to do all the work?

The villas are on one level with luxurious master bedrooms, big well-equipped kitchens, and wrap-around decks with spectacular views. The *casas* are two-level with peaked roofs, heavy Balinese offset doors, hot tubs on the upstairs balconies, and two downstairs bedrooms, each with its own huge bathroom. Two couples could easily share this space without getting in each other's way. There's even a washer-dryer – a good thing in this climate, but a rarity in Costa Rican lodgings. There are three pools, each with a bar. You can *drive* down the hill to the private beach if you don't feel like walking and even park on a paved surface.

If you don't want to cook, the friendly Buena Vista staff will deliver breakfast to your *casa* or villa. A new on-site restaurant is planned, but until it's finished you'll have to either use that nice modern kitchen or make your way back up the hill. The Barba Rossa is right next to Buena Vista's driveway and is famous for its sunsets as well as its food. Manuel Antonio is full of restaurants, and even the fancy ones don't require dress up. The driving can be a bit crazy after dark, though, so you might want to take a cab.

There you go. Your own house by the beach? No problem. Just don't tell your realtor.

Makanda by the Sea $$$$

Manuel Antonio   Honeymoons, Adults Only, Wildlife,
                                   Destination Restaurant

Photo © Alison Tinsley

Contact Information:
888-MAKANDA (in US); 506-777-0442 (voice); 506-777-1032 (fax)
info@makanda.com
www.makanda.com

Essentials:
6 Villas, 5 smaller Studios
English, Spanish
All major credit cards accepted
Secure parking
Swimming pool, Beach access
Breakfast included delivered to villa or studio, Restaurant, Bar
Room Amenities: AC, TV, Full kitchens, In-room safe, Private outdoor
space

How to get here:
Turn right off the main road in central Manuel Antonio, following
signs to Makanda. Bear right at the Y-intersection part-way down the
hill; Makanda is farther down on the right, one km from main road.

The howler monkeys woke us at 4 a.m., and then the rain came – a torrential downpour with crashing thunder. We were visiting Manuel Antonio in October at the height of the rainy season to avoid the dry-season crowds. By dawn the rain had slackened, and we could see the roiling ocean below. Our favorite room here – #1 – is completely open: there is nothing, nothing at all, between you and the Pacific but the sheer-white mosquito net around the four-poster bed and 100 meters or so of air. This morning, rainy misty air. We drank our coffee, put on yesterday's clothes, and set off down Makanda's steep but well-maintained stairway to the secluded and very private beach. Aside from a moored sailboat or two, you'd have no idea that a human settlement was even nearby.

Some luxury hotels can be stuffy and pretentious or make you feel like you have to act right or even that you shouldn't be there at all. Makanda isn't like that. Here it's just you, the jungle, the wild sky, and the roaring Pacific below. Everything around you is meticulously perfect, from the furnishings in your stylishly contemporary room to the instantaneous and personal service in response to your every need. Relax. You don't have to go anywhere or even think about anything. This is just to be enjoyed.

Makanda specializes in weddings and honeymoons and it's clear why. It was created for couples. The six villas and five smaller studios are scattered along a steep hillside, all facing the ocean, all with private spaces protected from their neighbors and everyone else. The villas themselves are enormous – about 1,000 square feet each – with full kitchens, huge closets and bathrooms, plenty of room for dining, relaxing, whatever. The grounds look like undisturbed coastal rainforest, but in fact 1,100 trees have been planted here giving Makanda a lush, dense and, especially in the rainy season, intensely green atmosphere. Birds, monkeys, sloths, and other Central Pacific critters abound. An infinity pool seems to hang in space over the treetops.

Breakfast at Makanda is served in your room by a very discrete waiter who raps ever-so-softly on your door. For lunch or dinner, drift down to Sunspot by the pool, with its hanging platforms and fluttering purple and yellow curtains. You'll think of Arabian Nights, one of the luxurious garden scenes with the Pasha's attendants somehow transformed into your engaging Rastafarian waiter. Pura Vida! It doesn't get much better than this.

Rafiki Safari Lodge $$$
Savegre River   Birding, Art/Architecture, Horseback Riding, Wildlife

Photo © Alison Tinsley

Contact Information:
506-777-2250 (voice); 506-777- 5327 (voice/fax)
info@rafikisafari.com
www.rafikisafari.com

Essentials:
9 Safari tents with attached enclosed bathrooms
English, Spanish
All major credit cards accepted
Secure parking
Swimming pool, River access, 750 acre private reserve, Horses and
    kayaks available
All meals included in room rate, Full bar
Room Amenities: In-room safe, Free WiFi, Private outdoor space

How to get here:
If you don't have a strong, high-clearance 4-WD and a good deal of
confidence, call from Manuel Antonio and they'll send a driver. If
you're confident and equipped, follow CR 34 through Quepos toward
Dominical. Just past the Rio Savegre bridge, turn left (inland) and
follow the dirt road through Silencio and then Santo Domingo,
following the occasional signs to Rafiki. Plan on at least 1 ½ hours
from Quepos. The road ends at Rafiki's front gate.

It's a bit of a safari just getting to Rafiki Safari Lodge. If you don't much like those one-lane wooden bridges with no sides or are uncomfortable driving your car through river crossings where you can't see the bottom, maybe you should hire a driver in Quepos and close your eyes for the tough spots. Once you're here, though, you'll be happy you came. A note in the guestbook has become Rafiki's informal motto: "Where the bad road ends and the good times begin."

The good times began for us with lunch – big plates of house-made South-African style sausages washed down with South African wine served on the wide verandah looking out over the jungle and the forested lower canyon of the Rio Savegre beyond. It was early afternoon, we'd been driving all day, and storm clouds were building. After all that food, we zipped up the mosquito flaps on our big South African tent and curled up in our king-size bed for a nap.

Sleeping in a tent always adds a certain sense of adventure, and it's even better when your tent has plenty of room, a hardwood floor, a beautiful big bathroom with hot water, and a WiFi link to the outside world. We emerged cleaned up and refreshed, just in time for drinks with our hosts before dinner. Rafiki promises braai – South African barbeque – but we weren't expecting perfectly-grilled very-rare tuna. Delicious!

Rafiki Safari Lodge occupies 750 acres of rainforest at the very top of the narrow Rio Savegre valley. Our fellow guests were all world-class white-water kayakers, there to surf a unique wave formed by the latest meanderings of the river's massive rocks. Kayaking and rafting on the Savegre are a Rafiki specialty; only a few kilometers separate perfect flat water for birding or just relaxing from raging Class-V rapids. Lautjie Boshoff, Rafiki's manager and resident biologist, will arrange a safari by water, horseback, hiking, or a combination of all of the above to fit your interests and adrenaline level. We opted for a natural-history hike and got an extended introduction to rain-forest geology illustrated by the previous hurricane season's rearrangements of Rafiki's landscape, as well as an introduction to local flora and fauna. Rafiki's wetlands are a perfect habitat for the endangered Baird's tapir, and reintroducing the tapir to these mountains – they were hunted out – is a Boshoff family mission. The lodge itself is step one of an ambitious plan to link wildlife conservation with sustainable tourism in the Rio Savegre valley, so by staying here you are contributing.

There is a lot to do at Rafiki so plan to spend a few days. After all, you'll have to tackle that road again to leave!

Dominical Area

South of Quepos there are no big towns on the Pacific coast until you get all the way to Golfito down past the Osa Penninsula, almost to Panama. A notoriously wretched, unpaved stretch of Costa Rica 34 links Quepos to Dominical and the south. It will be paved someday, but for now expect at least an hour's drive to Dominical, with hardened ruts when it's dry and unpredictable water crossings when it's not. The pavement begins again at the Rio Barú bridge where Costa Rica 22 comes down from San Isidro El General. From there south, Highway 34 is as pretty as can be. The route through San Isidro is the easier way to get here from San José or the central valley, at least until the new airport goes in at Palmar Sur where Highway 34 finally connects with the Interamerican Highway and ends its long run down the coast.

The Central Pacific's beautiful beaches continue, interrupted only by the rivers and the occasional rocky headlands, from Manuel Antonio all the way to Playa Tortuga and the small, still mostly French-Canadian town of Ojochal. South of there the mangroves begin, and there's no dry land until you hit the heel of the Osa Penninsula. While the beaches all face southwest, the surfers thin out after Dominical, and the long stretch of Playa Hermosa can be almost deserted. The developers are already at work; having lunch one day at the great restaurant at La Parcela point below Escaleras, we heard nothing but land deals being hyped. However, until Highway 34 is completed or the airport goes in, this is a remote area where you can still have the beach to yourself.

There are plenty of places to stay in the Dominical area, but you have to hunt to find some of them and, like anywhere in Costa Rica, they come and go. We're not much for the late-night party scene, but if you are, take the first right past the Rio Barú bridge for the cluster of hotels and hostels along Playa Dominical. A more upscale option down the beach past Uvita is Cusinga Lodge with its meticulous stonework and cabins built of local teak. We've never managed to stay there, but we can tell you that Chef David's macadamia pie is exquisite. We like two small B&Bs, Finca Bavaria south of Uvita and Diquis del Sur in Ojochal, but they're both up in the hills and if we're in this part of the world we'd rather be near the ocean. If you're coming with a big family or group of friends and don't mind a little four-wheeling, there are some splendid villas for rent up in Escalares. We also hear that La Parcela has four rustic cabins with unbeatable views and all-night music from the surf.

Bahari Beach Bungalows $-$$
Playa Matapalo   Oceanfront

Photo © Bahari Beach Bungalows

Contact Information:
506-787-5014 (voice); 506-787-5057 (fax)
andrealudwig@hotmail.com
www.baharibeach.com

Essentials:
4 Safari tents with attached bathrooms, 2 Rooms
English, Spanish
Visa, MasterCard accepted
On-street parking
Swimming pool
Restaurant, Bar
Room Amenities: AC (Rooms only), Refrigerator (Tents), Fan, Semi-private outdoor space (Tents)

How to get here:
In the town of Matapalo turn west off Highway 34 following signs to Playa Matapalo. The dirt road bends sharply north at the beach. Bahari Beach is about two km north of the bend.

When was the last time you camped on the beach and didn't end up with sand in your hair and a million sand-flea bites in places you'd just as soon not recall? If the answer is "never," head for Bahari Beach and try "camping" in one of their big South African safari tents with a comfy king-sized bed and a seamlessly-attached full-sized bathroom. There's plenty of room to hang up your clothes, and the polished concrete slab your tent sits on extends out to form your private patio. Your tent even comes with a fridge!

Playa Matapalo is a long, straight, southwest-facing, black-sand beach bounded by the Rio Savegre to the north and the Rio Hatillo to the south. You turn off Highway 34 at the dusty little town of Matapalo, a few thousand potholes from Quepos and we forget how many stream crossings from Dominical. You guessed it – this isn't the easiest beach to get to and you won't have to vie with a hundred other vacationers to get your board in the water or your blanket onto the beach. In fact, you may not have to vie with anyone. When we were there – early November we admit – there were a couple of people lazing in Bahari's pool and *no one* on the beach as far as we could see in either direction. A family of wild horses sauntered by, the eager little colts never straying too far from their moms. Other than that, it was just us and the surf. Definitely worth the drive.

Matapalo is good for swimming as well as light surfing, and Bahari Beach will rent you a board, a sea kayak, or a bicycle for getting around. There's not a whole lot of beachside development here – a few other hotels and a couple of bars – and you can ride on the beach for miles. Be on the lookout for wildlife; this is a relatively unpopulated area with several nature reserves nearby. The most developed is the Refugio Baru between the Hatillo and Barú rivers down toward Dominical, a center for work on the hoped-for Osa-to-Talamanca tapir corridor.

Bahari Beach has a nice upstairs restaurant serving lunch and dinner as well as breakfast. Considering how far you are from the nearest real town, it's a good thing. It's open-air with a great view out toward the beach. There are two rooms under the restaurant for those who absolutely must have air conditioning, but we recommend the tents, especially #2 and #3 which are right on the beach. After all, camping like this is a rare opportunity.

Roca Verde $$
Dominical   Oceanfront, Surfing, Happening Place

Photo © Roca Verde

Contact Information:
506-787-0036 (voice); 506-787-0013 (fax)
info@hotelrocaverde.com
www.rocaverde.net

Essentials:
10 Rooms
English, Spanish
Visa, MasterCard accepted
Secure parking
Swimming pool
Restaurant, Bar
Room Amenities: AC, TV in bar

How to get here:
Continue one km past the main Dominical exit on Highway 34; Roca
Verde is on the right (i.e. the ocean side).

Dominical is the southernmost surfer town on the Central Pacific coast. There are still some nice beaches south of here – especially Playa Hermosa just on the other side of Punta La Parcela – but soon you hit the mangroves and then the vast barely-populated Osa Penninsula and the even less-populated area southwest of Golfito. Dominical is closer to San José than Tamarindo, but the stretch of Highway 2 over the "mountain of death" has a bad reputation and the whole area feels remote. If you're heading down on Highway 34 from Jacó there's an hour of wretched driving after Quepos. The upside of difficult access, of course, is less crowding and a more relaxed atmosphere. We like Dominical and sort of wish they wouldn't pave the road. Well, maybe they could grade it now and then …

The first turnoff past the Rio Barú bridge takes you to "downtown" Dominical and the beach, but if you go just a little farther you'll get to Roca Verde. We wandered into the big open *palapa* bar on November 8, the day after the 2006 U.S. elections. We hadn't seen a TV for days and everyone in the area, it seemed, was glued to the one behind the bar. Most of the crowd seemed pretty happy with the news, even the Costa Ricans. We watched for a while and then walked out to the beach. The tide was just building and not many surfers were out. Time for an early beer, maybe. It's hard to think about politics in a place like this.

The Roca Verde is your basic beachfront hotel with ten rooms on two floors facing the ocean, a pool big enough for light laps or just cooling off in fresh water, and the big round *palapa* serving as bar, restaurant, and public sitting area. The rooms are spacious with private patios downstairs and balconies upstairs. All have bright murals painted on the walls – flowers, jungle plants, colorful fish. The upstairs rooms have a better view and fill up first, but chances are good that if you're staying here your first choice for a view will be the beach itself – it's just a few steps away.

The bar at Roca Verde is a classic – a big semicircle covered with murals of tropical sea-life, and leaping marlins and a whole school of tuna suspended from the ceiling overhead. Bits of marine paraphernalia decorate the walls. Every Saturday is disco night with dancing till three a.m. For those more inclined toward relaxation or with over-stretched muscles to cure, there's massage on the platform upstairs over the bar on Tuesdays and Thursdays. A special detox with noni juice was on offer when we were there. We've tried noni; it tastes awful, and we didn't want to even imagine what a detox regime with that stuff would be. But each to his own. It must be good for something or it wouldn't have such devoted fans. We'll stick to the standard massage and detox with a piña colada and a nice view of the sunset.

Costa Paraiso $$
Dominical   Oceanfront

Photo © Costa Paraiso

Contact Information:
506-787-0025 (voice); 506-787-0338 (fax)
info@costaparaisodominical.com
www.costaparaisodominical.com

Essentials:
1 Cabin, 2 Duplex Cabins
English, Spanish
All major credit cards accepted
Secure parking
Swimming pool
Breakfast included
Room Amenities: AC, Full kitchen, Fan, Semi-private outdoor space,
    Free WiFi

How to get here:
Continue on Highway 34 a little more than one km past the main
Dominical exit; Costa Paraiso is down a steep driveway on the right.

Two flat tongues of black rock, broad as freighters, jut into the ocean from the black-sand beach. From the prow of the southern one a ragged rock forecastle rises crowned by spindly palm trees. At low tide the ocean sloshes through the narrow space between these monsters. Their smooth, sun-soaked surfaces are perfect for some serious tanning. Twelve hours later their decks are submerged and rolling waves born somewhere off the Philippines throw thirty-foot towers of spray as they crash into what are now a pair of low islands. Welcome to Costa Paraiso, where this fury of water and rock is right outside your window.

If you're staying here at the southern end of Dominical you're probably here for the water. The Domenicalito beach stretches for two km south to the rocky point of La Parcela; nearly-flat Playa Hermosa extends anther ten km from there. Take a dip in the protected tide-pools among the rocks, wander the beach at dawn or dusk, try out the surf on Playa Hermosa, or relax in the pool with its grinning green gecko mosaic replacing the usual *delfinas* (dolphins). If you need more action, Uvita and the Marino Ballena National Park are only about 15 minutes down the road or head back north to Dominical proper for more surfing and the evening scene at the surfer bars.

The Costa Paraiso has five rooms in three separate cabins, all with kitchenettes. Toucan, in its own cabin, has the best view; we prefer Dolphin or Pelican with their larger kitchens. We have, as you've probably gathered by now, a thing about rooms or cabins with a proper kitchen, and all you have to do is stroll down to the little *palapa* overlooking the beach, with its lazy hammocks and adjustable lighting (!) to have an even better view than Toucan's. You could go for broke and sit out on one of those rock battleships rising out into the ocean. If the tide's coming in you're going to have to hang on, and at any time you're going to get wet, but this is as immersed in the Pacific as you can be while still on dry (well, sort of) land.

Costa Paraiso's new co-owner/manager Doug just sold an internet company in Calgary and some upgrades are in store for the Paraiso. A new *palapa* was going up by the pool in November, 2006, new plantings were in the gardens, and Doug will be offering breakfast to guests starting in 2007. Even better than all that, Doug is at work on a detailed map based on current satellite images of the beaches and towns running south from Dominical. Anyone who's wondered what the makers of many Costa Rican maps could possibly have been thinking, and if you're in this area that probably includes you, will be excited by this. We can't wait for him to finish and to get our hands on one.

Cristal Ballena $$$
Uvita Kid-friendly, Wildlife

Photo © Alison Tinsley

Contact Information:
506-786-5354 (voice); 506-786-5355 (fax)
info@cristalballena.com
www.cristalballena.com

Essentials:
23 Rooms
English, Spanish
All major credit cards accepted
Secure parking
Swimming pool, Spa
Breakfast included, Restaurant, Bar
Room Amenities: AC, Fan, Coffee maker, In-room safe, Private outdoor space, Free WiFi in bar/pool area

How to get here:
Continue south on Highway 34 from Dominical past Uvita. The Cristal Ballena is on the left, seven km south of Uvita.

The brand-new, four-star Cristal Ballena is perched on a steep hillside overlooking the Marino Ballena National Park. The view from our private patio made us just want to sit there, sip the drinks we had been handed on check-in, and watch the ocean go by. It wasn't whale migration season, but Chris, the manager, assured us that if they were out there we'd be able to see them from our room.

With its odd combination of plantation-style balconies and almost-Japanese arched tower, it's clear that the Cristal Ballena is not one of those luxury hotels that takes itself far too seriously. There's a pleasant sense of whimsy here, combined with fierce attention to detail and an atmosphere of unassuming graciousness. When we met Waldemar, the owner, at breakfast, we understood why; this is his environment and he clearly wants his guests to be perfectly at ease. Lots of little things have been done exactly right, like the unobtrusive clotheslines on the balconies and the switch that lets you turn the minibar refrigerator off at night. We wish other high-end hoteliers would think of things like this.

The Cristal Ballena occupies 12 hectares, most of it uncleared rainforest. Water for the enormous swimming pool comes from the river running through the property. There is a steep and intentionally-primitive "adventure" trail into the woods and a challenging California-style fitness trail down the hill in the garden. From the baying and moaning that woke us up about five a.m., there must be at least three or four separate troops of howler monkeys living here, arguing about dominance every morning. From our patio we later saw them casually moving through the trees having their breakfast after the sun was well up and they forgot about politics for another day. Chestnut-mandibled toucans chased each other through the trees at the edge of the jungle, male and female Cherries's tanagers courted, and a lone osprey surveyed the scene from the tower. Like the guests, they all seemed perfectly at ease.

If you don't care to drive, the Cristal Ballena will pick you up at the Palmar Sur airport. Should you require activities, the staff can arrange whale-watching, kayaking, horseback tours, sportfishing, or even surfing for you. There is Ayuravedic massage in case you're feeling creaky. Planning a wedding or honeymoon? Just call. The top-floor restaurant converts to a fully-wired conference center. If you're not into roughing it, or just want to hang out and be taken care of, this is the place for you.

Villas Gaia $$
Ojochal   Kid-friendly, Birding, Destination Restaurant

Photo © Alison Tinsley

Contact Information:
506-786-5044 (voice); 506-244-9205 (fax)
info@villasgaia.com
www.villasgaia.com

Essentials:
14 Cabins
English, Spanish
All major credit cards accepted
Secure parking
Swimming pool
Restaurant
Room Amenities: Ceiling fan, AC (some Cabins), Private outdoor space

How to get here:
Continue south from Dominical on Highway 34 for about an hour.
Villas Gaia is on the ocean side of the road, just before you enter the
town of Ojochal.

Five scarlet macaws flew overhead: once, twice, three times and then landed, squabbling vigorously, in a tall tree directly in front of us. We were ankle-deep in last night's rain, just off the grass-covered old highway from Dominical. Giovanni – Villas Gaia's gardener, guide, and general assistant to Luke, the owner/manager – led us onward into thick stands of bamboo and tangled coastal jungle, explaining as he went how the venomous *terciopelo* snakes sleep during the day and hence weren't cause for concern. Three smallish crocodiles lazed about in a slow-moving estuary. The big ones hang out down the coast in the kilometers-long mouth of the Terraba River, Giovanni said, but the mother crocs bring their young here to grow up in relative safety. Crocodile kindergarten – what a neighborhood! We picked our way back across the marsh on steps made of cut tree-trunks, crossed a hanging bridge, and climbed the steep stairs back to Villas Gaia. Time for breakfast. *Gallo pinto* with lots of hot sauce never tasted so good.

Villas Gaia snuggles into a strip of jungle between Highway 34 and a sharp drop-off down to occasionally-flooded bottomlands and Playa Tortuga beach, just north of Ojochal. There are 14 cabins – one three-bedroom "family cabin" where Luke and his family used to live and 13 one-bedroom cabins arranged in loose clusters that make for plenty of privacy. The furnishings are spare but comfortable; ten of the cabins are air-conditioned and the family cabin has a fridge and TV. Our cabin was not air-conditioned but was perfectly comfortable with just the ceiling fan in hot, humid November. Our broad front patio faced thick jungle; other patios look onto Villas Gaia's gardens. Cabins # 9 – 12 cluster near the pool with its waterfall and *palapa* full of comfy bamboo furniture. These cabins are the most popular so reserve them early.

Playa Tortuga is the transition point between the long strip of Central Pacific beaches and the wilderness of the Southern Pacific region. South of here, the mangroves start – 22,000 hectares of trees and swamp watered by the Terraba and the Sierpe rivers with rain collected from most of the Pacific side of the Talamanca *Cordillera*. A river of muddy brown fresh water pours into the Pacific just south of here, flowing northward along the coast for miles before it's finally absorbed by the currents. This is not a beach for swimming or surfing, but it is fascinating as a wildlife habitat and as an illustration of the powerful interactions between opposing bodies of water.

For a hotel in its moderate price range, Villas Gaia has a surprisingly good restaurant. Luke let us in on the secret – a world-traveled retired private-yacht chef consults on recipes and helps train the kitchen staff. Try the Thai curried fish. You may stay an extra night or two just for the food.

Osa Peninsula and the Golfo Dulce

Costa Ricans and ex-pats alike speak reverently of the Osa Peninsula, and it's easy to understand why. Aside from the cattle ranches along the eastern side of the Osa and the plantations just south of Golfito, this is wild country. The mangrove estuaries and coastal rainforests of the Osa are the largest remaining on the Pacific side of Central America, and they support enormous biodiversity. There are more plant, insect, and bird species here than in all of North America, and highly endangered mammals like jaguars, spider monkeys, and tapirs stalk the forests. If you've come to Costa Rica for wildlife, don't miss the Osa.

The Osa has thus far been spared the kind of dense, high-impact development that mars northern Nicoya and the Jacó and Manuel Antonio areas, and several local organizations are fighting to keep it that way. Many of the lodgings here are set on enormous private reserves, the conservation of which is supported largely by their guests. Groups of landowners have banded together to create protected corridors for wildlife that effectively extend the borders of Corcovado National Park or other publicly-owned reserves. Even small establishments seem to devote substantial time and money to reforestation, plantings that provide food for wildlife, or other conservation efforts. Visiting the Osa can be expensive compared to other destinations in Costa Rica, but you can be sure that at least some of the money you're spending is helping to preserve this magnificent piece of the world.

Do not expect all the comforts of home here on the Osa. Many eco-lodges, even the most luxurious, have limited electricity and no air conditioning, telephones or internet access. If you can't reach the front desk directly by telephone, it's probably because they communicate with their remote office – and everybody else not in shouting distance – by marine-band radio. Both Sansa and Nature Air have daily flights to Golfito and Puerto Jiminez and the best ways to get around once you're in the Osa are often by private air-taxi services or by boat. Getting 10 or 20 miles overland can easily take an hour and may be impossible if a river happens to be high. Don't even think about driving here unless you have a strong, high-clearance 4-WD and a good tolerance for crossing running water. One friend recalled a French tourist who arrived at his hotel in a tiny VW Bug. When he asked how on earth she'd made it, she explained that the car was really very light – only eight guys were needed to carry it!

We've come to expect a certain level of informality in the Osa. After one flight across the Golfo Dulce, we found that the pilot of our four-seater had no idea what the fare was. "I'm just filling in; I don't usually fly this plane" he said. We worked out a price that seemed reasonable all around, and he hopped back in his seat, bounced down the grass landing strip, and was gone. Hotel keepers will sometimes negotiate on rates, especially in the rainy season, and we've heard more than one story of guests without reservations being taken in and housed somewhere, anywhere, often for several nights. Need someone to pick you up at three a.m. in a remote location? Just ask, your host can probably figure some way to work it out. This is still the frontier.

Black Turtle Lodge $$$
Puerto Jiménez   Oceanfront, Wildlife

Photo © Black Turtle Lodge

Contact Information:
506-735-5005 (voice); 506-735-5043 (fax)
info@blackturtlelodge.com
www.blackturtlelodge.com

Essentials:
2 Cabins, Two 2-BR Treehouses
English, Spanish
Visa, MasterCard accepted (extra charge)
Off-street parking
All meals included in room rate
Room Amenities: Ceiling fan, Private (Treehouses) or semi-private
    (Cabins) outdoor space

How to get here:
Follow the road that leads to Playa Platanares from the east side of
the Puerto Jiménez Airport (the side opposite the "terminal"). Bear
right after passing Crocodile Bay Lodge, following signs for Pearl of
the Osa or Playa Preciosa. Black Turtle's driveway will be on your
right. If you reach the Iguana Lodge, back up.

We arrived at Black Turtle Lodge the morning after a nest of turtle hatchlings emerged. The owner, Nico, was exhausted but ecstatic. He took over the Black Turtle from its builders only two years ago and joined a turtle-conservation group that carefully reburies the precious egg clutches in areas that can be protected from poachers. Now the second of this year's clutches had hatched, and the tiny turtles had swarmed into the waiting waves. That morning, at least, he looked for all the world like a proud father.

The Black Turtle is a five minute beach walk from the Iguana Lodge, but the two have very different atmospheres. Black Turtle is set back from the beach and surrounded by dense jungle. There are two one-bedroom cabins that share a bathhouse, and two two-story, two-bedroom "treehouses" that have their own outdoor bathrooms. The treehouses rent as units and are designed for adults upstairs (with the king bed) and children downstairs (on two singles). The bathrooms are downstairs which we didn't much like, being old enough to need at least one trip down the stairs at night. Bedroom walls upstairs and down are all screen, so privacy is provided only by the trees; you indeed feel like you're sleeping in a treehouse, but this is not a place where the overly modest will be happy.

Nico serves meals family style on the porch of his house, the main building on the property. There is also a pleasant sitting area here with a library a good deal more literary than is found in most Costa Rican hotels. There's no bar, but wine is included with dinner and you can start with a glass while sitting around outside the open kitchen, relaxing and discussing the day's adventures. Guests are clearly meant to interact at the Black Turtle – it's like an intimate B&B, but with the bedrooms (and the bathrooms) spread around in the woods.

The Black Turtle is a bit rustic and a tad too intimate for Alison's taste, but it's my (and some of our friends') favorite place near Puerto Jiménez. For me, it's Nico's determination to keep the place as wild as he can and the appreciative response of the area's wildlife. A cast-out male howler arrived soon after Nico did, collected some girlfriends, and now there's a resident troop which we could see lounging in a tree right over our heads on our hot first afternoon. *Carablancas* (white-faced monkeys) pass through, exchanging insults with the howlers, on their way from the mangroves to the beach. Squirrel monkeys cruised Nico's banana plantings soon after sunrise and reappeared in late afternoon for another round of foraging. Nico has seen sloths on the property, and even an ocelot. Macaws, parrots, and fish hawks stop here on their daily rounds. And of course, there are the turtles.

Iguana Lodge/Pearl of the Osa $$$$/$$

Puerto Jiménez Oceanfront, Happening Place,
Wildlife

Photo © Iguana Lodge

Contact Information:
506-829-5865 or 506-848-0752 (voice)
info@iguanalodge.com
www.iguanalodge.com

Essentials:
4 Rooms, Two 2-BR Treehouses, one 3-BR House; 8 Rooms next door
at Pearl of the Osa
English, Spanish
Visa, MasterCard accepted (extra charge)
Off-street parking
Swimming pool
All meals included in room rate (Iguana Lodge)
Room Amenities: Ceiling fans, Private (Treehouses) or semi-private
(Cabins) outdoor space at Iguana Lodge

How to get here:
Follow the road that leads to Playa Platanares from the east side of
the Puerto Jiménez Airport (the side opposite the "terminal"). Bear
right after passing Crocodile Bay Lodge, following signs for Pearl of
the Osa or Playa Preciosa. Iguana Lodge is on your right, followed by
Pearl of the Osa.

Playa Plantanares may be the best swimming beach in Costa Rica. Its gentle arc faces east across the Golfo Dulce, protected by a reef about 100 meters out. The slope is perfect – wade a few meters out and you're in waist, then chest-deep water – and the incoming tide is just strong enough to build an occasional wave that breaks over your head. The sand is, well, sand colored, and the few rocks have been polished smooth. There's some driftwood to sit on, and the Iguana Lodge has also thought to provide a line of thatched *palapas*. Best of all, you're far enough from Puerto Jiménez that no one's likely to be here unless they're staying at the Iguana, the Pearl, or the Black Turtle next door. Walk a little ways north or south and it's as if you're on your own private beach.

The two casitas and two 2-bedroom cabins of the Iguana Lodge are separated from the beach by a light screen of palms, and the Pearl of the Osa restaurant with its upstairs rooms looks toward the beach across a broad grass lawn. The Pearl is the area's liveliest bar, so we can only recommend staying there if you're into staying up late or sleeping right over the party. The Iguana, on the other hand, offers privacy, manicured tropical gardens, and a beautiful thatched-roof *rancho* with downstairs sitting and breakfast areas and an upstairs formal dining room for dinner. The casitas and cabins have wood-frame bedrooms with walls of screen on three sides to let in air and the view. The cabins have a downstairs bedroom with a deck and an upstairs bedroom with a private balcony. Each bedroom has an attached bathroom with curved concrete walls and bright colors. How about yellow and blue with a bright pink shower to wake you up in the morning?

The upstairs and downstairs bedrooms in Iguana's cabins rent separately, so ask for an upstairs room unless you don't mind a certain amount of tromping around over your head. Besides, the upstairs rooms have more sea breeze and a better view. Friends traveling together might opt for both rooms of a cabin, but for larger groups Iguana also offers a three-story, three-bedroom tropical-style house situated just a few trees from the beach. The bottom floor is an open kitchen and eating area; the top floor is a spacious master suite. You can cook here yourself or join other Iguana guests for the nightly fixed-menu feast served in the upstairs dining room of the main *palapa*.

The Iguana offers a full assortment of toys including bicycles, boogie boards and kayaks, and even heavy rubber boots in case you care to venture into the mangroves on foot. (We wouldn't recommend this – take a kayak.) There is a small yoga platform by the beach, somewhat incongruously sporting a multi-function weight machine. As far as we can tell, though, the main guest occupations here are romantic sunrise and sunset beach walks and lounging in or near the surf.

Ojo del Mar $
Playa Matapalo   Oceanfront, Yoga/Meditation

Photo © Ojo del Mar

Contact Information:
506-735-5531 (voice)
ojodelmar@yahoo.de
www.ojodelmar.com

Essentials:
4 Cabins (3 with shared baths)
English, Spanish, German
Cash or traveler's checks only
Secure parking
Breakfast included, Restaurant.
Room Amenities: Ceiling fan, Private or semi-private outdoor space

How to get here:
Take the road from Puerto Jiménez toward Matapalo and Carate; this is the main coastal road around the eastern side of the Osa Peninsula. Ojo del Mar is on the ocean side about 40 minutes from Puerto Jiménez, across from bright-blue Carbonera school. Look for a sign with an eye. If you see Lapa Rios, you've gone too far.

Under a hanging brass gong, guitars and several sizes of conga drums stand ready in one corner of the bamboo-and-thatch dining *palapa* at Ojo del Mar,. We're not players, but we expect that on many nights there is music here under blazing torches or softer clusters of candles, with the sounds of the jungle for harmony and the gentle surf in the background. And afterwards, just the jungle, the surf and the night sky. There is something very peaceful about places like Ojo, with no electricity and hence no artificial lighting and no generator racketing through the night.

Ojo del Mar calls itself a "simple life retreat," and the atmosphere seems somewhere between a counterculture commune and a monastic retreat. Carefully arranged stone cairns (some cemented for greater permanence) line the paths, surround the beachfront yoga platform, and appear here and there among the trees. Painted gourds, shells, and bits of shiny metal hang as decorations. Walls are painted with stars, spirals, geometrical designs. A small stuffed teddy bear sits on a post, waiting no doubt for Christopher Robin or the Eternal Child in whichever guest stumbles upon it, picks it up, and reflects on the combination of playfulness and fiercely-defended innocence that Ojo embodies perhaps more than anyplace else we've encountered here on the Osa Peninsula or, for that matter, in all of Costa Rica.

Ojo del Mar's four cabins are all different, made of wood or bamboo, with porches, hammocks, and open-air designs. The two-story "beach house" offers a second, upstairs bedroom under its peaked roof. Each cabin sports a collage of decoration – painted eyes, colorful batiks, shell curtains, little piles of stones or arrangements of shells – some, no doubt, added by guests. Showers are outdoor but private, screened by partial walls or banks of dense plantings. Bathrooms are separate from the cabins, connected by paths through the trees. You'll need a flashlight to find your way if you're the sort who gets up in the middle of the night.

Yoga is an Ojo del Mar specialty, practiced on the lovely platform bordering the beach. It's a pleasure just to sit here, listening to the waves and feeling the constant breeze. Stretches are an extra.

The owner, Nico, serves vegetarian meals in the central *rancho*, favoring organic produce from her own gardens or neighboring growers. If you're headed off for the day, she can pack you a healthy lunch. For a taste of another lifestyle, take some of the money you've saved staying here and head up the road for lunch at Lapa Rios where you can see and be seen with the glitterati.

Bosque del Cabo $$$-$$$$
Playa Matapalo   Birding, Relax/Get Away, Wildlife, Hiking

Photo © Bosque del Cabo

Contact Information:
506-735-5206 (voice/fax)
reservations@bosquedelcabo.com
www.bosquedelcabo.com

Essentials:
15 Cabins, 4 Houses
English, Spanish
All major credit cards accepted
Secure parking
Swimming pool, Beach access, Massage
All meals included in room rate
Room Amenities: Ceiling fan, In-room safe, Private or semi-private
    outdoor space

How to get here:
Take the road from Puerto Jiménez toward Matapalo and Carate; this
is the main coastal road around the eastern side of the Osa Peninsula.
Bosque del Cabo is on the ocean side about one hour southwest of
Puerto Jiménez, just past Lapa Rios.

You may think it's nothing but fun flitting from place to place, staying in luxury hotels, eating fabulous meals, bathing in limpid pools under cascading waterfalls and being wakened in the mornings by wandering troops of howler monkeys. You'd actually be right. But every now and then the constant on-the-go gets a little tiring and a girl just needs a good massage. Bosque del Cabo was clearly the place to get it.

From the moment we pulled up the long, tree-lined driveway and saw the spacious lawns spreading out around the thatch-roofed lodge I thought, Aaaahhhh, I'm going to like it here. I sought out Jutta, the resident massage therapist, and she led me back into the jungle about 200 meters beyond the swimming pool to a small grove surrounded by huge trees. It was perfectly silent except for the sound of wind rustling the leaves and birds singing. Jutta told me that one day an ocelot emerged from the trees and padded by when she was giving a massage. I lay on my back on her table, gazed up into the lush green canopy, and surrendered myself to pure bliss.

The massage renewed me enough to join Chris on a hike down one of Bosque del Cabo's trails, across a small river (there's a waterfall further downstream) and up through primary rain forest, then back to our room by the tropical garden and the frog pond. As well as trails through the jungle, you can walk to the Pacific coast (only accessible during low tide) and to the Golfo Dulce where you can swim at one of several beaches and then arrange for the folks at Bosque del Cabo to pick you up. Bird-watching in the garden or from the lodge is fabulous and all types of jungle animals, even large cats like pumas, have been spotted in the 600+ acre forest reserve.

Eleven thatched-roofed, screened bungalows are situated in the gardens around the lodge, each with a private deck overlooking the ocean and a modern bathroom with an outdoor shower. The furniture is simple bamboo, elegant in its classic design. A ten-minute walk from the lodge, across a long suspension-bridge, the two open-air garden rooms are smaller and less luxurious (and less expensive), but tucked into the jungle in a way that makes you feel like you're on safari. If you're traveling with friends or family, you might prefer one of the three houses, two with ocean views, that Bosque also offers.

All meals are served in the main lodge (which made walking across the suspension bridge to our room after dinner a real adventure) and are simple but well-prepared. Before dinner, guests gather at the poolside bar to compare their day's activities. Dinner is served family-style and lunch can be a picnic prepared ahead of time for taking with you. Despite its proximity to the jungle, Bosque del Cabo feels country estate-like in its garden setting 500 meters above the ocean. It's the perfect place to renew yourself.

Lapa Rios $$$$
Playa Matapalo   Honeymoons, Wildlife, Birding

Photo © Lapa Rios

Contact Information:
506-735-5130 (voice); 506-735-5179 (fax)
info@laparios.com
www.laparios.com

Essentials:
16 Bungalows
English, Spanish
All major credit cards accepted
Secure parking
Swimming pool, Beach access
All meals included in room rate
Room Amenities: Ceiling fan, Private outdoor space, In-room safe,
     Breakfast delivered to your room

How to get here:
Take the road from Puerto Jiménez toward Matapalo and Carate; this
is the main coastal road around the eastern side of the Osa Peninsula.
About an hour from Puerto Jiménez, Lapa Rios is on the right, just
after you ford the river.

The *monos congos* (howler monkeys) launched into their morning howls at 3:30 a.m., with the still-full moon high above the trees. They stopped after 15 minutes and we drifted back to sleep until five o'clock when they started again, this time in earnest, this time to greet the dawn. As the sun rose, they crashed through the trees while Alison tested the fast setting on her new camera. As we watched and photographed, we also took odd shots of the toucans, Mealy parrots, aracaris, and Linneated woodpeckers that passed through our little circle of trees. No need to go looking for birds and animals here at Lapa Rios; they come to you.

Lapa Rios is the height of rainforest luxury, a destination for honeymooners and top-tier vacationers who didn't want to fly all the way to Tahiti this year. Someone hands you a drink the moment you walk in the door, then asks you what you'd like for dinner. Your bags are arranged in your spacious private bungalow by the time you walk down the trail (which can be quite long, depending on where you're located). Bamboo shades roll up to reveal walls of nearly-transparent screen and doors open onto completely private decks with rockers, lounges, and hammocks. Fourteen of the bungalows look down onto the Playa Matapalo beach, two overlook a steep jungle canyon. Coffee and warm milk are discretely delivered to your bungalow at 6 a.m. Meals are served in a beautiful open *palapa*, with a three-turn spiral staircase running up to a covered observation deck just below the roof's peak. The menu is varied, the food is excellent, and the Lapapalapa bar will mix up anything you might like. The staff is extraordinarily attentive; it seemed like everyone at Lapa Rios knew our names within five minutes of our arrival.

Lapa Rios is one of the oldest and, at 1,000 acres, one of the largest ecolodge reserves in Costa Rica. If you're here looking for wildlife there is little reason ever to leave the property. On a good day, all four Costa Rican species of monkeys can be seen from the deck of your bungalow or even from the restaurant. A one-hour trail down to a nearby waterfall and back to the main lodge is perfect before breakfast, and you can always walk to the beach. Most excursions into the jungle require a naturalist guide who knows the trails as well as the creatures. The night walk, in search of frogs and nocturnal mammals, is one of the most popular. Lapa Rios takes preservation and low guest impact seriously; you can even take a "sustainability tour" that explains such down-to-earth basics as the generation of gas for the kitchen stoves from yesterday's leftovers.

As we were saying good-bye after our morning with the howlers, we overheard a dainty young woman complain about the lack of air conditioning and the terrible long walk in her silver slippers to get to her room. This is Costa Rica, not Paris. Keep in mind that even at ultra-deluxe Lapa Rios, you're still in the jungle.

Luna Lodge $$$-$$$$
Carate   Wildlife, Birding, Yoga/Meditation

Photo © Alison Tinsley

Contact Information:
506-380-5036/358-5848 (voice)
information@lunalodge.com
www.lunalodge.com

Essentials:
3 Rooms, 8 Bungalows, 5 Tents with platforms
English, Spanish
All major credit cards accepted
Secure parking
Swimming pool, Beach access (It's a hike!)
All meals included in room rate
Room Amenities: Ceiling fan, Private or semi-private (Cabins) outdoor
    space, Internet access available (extra charge)

How to get here:
Fly to Carate. Or, if driving, Luna Lodge is at the end of the Coast
Road, about two hours from Puerto Jiménez. Turn up the hill just
past the Carate airstrip, cross the Carate river twice, and keep going
until you see Luna Lodge. You can't go any farther.

An urgent keening interrupted breakfast, and Lana ran out from the kitchen closely followed by several of the Luna Lodge staff. "The white hawk," she cried excitedly. "My power bird!" Two white hawks circled slowly above our heads, calling plaintively. We watched as they drifted in widening then narrowing circles, up the Carate's tree-lined canyon then farther east until they were out of sight. Lana later explained to us, during a break in our yoga session on her platform high above the lodge, that the white hawks appeared whenever she had difficulties. We viewed them as a good sign.

Lana Widmore has been a cook, a sailing captain, and a guide in both Australia and Costa Rica. With money earned for clean-up work after the Exxon Valdez oil spill, she bought a former fruit-tree farm up the steep canyon of the gold-bearing Rio Carate and created Luna Lodge. There are places that are off the beaten path, and then there are places like Luna, two hours of rough road from Puerto Jiménez, bordering the vast Corcovado reserve. The end of the line. From here, the only permitted form of transport is your own feet. Guests have been stranded at Luna when heavy rains rendered the Agua Buena river unfordable, at least until the weather cleared enough for the air taxi from Puerto Jiménez to land on the gravel strip on the beach at the mouth of the Carate. What a tragedy – a few extra days at Luna, days of isolation and utter calm.

If you are looking for lowland rainforest birds, you can't do much better than this. On our first afternoon we saw pairs of toucans, macaws, aracaris, kiskadees, and Red-lored parrots, all from the private front deck of our peak-roofed bungalow. I watched two scarlet macaws expertly eating not-yet-ripe almonds 15 feet above my head. The next morning in a short walk we saw more toucans, more macaws, plus trogons, brilliant sky-blue and black cotingas, manikins, and many other colorful little songbirds. And then the white hawks. Lana has even seen Harpy eagles here, fearsome birds with two-meter wingspans that can seize monkeys and sloths from the dense forest trees.

Luna Lodge offers a range of lodging options: beautiful circular bungalows with peaked roofs, bamboo walls, and open-air bathrooms; conventional "hacienda" rooms for those who prefer a more traditional and enclosed sleeping environment; and two-bed tents on wooden platforms set among the trees above the yoga platform. Bungalow #7 – where we stayed – is a steep climb but has the best view; #1 and #2 are the easiest to access for those who don't like steps. The hacienda rooms are right next to the main *palapa*; #9 has windows on two sides looking into the jungle. All the lodgings are placed so as to provide a sense of intimacy, and a direct connection to the surrounding jungle.

Cabinas Los Cocos $
Playa Zancudo   Downtown, Oceanfront, Birding, Fishing

Photo © Cabinas Los Cocos

Contact Information:
506-776-0012 (voice)
loscocos@loscocos.com
www.loscocos.com

Essentials:
4 Cabins with full kitchens
English, Spanish
Cash only
Off-street parking
Restaurants nearby
Room Amenities: Ceiling fan, Private or semi-private outdoor space,
    Full kitchen, In-room safe

How to get here:
Call Andrew at Los Cocos and arrange to be picked up by boat in
either Puerto Jiménez or Golfito. Otherwise, Zancudo is about an
hour's drive from Golfito; Cabinas Los Cocos is in town on the beach
side of the road.

Andrew slows the boat just enough for us to slide down the big waves that have appeared in the otherwise-flat Golfo Dulce, and then to skate up and over the crests. It's an El Nino year, and the rain runoff down the Rio Coto Colorado has been insufficient to carve a new channel; hence the river mouth is a broad, flat expanse of sand extending far out into the bay, and the incoming surf breaks as if on a beach. We clear the flats into the river proper and land. Zancudo has no airport, and it's a long, bumpy drive out from Golfito. The best way to get here is by boat and Andrew is our host at Cabinas Los Cocos, right on the Playa Zancudo beachfront.

The town of Zancudo occupies a six-kilometer spit of sand separating the mangrove-filled estuary of the Rio Coto from the Golfo Dulce. The palm-lined black-sand beach slopes almost imperceptibly into the sea. At high tide you can walk out 20 or 30 meters and be less than knee-deep. At low tide the water glistens on top of the sand, mirroring the sun during the day and the moon and stars at night. The frustrated currents of the gulf have piled generations of driftwood here, from worn bits of finished planks to huge sand-polished stumps with roots still twisting off in every direction.

An interesting ex-pat community has washed up in Zancudo as well. Susan England bought the land where Los Cocos now sits almost 30 years ago, and she and Andrew built a boat-service and tour business and then the *cabinas* in the years that followed. After Jerry Garcia departed this world for his final trip, their "Dead-head" neighbors Rick and Lori moved from California to open Sol y Mar, the place to head for breakfast, lunch, or after-dinner entertainment. Italian chef Alberto came about the same time. Let him know in the afternoon and he'll make you a fabulous dinner at his Puerta Negra restaurant down the road. Zancudo, it seems, is one of those nowhere places to which people migrate from whatever life they had before and then stay. Alison is reminded of her misspent youth in Brown County, Indiana, where the music was always good, life was not quite communal but pretty relaxed, everyone got by somehow or other, and the force of gravity exerted a strong pull on whoever thought about leaving.

Los Cocos has four cabins; two hand-built of mangrove logs and palm thatch, and two reassembled and decorated former banana-workers' dwellings from the old United Fruit operation on the Rio Coto. All have full kitchens. The biggest is #2, where we stayed. Upstairs from the broad front porch is an open loft with a second double bed, a completely private, hidden space. It's about 50 feet of sand and palm trees to the beach. Split coconut hulls edge the plantings of bananas and heliconias. Andrew's whimsical sculptures, carved from unset concrete, stand along the pathways with a Buddha or two keeping watch as well. The light breeze off the gulf rocks our hammocks. No worries. Maybe we won't leave tomorrow after all …

Tiskita Lodge $$$$
Punta Banco   Oceanfront, Wildlife, Birding, Hiking, Kid-friendly

Photo © Alison Tinsley

Contact Information:
506-296-8125 (voice); 506-296-8133 (fax)
tiskita@racsa.co.cr
www.tiskita-lodge.co.cr

Essentials:
10 Cabins
English, Spanish
Credit cards accepted in advance, Cash only at Lodge
Secure parking
Swimming pool
All meals included in room rate
Room Amenities: Ceiling fans, Private or semi-private outdoor space

How to get here:
Fly from Puerto Jiménez or Golfito. Otherwise, Tiskita is about three
hours south of Golfito, at the very end of the coast road. Follow signs
to Pavones and then to Banco. The road turns into Tiskita's driveway
just after it crosses the grass landing strip.

Tiskita Lodge is Closed Sept. 15 – Oct. 15

We were walking back to Tiskita's main lodge from our cabin when I sensed motion and whirled to face a beautiful blue snake almost two meters long eyeing me, its tongue tasting my scent from a distance. A bullet-shaped head – clearly nonvenomous – so the snake and I just watched each other for a few moments, and then it virtually flew across the path and into the woods. A *mica*, said Tiskita's owner Lisbeth, a racer, consumer of rodents and other snakes. Always a good omen.

Peter Aspinall homesteaded this land when he got out of school almost thirty years ago, and he and Lisbeth built Tiskita first as their home and then as a guest lodge over the course of two decades. Fruit trees are Peter's passion, and over 100 varieties, endemic and exotic, thrive in his carefully-tended orchard. On a long morning walk, he leads us through re-forested hillsides that had once been slashed and burned by small-scale farmers and then takes us further into the orchards, stopping to name trees and explain the lifestyle, ecology, and human uses of each. Peter nurtures trees from seed and plants constantly, sometimes to produce human-edible fruits, but also to provide shade, encourage forest succession, provide food or nesting sites for birds or mammals, and improve the heavy clay soils with nitrogen fixation. We cross a little stream several times – it marks a rough boundary between cultivated and wild land. Later we make our way above this stream's spectacular rock-faced waterfall to bathe in deep pools cut in the bedrock. Here we are surrounded by jungle. Tiskita is an 800-acre reserve, nearly all of it untouched rainforest.

Tiskita offers ten cabins, four individual (# 6, 7, 14, and 17) and the rest designed for families or groups with two or three bedrooms with private bathrooms in each cabin. All are different in details, but have ample porches, outdoor showers, and considerable privacy. Lisbeth installed outdoor showers even in the few cabins with fully-enclosed bathrooms. She explains that one needs to shower often in the humid tropics and, besides, it's more fun to shower outside. We reflect on the fact that many visitors to Costa Rica dwell in northern cities or suburbs and may never have taken their clothes off outdoors. Tiskita can cure that.

Over breakfast, we expressed our delight that we, who were staying in the cabin named Titi, were visited in the morning by a whole troop of *titis* – golden-furred squirrel monkeys who appeared suddenly just after dawn and then disappeared, heading deeper into the woods after about 15 minutes of rambunctious play. Lisbeth told the story of an elderly woman, the oldest member of a birdwatching group, who simply sat on the deck of her Tiskita cabin and saw as many different birds as did all of her friends who were searching through the forest. "It's always interesting," she concluded, "every day is different. You just have to be still and watch."

Send us your feedback!

If you've stayed someplace we recommend and have comments, if your favorite Costa Rican vacation spot isn't listed and you think it should be, or if you're a hotel owner and think your hotel should be in our top 100, let us know:

feedback@sleepingwiththetoucans.com

If you're and innkeeper and would like us to review your hotel thoroughly, anonymously, and confidentially, contact us at:

reviews@sleepingwiththetoucans.com

Feedback, new great hotels, ultra-low budget options, updates on road conditions, and other useful tips for travelers are on our website:

www.sleepingwiththetoucans.com

Index

About the Authors

Photo © Judd Pilossof

Alison Tinsley has been a Peace Corps worker in Africa, a fashion model and actress in Rome, an alternative high school teacher, a university writing instructor, and a real-estate broker. She's written speeches, lifestyle and travel articles, short stories, and testimony for the U.S. Senate. She's also had lots of pets.

Chris Fields has been a nuclear physicist, bioinformatics researcher, software entrepreneur, and university administrator. He's written a lot of research articles and marketing documents. He veered off the fast lane to become a painter, writer and bon vivant.

Rosie, the indomitable Toyota, has worked the fancy streets of Santa Fe, NM and San Miguel de Allende, Mexico. She finds the rough roads of Costa Rica much more to her liking and she appreciates her new tires!

Our many thanks to the friends who helped with this book or just put up with us: Cathryn, Phil and Janet, Kelly, Marcel, Judd and Liz, Berni and Nhi, Frank and Oriana, Sebastian, Maximiliano, Rosa and Yadira, Anthony and so many more we can't begin to list them all. Special thanks to Ann Rohovec – proofreader extraordinaire – and to Pam Porter for last-minute PhotoShop wizardry.

And to all of you, Happy Travels!

www.sleepingwiththetoucans.com